VOICES OF CHANGE IN THE
SPANISH AMERICAN THEATER

THE TEXAS PAN AMERICAN SERIES

Voices of Change in the

Spanish American Theater

AN ANTHOLOGY · *Edited and Translated by*

WILLIAM I. OLIVER, 1926 — comp.

UNIVERSITY OF TEXAS PRESS : AUSTIN & LONDON

The Texas Pan American Series is published with the
assistance of a revolving publication fund established
by the Pan American Sulphur Company and other
friends of Latin America in Texas.

International Standard Book Number 0-292-70123-3
Library of Congress Catalog Card Number 73-167285
© 1971 by William I. Oliver
Printed by The University of Texas Printing Division, Austin
Bound by Universal Bookbinding, Inc., San Antonio

Information about producing any of the plays printed in this
book can be obtained from Bertha Klausner, International
Literary Agency, Inc., 71 Park Avenue,
New York, N.Y. 10016.

CONTENTS

c.1

INTRODUCTION

"Spanish American plays?!"

The inflection of that question, which pushes the query into an
exclamation of superior disbelief—that inflection, more than anything else, goaded me to the preparation of this anthology. Today, it
is merely tiresome to complain about the patronizing superiority displayed by North Americans to their Latin American neighbors—but
because of that inflection some recapitulation of these pejorative
myths must be made. Latin Americans have for too long been char-
acterized as welfare recipients of our good will policies—quaint na-
tives with large hungry eyes who promenade across our television
screens whenever we tune-in a CARE commercial. They have had to
bear up under the "Seeee, senyoor" image of the lethargic Hollywood
extra eternally trapped in a siesta of uselessness—a race of Latin
Stepin Fetchits and Butterfly McQueens. North Americans have persistently thought of Latin America as a soft land from which to extract
rubber, oil, tin, copper, bananas, saltpeter, silver, balsa, and jumbo
shrimp—all at bargain prices and low labor costs. It has also been a
musical comedy fairyland, a pastoral grazing ground for hordes of
American tourists in hot pursuit of quaintness, picturesqueness, and

the ghost of Panama Hattie. We have come to believe implicitly this highly prejudicial image of the Latin American and his world. To many of us the very notion of a respectable exchange of thought and sentiment with anything south of the Rio Grande seems as insane as attempting to converse with marmosets.

While we have persisted in our belief of these myths about Latin Americans, the whole of Spanish-speaking America has, just as persistently, grown in resources, power, and population. Even more impressive than its prodigious material growth is the cultural and political upheaval that has been stirring beneath its social surface. The traditional socio-political inheritance of the Spanish and Portuguese colonial systems has begun to expire and in many countries it is sustained only by force of arms. The Cuban revolution, whatever one may think of it, spelled the death sentence of the old and somewhat aristocratic order throughout all of Latin America. I do not mean that all of Latin America is necessarily on the march toward communist government; I do mean that, whatever the political disposition of a country, it will inexorably lose its vestiges of aristocracy, *caciquismo*, and fascistic militarism. Latin American democracies are compelled increasingly to fulfill their political responsibilities—the days of nominal democracies in Latin America are numbered. The militarists, those chieftains of the oligarchies, are ruling (if not running) scared. Of course, some countries are adjusting to the socialist pressures with more success than are others. In some cases their adjustment to these pressures is far more sophisticated and effective than our own, but, no matter whether the adjustment is one of repression or conciliation, there appears to be little possibility of ultimately restraining the impetus of change toward a greater social freedom and a more equitable division of wealth.

Beneath the broad socio-political upheaval one detects the ferment of yet other changes. The Catholic church, though still powerful, no longer holds dominance over the minds of the people as it once did. Increased educational opportunities, the direct exposure to Marxist ideologies, the increased need for and practice of birth control—all have begun to loosen the grip of the church. Programs of social welfare and economic improvement (some sponsored by the United

States, others by the United Nations, and a very good number of national origin) have shaken the old allegiance to the church on grounds of its antiquated program of stop-gap charities and doles. The church itself has begun to split its staves. It was in Chile where a group of progressive Catholic clergy invaded and took over the cathedral for a whole day to protest the Pope's visit to Colombia, maintaining that this visit was a regressive rather than progressive event; it was also in Chile that an international congress on birth control was celebrated and officially recognized by the president of the country, who addressed the congress at its inaugural ceremonies. Finally, it must be remembered that it was Perón, not Castro, who first attempted to legislate against the powers of the church.

Increased educational facilities have created an ever-growing middle class and a concomitant movement toward a less agrarian and a more technocratic society. Labor unions are beginning to acquire real power for the first time. This socio-economic change has not tended to quell the hunger of the people for greater freedom and self-determination. Quite the contrary, it has exacerbated it. Under its persistent demands, Latin American governments make ever more stringent demands of the foreign powers that control their industries, their mines, and the growth and export of their agricultural mainstays. Time and again the pressures of increased numbers of educated citizenry, the burgeoning ranks of candidates for the affluence of the middle class, have forced governments to "nationalize" industries and firms owned by foreign capital.

Urban growth has been alarming. If it is true that all transcendence in this life involves us in a measure of painful responsibility, it will come as no surprise that the growth of Latin American cities has given rise to a new swarm of problems that often seems to outweigh the economic progress which the cities themselves have fostered. The major Latin American cities are overwhelmed by an invasion of *campesinos* from rural communities—persons not yet capable of taking their place in the technocratic existence of the cities. In turn, this invasion places an increased burden upon the agrarian community to produce more food in order to support the hungry cities. This food, of necessity, must be produced by new methods of farming and machinery that displace the remaining farm hands and push them into the already overcrowded cities to multiply the need for more food. The education of these waves of people that flow into the cities is not rapid enough to train them to take their place in an urban community of a technocratic nature, *but* it is sufficiently rapid to whet their appetite for the good things of urban life. The agonizing problems of burgeoning economic growth and the population explosion in Latin America begin to resemble those of the Roman Empire.

The world of Latin America is increasingly polarized. The old and rigid social order of the colonial world is confronted by that of the new technology. The needs of the exploding cities seem to militate against the growth of the agrarian society. The old religious unity of Latin America erodes through its own efforts to solve new problems by means of old panaceas, and the more the church resists change, the weaker it appears to those she wishes to protect within her ranks. The more the military oligarchies try to force the citizenry to conform in the old ways, the more they jeopardize the longevity of their power by provoking the people to organize in orderly or cohesive rebellion. The more the nations educate their people to meet the demands of expanding industry and commerce, the less those people are prone to submit to the social and economic stratification of the old order. Change in Latin America began as it did in the United States, through revolution, but the subsequent changes have tended to retain the pattern of violent confrontation and have not acquired the gentler tendencies of rebellious evolution. The new temper of violent rebellion, if not revolution, in the United States should make North Americans more curious about and more acutely aware of the societal changes that are occurring south of our border.

It is the vibration of these volcanic changes that led me in my search for plays. I was not interested in the conventional dramas that continued in the old traditions of folkloric realism, sentimental melodrama, and facile comedy. I was surprised to discover how few of the current plays express the revolutionary changes of contemporary Spanish America or how many of the plays smothered the boldness of their thematic statement in sentimentality. Most infuriating of all was to encounter plays obviously inspired by a spirit of rebellion and intelligent criticism which capitulated in their third acts to the old shibboleths of the establishment. It soon became apparent that the theater was not so aggressive in its pursuit of change as were other aspects of Spanish American culture. However, there were some encouraging signs of artistic ferment. I sought for and I believe that I found plays that could be translated culturally as well as linguistically. Some situations will not retain their value and dramatic charge when performed within a different national or cultural audience pattern of response; some plays will lose their verbal potency in translation (this is definitely the case with García Lorca's plays, which become quite flat and prosaic in English translation). This stipulation with regard to translation narrowed my scope considerably. Finally, I was in search of dramas the style and form of which indicated a healthy break with the old realistic, sentimental, and melodramatic conventions of Spanish American theater.

In my search I learned a great deal about the ways in which the theatrical milieu of Spanish America determines its drama. Having grown up in Panama, where, until recently, drama has never been a strong cultural activity, I was impressed by the enormous quantity and high quality of the theater available in such centers as Mexico City, Santiago, and Buenos Aires. I was equally concerned by the relatively low profits that accrue to the pursuit of the playwright's craft. Few playwrights if any can make a living solely from their plays. Runs are short, while profits are low and are cut into too many slices. It is easier for actors to make a steady living than it is for a good playwright. Personality stars acquire a following similar to that of the old Hollywood idols. Though few, some of these actors have been known to develop companies that churn out productions tailored to the particular charms or skills of the star. In these cases the star makes more than a modest profit, while the playwright and the other actors of the company often make no more than a living wage. Playwrights who endeavor to write works that stand on their own merits encounter problems quite different from those known to the profession in this country or any other major theatrical center in the occidental world. Even a successful drama pays the playwright very little if his profits are extracted solely from box office receipts. Most playwrights rely heavily upon patronage and bonuses such as prizes and, above all, upon government employment and subsidy. It is generally admitted that, aside from occasional prizes, the only compensation a nation can give its playwrights lies in an appointment to some foreign office of the state department. This insures the playwright a healthy salary and the ability to travel, but it does not cure one of the major difficulties that beset him: by and large his plays remain locked hermetically within his own country. There is not yet an adequate theatrical exchange even among Spanish American countries themselves. Plays from Europe and the United States are produced with regularity, but productions of plays from other Spanish American countries, no matter how good, are infrequent because they displace the works of local authors. From a chauvinist point of view, foreign Spanish American plays are undeniable liabilities.

Playwrights also have to cope with serious problems of censorship. Sometimes the censorship is official and direct, but more often than not the most pernicious censorship lies hidden in the prohibitions that are built into the compromise struck between most playwrights and their audience. In order to succeed, the playwright is forced to remain within the limits of tolerance set by his audience. Latin audiences for good drama are by and large middle class to rich and are more conservative in their tastes than those of Europe and the United States. A playwright who wishes to change the conventions of his theater or to speak against the evils of his time runs the risk of offending the very people who support him. The audience of the Latin playwright tends to be conservative and sympathetic with the establishment, and, like many conservative audiences the world over, it tends to seek a pleasant and undisturbing theater. As a consequence of audience pressure, many playwrights capitulate to vulgarity and pander their daring for the sake of necessary approval. It must be recognized, however, that these strictures on the artistic integrity and thematic mobility of the playwrights are beginning to loosen as the socio-economic fiber of the country becomes richer and more complex.

Among the most disturbing tendencies in Spanish American drama is the Latin's endless hunger for sentimental and romantic plots. This may be an inheritance from the melodramatic ancestry of the nine-

teenth century, but it is nonetheless a sign of cultural or ethnic pre-
disposition. Both audiences and authors seem to suffer from an irresistible weakness for the tender sentiments. I have read and seen
several plays that promise to develop into hard and strong theater
but that collapse or, rather, melt in their third acts into a placid puddle
of romantic sentimentality. Love triumphs over any adversity and all
differences of opinion. Love is given as a magical force capable of
resolving all difficulties including those of thematic honesty and sound
plotting. Love vanquishes all and even overrides the empirical facul-
ties of the audiences' critical posture. Nonetheless, there is an increasing measure of irony and toughness in Spanish American drama. If
playwrights do not often seek to challenge their audiences' predilec-
tions in open confrontation, many of them have learned to undermine
their audiences' penchant for the sentimental by means of irony. I
found it encouraging to hear playwrights such as Griselda Gambaro
and Emilio Carballido attack this sentimental propensity more vitu-
peratively than ever I did.

Low profits, short runs, and the demands of an audience for lots of
easy entertainment—these three conditions have remained constant
in Spanish American theater. In fact, they have a historical lineage
that goes back unbroken to the Spanish Golden Age of the Seven-
teenth century. Together these three factors conspire to evince a very
damaging response from the playwright: facility. Authors find themselves compelled to write plays with the indecorous fecundity of rabbits. In order to live and in order to please, they write quickly and
prodigiously, but not carefully and with the seriousness of attention,
the thrust of the intellect, that marks the great figures of modern
drama. Their audiences do not seem to object so long as the play
entertains, so long as there is a thick veneer of wit and a display of
facile originality.I have sought out only those authors who have taken
time to "finish" their works with the attention requisite to sound
craftsmanship. I have insisted upon works that reflect their authors'
respect for the theme and form of the play—works that are invested
with careful signs of the author's pride.

There are now definite signs of progress and change in the theater.
Yearly in Havana a Congress of the Arts is sponsored by the Casa

de las Americas. Plays and theater artists from all over Latin America
convene and participate in this Congress. ILAT (Instituto Látino
Americano del Teatro) is also making concerted efforts to promote
exchange of theatrical talent and energy. However, neither of these
projects is adequate—each is restricted either by political reserva-
tions or economic limitations. The various Latin American nations
continue to support their own playwrights on chauvinist grounds and
at the expense of critical standards of dramatic excellence. Naturally
enough, authors tend to continue to protect their plays and themselves by writing folkloric realism—the more national and identifiable
the subject matter, the more apt the play is to succeed at home and,
by the same token, the less it is likely to succeed abroad. For these
reasons one *must* applaud the efforts of ILAT and the Havana Congress of the Arts—they both help to break down the regionalism of
Latin American theater. However constructive these two festivals
may be, as one who wishes health and growth to Latin American
drama I am afraid that they are as yet inadequate correctives. I find
their efforts truncated—the ILAT, because it lacks adequate funds,
and the Havana conference, because it lacks the eclecticism to promote the stylistic and thematic mobility necessary to the growth of
truly profound social change or incisive drama.

     What Latin America needs most is recognition in the major theater
centers of the Northern world. Only such full recognition can au-
thenticate this drama in the eyes of the artists who create it. It has
been my hope to discover plays that could stand on their own merits
and side by side with the best of current fare in New York and Europe.
I have rejected "literary dramas"—that is to say, plays that relied
more on the page than the stage for their effect. I have sought plays
that displayed impatience with old forms and worn-out conventions.
I have looked for works that expressed an impatience with the intransigence and weakness of the old social system as well as the dramatic values that it cherished.

     If I have not included a post-Castro Cuban play it is because I
have not encountered one that was provocative both thematically and
technically. This does not mean that there may not be good Cuban
plays, it just means that the plays I have read were unexepectedly

dull in their plodding realism or insufferably gauche in their relentless didacticism. Now that channels of communication between Cuba
and our world are beginning to be more free of governmental inter-
ference, it may be possible to discover some notable Cuban plays. I
must say none of the Cuban plays that I saw in South America, such as
La Casa Vieja or others that I have managed to read, meet my standards of excellence. I *have* included *The Day They Let the Lions Loose*
by Emilio Carballido—a Mexican play that won the prize for drama
at the Havana Festival of the Arts in 1963. Though I have made
reference to the very real climate of political unrest that exists in
Latin America, I have not found plays that were both strong and
skillful in the revolutionary genre. I admit that I have encountered
some plays that promised to fulfill my expectations in this category,
but I was disappointed in their ultimate effect. Some of the best of
these were written by authors whose works are included in this
anthology. In one instance that I recall, the play, an episodic piece
comparable in structure to Brecht's *Private Life of the Master Race,*
was obviously awkward and truncated. Mandatory thematic develop-
ments were left out of its structure. This is not to be wondered at,
since the full statement of the author's thought could not safely be
made in his own country. Another instance involved a text submitted
to me in one of its preliminary drafts. The piece, though unfinished,
promised to develop so effectively that immediately I made a translation of the early draft. Subsequent revisions, however, all softened
the moral-existential critique made by the plot until the play became
utterly toothless, incapable of biting into the blandest of problems.
Finally the play disintegrated to so innocuous a level as to be awarded
a prize and production in the "national theater." What is appalling to
me in this instance is that the end result was a denial of the author's
initial burst of intelligent protest and heartfelt conviction. I did not
find these two disappointments discouraging—to the contrary, they
confirmed me in my purpose.

Direct assault is not the way of Spanish American drama. In this
respect the Spanish Americans have maintained a close parallelism
with the techniques of the best Spanish drama. Their best criticism
tends to be slyly couched in humor and surrogate situations. However,

more and more we find playwrights openly declaring themselves against the injustices and stupidities of life without resorting to protective subterfuges. It is my conviction that Spanish American theater will burgeon in importance once its existence is recognized by the theater centers of the United States, France, England, and Germany. I realize that such recognition is predicated on the efforts of the playwrights in question as well as those of the producing centers—but the initial gestures should, it seems, be made by that factor in the recognition that possesses the greatest mobility. This recognition would encourage Latin playwrights to universalize their writing in style and theme. It would free them from a dependence upon official support and a subserviance to audiences of timid tastes and intolerant biases. This anthology is humbly but energetically dedicated to that end.

WILLIAM I. OLIVER

The Day They Let the Lions Loose

BY EMILIO CARBALLIDO

Emilio Carballido is one of Mexico's leading authors, having written a large number of plays, novels, and short stories, as well as scenarios for various films. His playwrighting underwent a very real sea-change when he traveled abroad in the Mexican foreign service. His present work reflects an encounter with the techniques of modern European theater, such as the Berliner Ensemble. In 1966 Sr. Carballido enjoyed a great success with *I Too Speak of the Rose.* It is an epic drama with expressionist controls that explores human possibilities from political, psychological, moral, and metaphysical points of view. All of this seems ponderous, but quite the opposite is the case. More recently his play *Medusa,* a contemporary interpretation of the Perseus myth, was chosen as the main theatrical offering in Mexico City during the period of the Olympics. It was my pleasure to direct the first production of this play for the Latin American Festival of the Arts at Cornell University.

The Day They Let the Lions Loose won first prize in the Havana Congress of the Arts held yearly by the Casa de las Americas and was produced in Havana in 1963. Perhaps more clearly than in *I Too Speak of the Rose* one can detect in this play the influence of European and Oriental techniques on Emilio Carballido's craftsmanship. This reworking of the Cinderella story is a delightfully serious frolic that indicts the authoritarian and dogmatic pattern of Mexican education, the plight of woman in the Latin American familial structure, the national inability to recognize and effectively reward the Latin American artist, the thingification of all life by an outworn and inhibitive culture. We all deplore revolution and the factors that make it necessary, but in *The Day They Let the Lions Loose* Carballido has given us one of the most charming interpretations of revolution that I have read. Despite this charm, I respect him for not having falsified the issues that contribute to repression and revolutionary aggression.

During a recent conversation with Sr. Carballido I was surprised and not a little amused to discover that he was not at all aware of the similarities between his plot and that of the Cinderella story. I see this not as a sign of critical naiveté in Sr. Carballido's work but, rather, as proof of his genuine narrative gift, his very real jongleuristic talent.

CHARACTERS:

The Aunt	*Two Birds*
The Neighbor	*Two Bears*
Ana	*Two Lions*
The Man	*The Woman*
The Teacher	*Policemen*
The Young Girl	*Passerby*
Godínez	*The Photographer*
López Vélez, Gerardo	*The Police Lieutenant*
Ten or Twenty Boys	*The Woman's Two Sons*
Two Monkeys	

In the woods of Chapultepec and its environs, autumn, 1957.

NOTES ON SCENERY AND PRODUCTION

The designer should invent scenery that is enormously eloquent and simple. The use of a revolving stage is unnecessary and is, furthermore, obviated by the large spaces required for the various scenes. In the scene on the island, however, the trees must create a mysterious and intimate space.

The cat is not real; it is mysterious but must never be a live cat.

The swan must be exaggeratedly delicate and poetic—reminiscent of Pavlova and Tchaikovsky.

Flies should be used for changes. Various borders of painted trees can be dropped in and taken out. The backdrop should be a cyclorama of blue curtains. The practical tree should be executed with great simplicity and there should be some sort of ladder at the back of it.

The lions should be played by two actors per lion, so that they will be large enough. Their cages should be on dollies.

*Changes from scene to scene can be made with light or blackouts;
a curtain should never be used.*

*As for the projections necessary for the interlude, "A Day With
The Lions," the ideal thing would be a animated color cartoon. Almost
perfect would be a color film made by the actors themselves. The
interlude can also be done with slides drawn or photographed in color.*

*The nautical battle on the lake is handled by having six policemen
cross the stage at the end of the previous scene on their way to the
lake; each one holds the end of a wide band of blue cloth. This is done
while the child and the loudspeaker are disappearing. These long
strips of cloth extend from one side of the stage to the other and are
undulated constantly to represent the water. The boats have holes for
the legs of the occupants and hang from suspenders around their
shoulders. Tie-ropes are necessary for the removal of these boats,
which are overturned. Also, they must be designed in a way that
permits the occupant to get out of the boat with ease.*

*The lights should be strong and unreal and violently colored—not
general lighting. However, there should never be any difficulty in
seeing the figures and faces of the actors.*

*The actress who plays the Neighbor should keep in mind that the
character is genuinely fond of the Aunt; if the thought ever crossed
her mind that she might inherit the home, it was an idle thought, of
secondary importance.*

ACT ONE

SCENE ONE

*A room with a balcony. The Aunt is in bed and the Neighbor stands
at the foot of the bed.*

AUNT: Oh! Oh!

NEIGHBOR: Does it hurt much?

AUNT: The pain is terrible! It runs up my back, then it grabs me
around the shoulders, after that it digs into my joints, and when it

goes away for a bit it comes back around my heart! And when it goes away for a while I feel such a pounding in my temples! It leaves me soaking in a cold sweat.

NEIGHBOR: That's a most unusual pain.

AUNT: And I've been suffering from it for fourteen years. Anita!

ANA'S VOICE (*off stage*): It's almost ready!

AUNT: My throat's already dry and if you don't bring me that tea in a hurry my palpitations will start again!

NEIGHBOR: They can say what they want about dandelion tea, camomile tea, or even tea made out of holy grass, but as far as I'm concerned there's nothing to compare with the iguana root. One of my uncles was dying of asthma and it cured him, like that!

AUNT: But I don't have asthma!

NEIGHBOR: And I've had a pain here ever since my fifth one. It wouldn't go away until I started taking iguana root. Blessed be the remedy! There's nothing like iguana root!

AUNT: Anita!

NEIGHBOR: I know she's there; I can hear her talking.

AUNT: There's something wrong with that girl. She's always talking to herself.

NEIGHBOR: I had to walk the third one to the school bus to keep him from breaking the glasses of the sixth one. He's so rambunctious, that one.

AUNT: I can hear him screaming over here when you spank him.

NEIGHBOR: Oh, the one who screams is the fourth one. I have to tie him up—and he screams—just to bother me.

AUNT: One of these days the rats are going to eat him up.

NEIGHBOR: No, they'll bite him, but they won't eat him.

AUNT: The sun is coming up behind that potted plant, that means it's seven o'clock.

(*Sound of a child screaming.*)

NEIGHBOR: Listen to him scream! Fat good it will do him, I'm staying right here.

(*Sound of bells from a distance.*)

AUNT: Ana, they're calling for second mass. She's deaf! She won't

answer! And now the sun's going to hit my eyes! Draw the blinds
for me, will you, dear?

NEIGHBOR: Of course, it's a pleasure.

SCENE TWO

(*The kitchen. Ana is petting a cat.*)

ANA: Nice kitty—but dirty kitty. A tassel full of ashes, that's what you
are! When I touch you, my fingers turn gray. Your paws are cold.
The fire in the oven must be low. At any moment now my aunt is
going to scream for her tea, and then she'll want me to go to mass
—since she can't go. The neighbor brings her so many different
kinds of herbs and teas. I don't know how she knows so many:
chicken grass, doe's weed, iguana root! I wonder why there's so
many herbs with animal names.

AUNT'S VOICE (*offstage*): Anita!

ANA: It's almost ready! Last night a lady cat came howling for you—
three colors, and blue eyes! But you're too little to have a sweetheart. After mass I'm going to market. You be very quiet while
I'm gone because if my aunt finds you she'll throw you into the
street. There's your cinderbox so you won't mess up the oven.
Remember, no noise. How could you live in the street? You've got
to grow up first so you can be a great big cat and fight them all—
fight off all the other cats, never let them take your sweetheart
away.

AUNT'S VOICE (*offstage*): Anita!

ANA: I won't answer her. Her tea's almost ready anyway. Oh, how I'd
love *not* to go to market. The women who sell vegetables say such
awful things! And that man who peddles cheese, and his wife! I
really don't think people are the way they say. Who knows? But
even if they are, they shouldn't scream it that way from one side
of the street to the other. You're not going to turn into one of those
awful cats that goes around howling and doing terrible things on
the rooftops, are you? Though—I wouldn't want to keep you from
doing anything you wanted . . .

(*Sound of the child screaming.*)

The neighbor's oldest child has such a dirty mouth, sometimes I hear him scream such things! Oh, my, such things! Filthy words, and all the rest! He's not screaming at anyone in particular; he's all alone, in the center of the patio, screaming for hours just for the fun of it!

(*Sound of the bells in the distance.*)

AUNT'S VOICE: Anita! They're calling for the second mass.

ANA: Oh, that tea is taking forever to boil. It must be very hard to live the way those people do. I never could, never wanted to, really. Well, I didn't want to very much. It's been so long. I remember once, a long time ago . . . You forget things for so many years, ten—twenty—forty years, swallowed in smoke. Then the wind blows and there they are again. One morning I woke up and I remembered, just as clear, the brick floor at home. I hadn't learned to walk yet, I must have been, oh, no more than two. And that was sixty-five years ago, nowadays I forget things that just happened, but I remember others that happened so long ago. Yesterday I remembered to buy scraps for you but I forgot the chicken for my aunt. (*The tea boils over.*) I don't know why I forgot it, because I like chicken very much. It's a pity she never has any left over. I'd love to eat chicken every day. On the other hand, she doesn't like it any more. I'm off to church now. You be good and don't cry, and try not to get your tail dirty.

(*The Aunt enters.*)

AUNT: Ana, that's a cat!

(*Ana cries out and retreats, hugging the animal to her.*)

No wonder. (*She goes to the stove*). I thought you were dead. There I was, waiting for my tea, and nothing! What's the girl doing all this time? She's playing with a cat! Who owns that animal?

ANA: It's a very clean cat.

AUNT: With all that hair? Ana, whose cat is that? Don't you lie to me.

ANA: He doesn't do anything. He was so tiny and they left him outside.

AUNT: You mean to say that cat has lived in my house?

ANA: He doesn't make any mess or anything. Look how pretty he is.

AUNT: Give him here. (*She pulls the cat away from Ana.*)

ANA: Oh! You are going to hurt him!

AUNT: No wonder the whole house stinks of pee with that little beast going around piddling on everything. Help, he's scratching me! (*The Neighbor comes in.*)

NEIGHBOR: What's happening?

AUNT: This animal has been here all the time and I didn't know about it!

NEIGHBOR: What a big cat, and how fat!

ANA: Give me my cat!

AUNT: That's all we needed! Don't you scratch me, you beast, or I'll twist your neck off.

ANA: He doesn't scratch. He's very good. Let him be!

AUNT: And let me catch my death of asthma?

NEIGHBOR: Oh, that's very true, cats cause asthma.

AUNT: Do me a favor, take it away and get rid of it! Throw it out!

ANA: Throw it out? But he's so tiny.

NEIGHBOR: Now, Anita, if you don't mind my saying so, these animals do cause asthma and they steal things. Why, one of these days he might bite your aunt and then the wound would become infected, God forbid! I'll take it away. Cat bites are very dangerous. Your poor aunt, God forbid!

AUNT: Oh, yes, dear, please get rid of it—because this woman doesn't care about me! I don't matter at all! Even though I brought her up as though she were my very own daughter. Ungrateful girl! (*The Neighbor goes out with the cat.*)

ANA: Where are you taking it?

AUNT: Where do you think you're going? You stay here! You stand still there, do you hear me?

ANA: Tell her to bring it back! You should be in bed, not wandering around like this. You'll get sick—but when it comes to spying on me, you're not sick at all!

AUNT: Throw it away! Far away! Where are you going? I told you to stay here.

ANA: Go and lie down! Why can't I have a pet if I want it? I'm not a little girl any longer. What harm has it done you?

AUNT: Don't scream in my ears. (*She goes out.*)

ANA: It's a clean little cat. Auntie, let me keep the kitten. When you

die I won't feel anything. There won't be anybody in the world
who'll miss you. I won't miss you one bit and I'm going to fill the
house with cats, and I'm going to put them on your bed so they
can pee on it! Oh, I wish I were dead! Auntie, let me keep the cat!
Let me have that kitten! (*She hesitates for a moment and then goes
out.*)

SCENE THREE

*Music. Chapultepec, at the edge of the lake. Early morning light,
mist; a swan goes by, from left to right; somebody whistles a long
tune, leaves fall, footsteps. Ana enters.*

ANA: It's cold and so damp. She came this way, I saw her—but then
I lost her in the trees. She ties up her son and leaves him all alone,
and now she's going to kill my cat! If I'd gotten pneumonia it
would serve her right! I'm going to cry. (*She cries*). It was such a
pretty cat. (*She cries.*) I wonder how many people have drowned
in this lake. (*She cries and sighs.*) Oh, after a while you learn to
put up with anything. (*She sighs.*) The woods seem deserted.
Smells like a river. (*Sounds of ducks.*) I wish I had some bread. I
could feed the ducks. (*The Man, very poorly dressed, rises from
among the bushes.*)

MAN: You could give the bread to me. The ducks are fat and well fed.
I'm not.

ANA: Oh!

MAN: I don't often ask for help, Madam. As a poet said, there are
certain birds that can cross the swamp and never soil their feathers.
My plumage is of that sort. I spent the night under the stars and
have come to sun myself a bit, but as you can see, there's no sun.
And now it's time for me to have some coffee—hot coffee!

ANA: I haven't had any coffee either.

MAN: Well, I wasn't referring to you, but ah . . . haven't you had
breakfast either?

ANA: No.

MAN (*disappointed*): Oh. Well, no one seems to come by here. If
you want to find something, you'd do better at the embarcadero.

You'd better get a move on. (*He goes back to his place.*)

ANA: What happened? Where is he? What are you doing in there? You're going to get sick. It's very damp in there. (*The Man coughs.*) You see? You've already got a cough!

MAN (*rising once more and coughing*): Hard work is hard on one.

ANA: Work?

MAN: Of course. It's still a bit early, but later in the morning the bushes are full of lovers. They stretch out here and there and everywhere! Then all of a sudden I show myself and preach a sermon. They like it so much they pay me money!

ANA: That's strange work.

MAN: It helps me to eat a little better and sleep a little better from time to time. Did they take you to jail?

ANA: Me? Why?

MAN: I wondered where you spent the night, you're so neat.

ANA: At home, of course.

MAN: Home? Then what are you doing here?

ANA: They took my ... nothing. It's time to go to mass.

MAN: Forgive me, but then are you going to have breakfast—later?

ANA: No, I'm not going back home.

MAN: No? Pity. I'd like a little something warm.

ANA: If there were some food hereabouts ...

MAN: There isn't.

ANA: If there were a fire I could make you some eucalyptus tea. Whose tin can is this?

MAN: Mine.

ANA: Bring over some eucalyptus branches. Eucalyptus is very good for a cough, and it tastes nice. You go gather wood.

MAN: But it's all wet. (*They start searching together.*)

ANA: These branches aren't so wet, and there's another one over there. (*She laughs.*) Let's see if we can't fix breakfast. (*They gather the branches downstage.*)

MAN: Eucalyptus tea! There's always something new. (*He looks up at a branch of the tree.*)

ANA: Oh, but that's not eucalyptus. This tin can is very dirty. (*She rinses it out; the swan goes by again, from left to right.*)

MAN: "Take the swan of deceptive plummage—and wring its lovely neck . . ."

ANA: Who, me?

MAN: No, I'm simply quoting a poet.

ANA: At home my sister Rosa used to kill the chickens. Then, later, my aunt taught me to kill them—and clean them.

MAN: I know how to kill chickens. (*He pantomimes the process.*) But I don't know how to clean them.

ANA: Some people people like dark meat but I prefer white.

MAN: So do I.

ANA: Well, it's a young swan; you can tell by its beak—and it's fat, too. (*They look at each other; the swan pecks a few grains of corn.*)

MAN: And you haven't eaten either . . . (*He smiles.*)

ANA: No.

MAN: Excuse me. (*The swan goes off, the Man follows it. Silence. Then the hideous cries of a bird. Silence.*)

ANA: I never did believe those stories about swan songs. (*She dries the tin can with her skirt, and goes off.*)

SCENE FOUR

The cages at the zoo. On stage can be seen the gorillas, a few exotic birds, the bears, and the lions, a pair of them. All is calm. Then the Teacher enters. He is young and dressed in a white uniform.

TEACHER: Hup, two, three, four. Hup, two, three, four, now keep in step, two, three, four! (*The Teacher is followed by ten or twenty students, who come marching on two by two, arranged by height and military ensignias. The animals become very excited; they roar and make ferocious noises. Then later on they simply look about and observe.*)

Class, halt! Now, right face! In your place! At rest! Now let me see—Godínez, one step forward, march! Now let me hear what you know about these animals.

GODÍNEZ: Well, this is a . . . a . . .

TEACHER: Why are you squirming about that way? (*The other boys laugh.*) Keep your military bearing. Now, let me hear what you know about those animals.

GODÍNEZ: Well—they're monkeys. (*The others laugh.*)

TEACHER: Silence! Simian anthropoids, not monkeys. The classification . . . the classification!

GODÍNEZ: Well, you see . . . they were easy to pick out in the book, but these are for real, and that makes it kind of hard to tell.

TEACHER: "Real," not "for real"! And a zoo is just like a book! And nature is just like a zoo! All it needs are bars. And here it is now, all before you—with bars. Now tell me what these animals are.

GODÍNEZ: Anthropoid apes.

TEACHER: And what is the meaning of anthropoid?

GODÍNEZ: Well, they are kind of like men.

TEACHER: Correct. The zoological scale is perfectly graduated and it ends with the rational animals—men. You are an animal. (*Laughter.*) Silence. I am an animal. (*More laughter.*) Who laughed? One step forward. You, I saw you laugh. One step forward, march! Your name?

BOY WHO STEPPED FORWARD: López Vélez, Gerardo.

TEACHER: Now, let's see, López, tell me just why you think you're not an animal.

LÓPEZ VÉLEZ: Oh, no, I'm an animal, all right.

TEACHER: Then why did you laugh?

LÓPEZ VÉLEZ: Well, because I don't have any . . . ah . . . any classification . . . or my oh, my, ah . . .

TEACHER: You are a homo sapiens, a mammiferous vertebrate. The particular facts of your life are on file in the civil register and the archives of the school. At this moment you are undergoing a process of domestication but you will be locked up into a cage at the first sign of bestiality. In school, in the laboratories, and in the offices of the government we know all that it is possible to know about you and your relatives and, for that matter, all beings on the zoological ladder.

LÓPEZ VÉLEZ: My father told me that no one knows anything about anything. That everything is really quite strange.

(*The Young Girl, who is rather plain, comes on stage.*)

TEACHER: How is that? Please explain.

LÓPEZ VÉLEZ: Well, that babies are born the way they are . . . well, kind of by chance . . . you know, with two eyes, and two ears, and everything in its place . . . and no one seems to know why.

TEACHER: By chance! Everything that happens in this world is clear and intelligible!

LÓPEZ VÉLEZ: My father says that no one really knows why. And that it wouldn't be very strange if from one moment to the next we'd turn into tadpoles, or into lions, or that something else would be born instead of children.

TEACHER: Would you be so kind as to tell your father he's talking nonsense. (*Laughter.*) Everything has been foreseen and everything is known. I myself could explain everything . . . (*The Young Girl coughs. The Teacher turns and sees her.*) Attention! López, one step backward. March! Batallion, about face. March! Parade rest! (*He approaches the Young Girl.*)

YOUNG GIRL: I love the way you give orders. (*He caresses her.*) I'm not interrupting you, am I?

TEACHER: No, no, no, of course not!

YOUNG GIRL: Can we sit down?

TEACHER: The bench is dirty.

YOUNG GIRL: A little.

TEACHER: You sit down. My uniform is white.

YOUNG GIRL: It would be nice to know things like you know.

TEACHER: That depends. The more people you know, the more difficult it is to keep order. Look at them! Within a year they'll be studying Greek roots and Latin roots; and then it will be all the more difficult to make them keep in step. But the moment they learn psychology, there's no holding them! The ideal system would be to keep them from learning what they don't need to know.

YOUNG GIRL: How handsome you look!

TEACHER: The uniform suits me, doesn't it?

YOUNG GIRL: Is it true you know everything?

TEACHER: Well, almost everything. All that's needed.

YOUNG GIRL: I've been trying on my dress for the dance. It's very pretty.

TEACHER: You're wearing a little too much rouge.

YOUNG GIRL: No, it's the heat.

TEACHER: Tomorrow they're going to issue us dress uniforms.

YOUNG GIRL: Oh, how wonderful, how wonderful!

TEACHER: It's nice working for an institution like this. Everything one could need—and discipline, to boot!

YOUNG GIRL: When we get married, will you get a raise?

TEACHER: Certainly.

YOUNG GIRL: Oh, wonderful!

(*One of the birds throws something at her.*)

TEACHER: What was that?

YOUNG GIRL: I don't know. Oh!

(*The gorilla throws something at her.*)

TEACHER: It was one of the monkeys! I saw it! (*He throws a stone at the gorilla and the animals retaliate with a rain of shit and garbage.*) Here, here, behind this tree!

(*The boys scream and throw things at the animals.*)

You there, attention! Attention! Don't break your ranks.

ONE OF THE CHILDREN: But they're throwing things. They're throwing shit!

TEACHER: Take it, like men!

YOUNG GIRL: Are you coming tomorrow?

TEACHER: With another class. At the same time.

YOUNG GIRL: I'm going now. Oh, dear me!

(*This time it was López Vélez, Gerardo, who threw.*)

TEACHER: I think it was the monkeys.

YOUNG BOY CORPORAL: It was López, lieutenant.

TEACHER: Oh! Well, then, till tomorrow at the same time! (*He kisses her. The Young Girl goes off, waving good-bye. The Teacher returns to the children.*) Attention! Right face!

CORPORAL: It was López, lieutenant. And what's more, he said his father wasn't stupid and that you were! He's got a slingshot!

TEACHER: Well, take it away from him, disarm him.

(*The Corporal goes to take the slingshot away from López Vélez, who in turn gives him a push.*)

López, two steps forward. March! Did you hear me? Two steps forward! March! If you don't obey me, I'll make you. I said, two steps forward! March!

(*López Vélez backs away and runs off.*)

López! Remember that this is a military academy! You're deserting! That's treason!

(*López Vélez, Gerardo, is behind the lion cage. The Teacher goes for him. Some of the students, spurred on by the example of López Vélez, throw things at the beasts, who become excited and return their fire. The Teacher approaches López Vélez, and López Vélez opens the lion cage. The beasts roar and escape. The Teacher retreats, screaming.*) Attention! Attention! About face! Double time, march! (*He runs off.*) (*The children see that the lions are loose, and run off screaming. We now have the dance of the liberated lions, supported by a chorus of the other animals.*)

SCENE FIVE

By the edge of the lake. Ana and the Man have made a fire and are roasting the swan. There are white feathers on the ground.

ANA: May I use your knife, please? (*She tests the swan.*) It's not done yet.

MAN: Rare meat is better for you.

ANA: I stuffed it with laurel leaves. It's a pity we don't have any salt.

MAN: Oh, that's very poetic: the swan, and laurel leaves . . . You know, if we'd had some banana leaves, we could have barbecued the thing.

ANA: I'd settle for a little salt.

(*Two boys enter running.*)

ONE BOY: The lion, sir! The lion!

THE OTHER: They're coming!

(*There are roars off stage; the boys run away screaming.*)

MAN: I think it's done now.

ANA: Those boys were just playing tricks. (*She tastes the swan.*) We could also use a little bread.

(A lady enters with a little basket over her arm. She is screaming, and faints).

MAN: Look, Ana. That lady's sick. You keep turning the swan. Ma'am. Ma'am. Oh, dear me, let me see, maybe if we gave her some tea or if we sprinkled water on her face.

(Roars offstage.)

She's got bread in her basket and salt and lots of other things too.

(The lions enter. The Man climbs a tree. Ana retreats as she sees them approach.)

Climb the tree!

ANA: I don't know how.

MAN: Neither do I!

(Ana hides behind a tree. The lions dance and roar. They see the Woman lying on the ground. The Woman wakes up, screams, and faints once more. They approach the swan and sniff it.)

ANA: Shoo! Shoo! You, animals! Leave that swan alone!

MAN: They're going to eat it!

ANA: Well, throw something at them.

(The Man throws some branches at the lions.)

MAN: They're going to eat it! Get rid of them! Get rid of them!

ANA: Shoo! Get away from here! Shoo! Off with you! Off with you! *(She leaves her hiding place and goes towards one of the lions and hits it. The lion raises its paw and swats at her. She retreats, screaming and covers her face.)* Oh my, oh my, oh my. *(She looks at the lion.)* He didn't bite me! *(The lions move toward the swooning woman.)* Oh, but now they're going to eat the lady. Oh you animals, go away! *(She pulls them off and makes them back away from the Woman.)* Now, gently does it, gently, gently! You just lie there. That's right, be nice little kittens and lie there. Dear mother of God, they're not biting me. They are just the nicest little kitty-cats, just as nice as could be! *(She scratches their necks. The lions stretch like kittens and obey her.)* There, there, there. Now you be gentle; you be quiet now, calm down . . . you're pushing me around too much! Oh, my, such rough little pets!

(The Woman comes to.)

WOMAN: What time is it?

MAN: It must be around nine o'clock.

WOMAN: Oh! There they are!

ANA: Don't be afraid. They won't harm anyone. (*She goes to the swan.*) The swan's done now. Ma'am, would you mind lending us your salt?

WOMAN (*hysterical*): I never go out! Never! My two sons are married now and I've been a widow for years. But today I wanted to go for a little picnic in the woods...

ANA: There, there, now, don't cry. They're not going to hurt you. Let me have your buns so that I can feed them. May I use your salt? Come over and join us. I will give you some tea. (*She serves it to the Woman; then she calls to the Man.*) Aren't you going to come down? Breakfast is ready.

(*The Man climbs down very cautiously. Ana sets out breakfast. The lions stretch out at her feet. The Man sits down and waits for his plate.*)

END OF ACT ONE

(BLACKOUT)

As soon as the blackout is complete, one sees the projections: the first one reads

MUSICAL INTERLUDE:
A DAY WITH THE LIONS

NUMBER ONE: Autumn leaves.

NUMBER TWO: The Woman's empty basket, and the bones of the swan, and the tails of the lions.

NUMBER THREE: A bandstand.

NUMBER FOUR: Discarded music stands; sheet music; dented and broken instruments; in front, the manes and the ears of the lions, as well as Ana's hands holding them back.

NUMBER FIVE: The peacocks.

NUMBER SIX: Place where the peacocks had been, full of feathers and bones.

NUMBER SEVEN: A hot dog stand.

NUMBER EIGHT: The same hot dog stand with all the merchandise in total disorder, half eaten by lions and humans.

NUMBER NINE: The lion tails, forming an X; beneath, the Man's feet, Ana's feet, and those of the Woman, in a semi-circle, their toes pointed upward. (We hear the melody that the Man likes to whistle.)

NUMBER TEN: Yellow branches against a blue sky.

NUMBER ELEVEN: More autumn shrubbery.

NUMBER TWELVE: Wild and beautiful view of the woods of Chapultepec.

NUMBER THIRTEEN: Several shots of autumn trees.

(The Man yawns, the Woman yawns, the lions roar, the humans giggle. We hear a loud roll on the drums, as in a circus.)

NUMBER FOURTEEN: There is a rapid pan from above to bars outside the park. (We hear a police siren.)

NUMBER FIFTEEN: We see six, seven, eight shots of police weapons. All of them from different angles but aimed toward the woods.

NUMBER SIXTEEN: A slow pan from within the woods of the bars surrounding the park. They bristle with weapons, all pointed in toward the woods.

NUMBER SEVENTEEN: A sign that reads "Danger!—the woods are surrounded by the police—they will attack at any moment."

(The projections are over, but the music continues, having changed in character so that it becomes the music that introduces the next act, which should begin without any interruption.)

ACT TWO

SCENE ONE

Siren sounds. Percussive music. The fence and gates around Chapultepec. There is a cordon of policemen. People pass by, stop to look at the commotion, and are then moved on by the police.

A WOMAN: What's happening?

FIRST POLICEMAN: On your way, lady, on your way.

ANOTHER WOMAN: They must be making a movie.

ONE OF THE PASSERSBY: Let's get out of here. The lions have escaped.

FIRST WOMAN: You see, you can never tell what's going to happen in a park.

SECOND WOMAN: It's a good thing they've got bars around the park.

(*They go off. The Neighbor comes in, running.*)

NEIGHBOR: Excuse me, sir.

SECOND POLICEMAN: Where do you think you're going?

NEIGHBOR: There's a lady in there and I've got to give her a message.

SECOND POLICEMAN: Impossible!

NEIGHBOR: And why, pray tell?

SECOND POLICEMAN: The lions are loose.

NEIGHBOR: I must see this lady. I have a very important message.

SECOND POLICEMAN (*shoving her*): On with you, on with you! Move on!

(*The Teacher enters. He is pushing the large tower of loudspeakers. It is crowned with four speakers.*)

TEACHER (*speaking into a microphone*): Attention, everyone! Stay away from the woods of Chapultepec. The lions are loose. The government will pay a large reward to anyone who captures them, dead or alive. There is also a small recompense for anyone who turns in the young deserter from the military grade school. This deserter must be tried by martial law. Any civilian willing to help in this dangerous mission will earn the eternal gratitude of his country.

(*While the Teacher is speaking, the Neighbor, who had moved on a few steps, takes advantage of the shift in attention and sneaks into the woods, behind the backs of the policemen. The Teacher finishes his announcement and goes off. He can be heard as he moves off: "Attention! Attention! Stay away from the woods of Chapultepec: the lions are loose . . ." A police lieutenant enters. They all salute him.*)

LIEUTENANT: Attention! We have just received new orders from headquarters. We are to organize a giant hunt through the entire woods. We must capture those lions dead or alive before dark.

(*Some of the boys come running terrified out of the woods. They are captured.*)

ONE OF THE POLICEMEN: Call the teacher!

(*The Teacher comes running on with his tower.*)

POLICEMAN: Is it one of these?

TEACHER: No. Attention! Where have you been all this time? Why didn't you come out before?

ONE OF THE BOYS: When you ran off, we got lost.

TEACHER: I did not run off! I led the retreat. Where's your classmate? The deserter? Have you seen him? Well? Why don't you answer?

ONE OF THE BOYS (*lying*): No, we haven't seen him.

TEACHER: I don't believe you. Arrest them!

LIEUTENANT: What do you mean, arrest them? Who are you to give orders?

TEACHER: Here are my credentials. They are refusing to denounce an enemy of the state.

LIEUTENANT: These aren't credentials. This is a transfer ticket for a streetcar.

TEACHER: A transfer? What do you mean?

LIEUTENANT: Let's see if you can identify yourself.

POLICEMAN: Yes, let's see if you can identify yourself.

(*The Teacher looks in all his pockets.*)

TEACHER: This is highly irregular! You are a civil authority, and I am military!

LIEUTENANT: We'll see about that. Keep an eye on him. Attention! Advance!

(*The rest of the policemen walk off into the woods. While the Teacher looks through his pockets, the boys go off.*)

TEACHER: Ah, here it is, here are my credentials! Here they are! Wait for me! (*He and the policeman go running off after the rest. The Teacher stops short, runs back for his tower, and then goes off with it.*)

SCENE TWO

A clearing in the woods. The bench and some swings. Thrown on the ground, an organ grinder's organ, an organ grinder's hat and stick. The Woman comes on.

WOMAN: Of course, you couldn't know this, but I'd never come to the
woods by myself before. My parents used to bring me, or my
parents and my sweetheart, or my husband, and then I used to
bring my boys—but like this today? A whole day alone in the
woods? Never. I always have so much to do—clothes to wash, iron-
ing, food to cook, oh, of course I listen to the radio, sometimes I
read, but not often. My boys kept me so busy. But now that they're
married, they don't need me as much. My daughters-in-law are so
stupid. There's nothing like a mother. It's just that sometimes—
haven't you felt suddenly that . . . that there's something missing?
I have so many things to do every day of my life. I take care of the
house all by myself and every day I do so many things—just as I
will do them again the next day, and the next, and the next. And
then, all of a sudden, I feel as though all my life long I have never
done a thing, not a thing, and then I have a terrible need to look
for something, something to do. So I buy plants and take care of
them. I have pots all over the place. They're lovely, all of them in
bloom. I've got canaries, too. And they sing a lot. But then I have
to water the plants every day. And I wash the birdcages. And when
night comes, I'm exhausted. And I still feel as though all my life
long I have done nothing. Tell me, haven't you ever felt that way,
ever? Oh, dear me, here I am, talking to myself. It's dark. The
trees are purple. The sky is violet. (*She sits in a swing and rocks
back and forth.*)
(*Ana and the Man enter. They are pushing food-vending carts of
aluminum and glass, with little lights inside.*)
ANA: We found these carts and they were full of all kinds of good
things to eat.
MAN: But the lions ate them all.
WOMAN: Where are the lions?
ANA: Playing on the merry-go-round.
WOMAN: You left me alone talking to myself.
MAN: You shouldn't have given it all to the lions.
ANA: Don't complain—you ate more than your share!
WOMAN: Those little carts don't give off much light. When it gets dark

this way, you start thinking things and get sad. When I'm at home, at this time of day—I'm always alone. I go about the house and turn all the lights on.

ANA: I see a lot of lights over there but I don't know how to turn them on.

MAN: I know. (*He goes off, left.*)

WOMAN: Do you want to swing with me?

ANA: Yes, a little. (*She sits on one of the swings.*)

WOMAN: In that black dress I can barely make you out. Are you in mourning?

ANA: Almost always. If it isn't one relative, it's another. I wore mourning for six years for my parents; for my sister, three. Aunts, uncles, nephews, and nieces, two years each. Six months for first cousins; and for close friends of the family, three months. I've gotten used to black.

WOMAN: Oh, don't talk to me about dead people! You die and you haven't done anything. You have children; you bring them up and they get married on you; and is that what you wanted to do with your life?

ANA: I never got married.

(*Lights come on, stage left. They whirl about in the patterns of the fairground spectacle. The Man comes back.*)

MAN: That's a little livelier, isn't it?

WOMAN: I don't like it when the shadows move around like that.

MAN: What we need is a little music.

ANA: There's a little barrel organ over there.

MAN: That's just what we need. But it doesn't sound loud when you play it on the ground.

(*He puts it on top of the bench. The Man starts playing the barrel organ; and the lions come in, excited and moving about nervously.*)

WOMAN: Look at your lions, what's wrong with them?

ANA: Music affects them that way sometimes. When my sister used to play the piano, she played it very well, all the pets around the house used to get very excited: the canaries sang and the dogs went around the house from one side to the other. Sometimes she played things they didn't like, and then they paid no attention. There are a couple of pieces that made the dogs howl, the way they do when the moon comes up or when someone dies.

MAN: If the lady would play for a while, we could dance, you and I. Would you do me the honor?

ANA: Oh, dear me, I don't know how to dance.

WOMAN: I love to dance.

MAN: Then if you would be so kind as to, ah . . . play for us? (*Ana takes the handle of the barrel organ. The man and woman dance.*)

WOMAN: Didn't you ever go to dances?

ANA: What was that?

WOMAN (*over the music*): I said, didn't you ever go to dances?

ANA (*replying over the music*): Oh, yes, I went to dances, but I sat in the corner all the time because my aunt wouldn't let me dance. I used to sit talking with the old women. But I did dance once! Oh, I can see it as though it were yesterday. Such a handsome boy! Such a nice boy! He asked me to dance and I said yes, in spite of the fact that my aunt pinched me and hissed at me. "You just wait, you'll see," but I went out and danced anyway. I was very pretty then. Oh, the poor boy, the way I stepped on his feet! But he put up with me for that whole dance.

WOMAN (*over the music*): I don't like these waltzes. I was best at the Charleston. (*The lions jump and move about without necessarily turning their movements into a dance.*)

WOMAN: My husband couldn't dance. I never danced after I was married. And then after I became a widow I was too old.

(*Shouts in the distance. The lions roar.*)

ANA: Oh, my God! (*Silence.*)

MAN: They're hunting the lions.

WOMAN: Oh, you beasts, go away,

ANA: Oh, the poor dears; let them be!

MAN: Let's leave them here and go away.

ANA: Leave them here? (*The lions roar and rub up against Ana. Sounds of sirens and shots.*)

MAN: Well, you're certainly not going to take them with you.

ANA: But how can we leave them? Oh, you poor little things, why did God make you so large?

TEACHER (*speaking over the loudspeakers, from a distance*): Attention! Attention! We have discovered the remains of a roasted swan. Considering the fact that it is impossible for lions to light a fire, we have come to the conclusion that they are accompanied by several accomplices.

LIEUTENANT (*speaking from a loudspeaker some distance away*): A reward for anyone who captures the lions, alive or dead.

WOMAN: You mean to say they think we're accomplices? Oh, I don't believe it.

MAN: I don't think a swan is such a serious matter. Oh, come on, lady, leave those lions and let's get out of here.

ANA: Oh, you poor little animals! They can't kill them; I won't let them!

TEACHER (*speaking through the loudspeaker some distance away*): We continue to find signs of destruction caused by the lions. Two food peddlers report the loss of their carts and all of their merchandise. The keepers of the grounds report the death of one swan and two peacocks.

MAN: The musicians haven't said anything yet, have they?

ANA: No, not yet.

TEACHER (*speaking through the loudspeaker*): All damages and their corresponding fines will be served upon the accomplices. Any person who has contact with these lions and does not denounce them will be considered an accomplice!

WOMAN: Oh, but that's not fair. We haven't met anyone we could denounce them to! He's no right to go around accusing lions. (*Sounds of several shots.*)

ANA: What are they shooting at?

MAN: The lions—and us!

ANA: But that can't be!

(*Sounds of sirens. They are caught in the beam of a searchlight.*)

WOMAN: They're coming from that side!

ANA: And from over there, too!

MAN: Let's go to the lake.

WOMAN: Oh, it's awfully dark. We'll get lost. (*The lions roar; she screams.*) Oh, be quiet, animals, be quiet!

MAN: Let's go; and please be as quiet as possible.

WOMAN: It's time for supper. My boys will be coming home and there won't be anything to eat. My daughters-in-law have gone off to the doctor—or so they say, but I think they go to the movies! The kitchen must be dark and cold, and no one is listening to the radio in the living room. I might just as well be dead!

MAN: Will you please shut up!

ANA: Come along, now, and quiet, very quiet . . .

(*They move off with the lions in tow. We hear the silence and see the beams of the searchlights. López Vélez enters cautiously. He comes in from left. The Neighbor enters from upstage.*)

NEIGHBOR: Anita! It's all so deserted. Beasts and bullets and search-lights . . . Praise the Lord and fill my soul with joy . . . Anita (*She is about to go off.*) Boy, little boy, listen to me!

(*The boy López Vélez runs to her.*)

LÓPEZ VÉLEZ: Lady, you know how to get out of here?

NEIGHBOR: Of course. There are walks all over the place. Have you seen a little lady in black?

LÓPEZ VÉLEZ: No.

NEIGHBOR: Oh, dear, I don't know what to do. What were you doing here riding the merry-go-round all by yourself?

LÓPEZ VÉLEZ: Well, it was running, and . . .

(*A shot very close, and from the distance the roar of a lion. There is a sound of shattering glass and the light in one of the food-vending carts goes out.*)

Are you coming with me?

NEIGHBOR: I can't, you go on.

(*More shots. The boy goes off.*)

Praise the Lord and fill my soul with joy! (*And she goes off after the boy.*)

(*The police enter, slowly, as though closing in on something. More sirens and searchlight beams. We have the dance of the police cordon. One of the policemen empties his revolver in the direction of the merry-go-round and fair, bringing about a blackout except for the light of the food-vending carts.*)

LOUDSPEAKER OFFSTAGE: Attention, attention, the fugitives have been sighted heading for the lake. Watch all rowboats, sailboats, and launches.

(*The police go upstage. There are shots offstage as they end the dance.*)

VOICES OFFSTAGE: We wounded one of them! He fell somewhere around here.

VOICE OFFSTAGE: Pick him up, pick him up! Be careful! Be careful!

(*Some policemen back on, looking offstage. We hear the voice of the Lieutenant offstage.*)

LIEUTENANT: Now look what you've done. Can't you tell the difference between a lion and a human being?

THE VOICE: Let's get him to the light. Get him to the light! It looks serious.

(*Policemen enter, carrying the Teacher.*)

A POLICEMAN: Who shot him?

ANOTHER POLICEMAN: Who knows?

ANOTHER: Lay him on the ground.

TEACHER: Not on the ground! My uniform will get dirty.

POLICEMAN: It's already stained in three places.

ANOTHER: Don't tell him. Put him . . .

ANOTHER: Well, where will we put him?

ANOTHER: Put him on the swing.

(*The Teacher is placed on the swing, and he rocks back and forth in pain.*)

TEACHER: I don't understand anything. Everything seems so strange.

(*He dies. Two or three policemen take off their helmets. The siren sounds once more.*)

CURTAIN.

END OF ACT TWO

ACT THREE

SCENE ONE

Music: a nocturne. An island in the middle of the lake. Nighttime.

*The sound of ducks. A small fire. The Woman and the lions are
sleeping next to the fire; Ana and the Man are awake. Silence.*
ANA (*singing softly*):

> If you marry a soldier,
> will you be happy
> marching by his side . . .
> will you be happy
> marching at his side . . .
> The hour is coming,
> the trumpets are calling,
> the drummers are drumming,
> pán, paran, pán, paran, pán!
> And what of you, my dear, what of you?
> You stay home and cry
> over and over and over again.
> Good-bye, good-bye, good-bye!

(*Another silence.*) I've forgotten the rest of it. Mother used to sing
it. She was a tiny woman, dark, with hair that came down to the
small of her back. Died in 1899, and I felt so bad about it, because
she always wanted to see the new century. "The twentieth century
is going to be marvelous!" she used to say. But I don't think she
knew what a century was.

MAN: There are some people who see the birth of a century and there
are others who see its death. I was born after the century started
and I'm not going to see it end. It's just like comets: some people
are born between comets and they never see one.

ANA: I saw a comet once. It trailed halfway across the sky. I remember
it clearly.

MAN: There are always people who are born in between great periods.
They see the world get sick and waste away. They see the end of
things without ever seeing the beginning. It's sad.

ANA: Well, I'm not sure when a period begins and when one ends.

MAN: One never does know; until it's over—much later. And then the
period is measured from the death of someone, or the time when
someone said something, or the publication of some book or other.

·

ANA: I never understood any of those things. I haven't read much. My aunt is very careful about what books are brought into the house. She reads them all and decides which ones are good ones and which ones are bad.

MAN: Why?

ANA: To keep my soul from sickness.

MAN: I suppose her soul is very healthy.

ANA: I don't know.

MAN: Oh, that's the way it goes. I've written many things but I never did what I wanted to do.

ANA: I've heard that they never let poets work.

MAN: No, no, no, you've got it all wrong. *I* didn't *want* to work! I wasn't one of those "immortal poets," as they say. I just knew how to improvise verses at weddings and birthday parties. I used to make up all kinds of wonderful verses for Independence Day. They were so good I had everybody in tears. I'd make my money and then I'd go on to another party. I was always surrounded by firecrackers and flags and bells. Once I won a golden flower—pure gold! I pawned it to buy champagne. That's the kind of poet I was; and everybody cried with joy at the things I spoke. One time I even improvised for Amado Nervo. You know him?

ANA: No, I don't believe I do.

MAN: An immortal poet, a real bard! It was a great party. He came up and hugged me and said that I had the real spark, right here! He pointed with his finger right here! He said I had the spark! Everybody heard him: the other poets who were not as good and all the important men—gathered together in the heat of poetry and wine! And because of that they made me a secretary of the exchequer. Imagine giving a farm to a tribe of gypsies, or what's worse, forcing those gypsies to *work* that farm. Since then I've had several jobs— and I've been in jail.

ANA: In jail?

MAN: There were so many people who wanted to help me! And then one of them decided that—for my own good—I should be treated more severely.

ANA: How can that be?

MAN: Well, it's all true. That kind of thing happens!

ANA: My aunt used to say you always kill the thing you love. She thought that would cheer me up. "A young girl's future is simply charged with promises!" she used to say. And I said, "And now? Now, today?" But she was always thinking of my future. Even now she has a townhouse that she says will be mine—when she dies. If at least I had been able to learn what I wanted. I never really did know much about my body—or why I dreamed. I never traveled; I never met all the people I wanted to meet or saw any of the places I wanted to see.

MAN: Well, I've been able to travel and I've been able to read—I haven't always been able to eat.

ANA: I've always eaten.

(*One of the lions rumbles and growls.*)

MAN: What's wrong with him?

ANA: He's having a dream.

MAN: Isn't that strange. I wonder what lions dream about.

ANA: That's simple. They dream smells and movements. They dream the feeling of the leap or the way meat feels between their teeth.

MAN: How do you know?

ANA: I used to have a cat and we knew each other very well.

MAN: What did the cat think of you?

ANA: What *we* think about each other. That's to say, he didn't think. I was a combination of smells and sizes and feelings that were at his disposal. He used to look at me in little bits; never all at once. When I think things, I think words. I talk inside. *He* used to think in very strong reactions, attractions, repulsions, his way of living was like a great warmth.

MAN: But I don't see any difference. We think that way.

ANA: No, we don't.

MAN: Tell me, then, just how do you think we govern ourselves?

ANA: Well, there are officers and the president. I don't rightly know. That is to say, I do know, but . . .

MAN: You know it in detail, but not all at once.

ANA: That's right.

MAN: You see.

ANA: But not everyone is like me. Or are they?

(*The lions get up and roar.*)

MAN: Now what?

ANA: They heard something..

MAN: I wish I could hear the way they do—nothing: silence.

(*The lions roar, then move upstage.*)

ANA: You're right. There's so many things we can't hear or see . . .

(*The lions growl toward the left, then the front, then the right.*)

MAN: There must be something circling the island. Did you know that there are machines that hear better than any lion or any ten lions?

ANA: Machines for listening?

MAN: And for seeing too.

ANA: And they see and hear everything?

MAN: No, actually they see and hear very little. In a way they're just about as deaf and blind as we are. There, now! I heard a splash.

ANA: I can't hear a thing.

(*There are more splashes. The lions roar.*)

ANA: You're right. There's someone there.

(*The Woman screams and wakes up. She begins to cry.*)

MAN: Don't cry. What's the matter?

WOMAN: I had such a sad dream!

A VOICE FROM THE DISTANCE: Anita!

ANA: That was my name!

MAN: Don't be afraid. I heard it too.

ANA: It came from over there.

MAN: It's someone calling from the lake.

(*They cross through the bushes to the edge of the lake and look out. The rowboat enters up left. In it are López Vélez and the Neighbor.*)

NEIGHBOR: Stop rowing and be quiet. Anita!

ANA: Who's calling me?

NEIGHBOR: There she is! Anita, what's the matter with you? Your aunt is waiting for you. You've got the poor woman's soul hanging from a thread.

ANA: Who told you we were here?

NEIGHBOR: This little boy saw you get in the boat. He came and told me. He said, "They ought to be on the island by now." And you see, here you are. Quite frankly, I don't know what you're doing here. If it hadn't been for me, your aunt wouldn't have eaten anything; the poor thing would have starved. She told me not to come to look for you, but I thought to myself, "Now, how can I help it?" Because, after all, your aunt has gotten much worse, with all this excitement, of course. And so I came to tell you anyway. Come go with us.

ANA: No.

NEIGHBOR: What do you mean, "No"? You can't just leave your aunt that way. Who's that with you? A man?

(*A lion comes up next to Ana. The Neighbor screams. The lion roars.*)

NEIGHBOR: Start rowing, little boy! Faster!

(*López Vélez and the Neighbor leave.*)

MAN: Are you really never going to go home?

ANA: Never.

MAN: Why?

ANA: I don't know.

MAN: Don't you?

ANA: This day has been unlike any other day in my life and I want more days like it. I'd hate it if this were the only one. I'm so old and I've learned things today. I can learn more things! What on earth would I do at home after today?

MAN: What on earth will you do out here?

ANA: The woman is still crying. (*They go back to the fire. Ana pats the Woman on the shoulder.*)

WOMAN: I had such a sad dream. I dreamt I was in a dress shop and there were lots of lovely dresses with feathers and furs; and there were uniforms and swimming suits of all styles. But I wanted something else. Then suddenly I saw a housecoat and an apron. They were lovely! But they turned out to be the housecoat I wear around the house and the apron I wear in my kitchen. I liked them so! And I had to fight and fight and fight because they wanted to throw them away.

ANA: Did they give them to you?

WOMAN: When I left I had them with me.

ANA: Then what are you crying about?

WOMAN: It's just that it was very sad. And then came something worse . . . I was dead and my sons were crying for me—they were very sad; they were crying! They missed me terribly. I wanted to devote the rest of my life to them, but it was too late! I was dead! Oh, I want to go home!

MAN: You can't go home. Go to sleep.

(*Sound of a siren.*)

WOMAN: Oh, there goes that siren again. What am I doing here? I'm cold and it's late. How will I ever get back? How did I get on this island? All I did was to go for a little picnic in the park, and . . .

MAN: One never knows when the lions will be let loose.

WOMAN: I want to go home!

ANA: Well, go!

WOMAN: You're right; I have to go. Oh, my boys, I'm coming, my boys! (*She goes off running.*)

MAN: You think she'll try to swim it?

ANA: No, she'll probably take the rowboat.

MAN: She can't! She doesn't know how to row, and if she took the boat *we* couldn't get off. (*We hear the splashes of the oars.*)

ANA: Look, she knows how to row now.

SCENE TWO

The edge of the lake. We see the tower of loadspeakers. Bright lights; reflections from the water. There is a body on a stretcher. The Young Girl enters.

YOUNG GIRL: I'm here. I had to change my dress. I feel more comfortable this way, in black. My mother's crying. She keeps saying that you were such a good catch. Daddy brought me here. I'm suffering so. Our children would have been handsome, just like you, and they would have studied under you at your school. And now they won't even be orphans: they were never born. And some noisy family is going to move into the house we would have rented and they're going to break the windows and tear the curtains.

Every day I tried to be more orderly and more serious just to please you. We would have been so happy. You don't know how I'm suffering. Tomorrow there will be someone new at the school to take your place; and he'll teach the boys just as you did. They'll pay him your salary and they'll give him all your attendance lists. I was the only one to whom you were indispensable! I suffer and suffer. Even though I love you very much, I wish I were suffering less. They say that after a while you get numb and you don't realize things. But I know you're here, stretched out. I saw your face and you were very handsome, as white as your sweater, dead . . . dead. Crying wasn't difficult for me. I cry and cry. My eyes are sore from so much crying. I'm not as upset now. But for a while there I banged my head against the floor and scratched the ground because I suffered so—because I *suffer* so. See my tears? Hear me sob? But now I'm beginning to feel a little better. (*She cries and listens to herself.*) They say it's good to cry this way.

(*The Photographer and a policeman come on. The Photographer takes a flash picture of the corpse and the Young Girl.*)

PHOTOGRAPHER: And this one?

POLICEMAN: Killed by the lions.

PHOTOGRAPHER: Someone told me he was shot three times.

POLICEMAN: I don't know anything about that. Have you spoken to the chief of police?

PHOTOGRAPHER: Yes.

POLICEMAN: So?

PHOTOGRAPHER: He was killed by the lions.

(*The stretcher bearers come on. They remove the corpse. The Young Girl follows them off, sobbing. The Photographer takes another flash picture. The Photographer and the policeman move off. The lights move about. A group of policemen come on. Two of them are carrying the Woman, others lead the boy López Vélez and the Neighbor.*)

LÓPEZ VÉLEZ: You must give her artificial respiration.

(*They do so.*)

WOMAN: Oh, oh, oh . . .

NEIGHBOR: She's coming to.

LÓPEZ VÉLEZ: I saved her.

POLICEMAN: What were you two doing on the lake?

NEIGHBOR: The woman was drowning. And the boy jumped in the water and pulled her out.

(*The Photographer returns.*)

WOMAN: I've got to go home. All this is going to make me sick. My ribs have turned to ice and I feel dirty all over.

POLICEMAN: What were you doing in the water?

WOMAN: I fell out of the rowboat.

LÓPEZ VÉLEZ: Then I saved her.

(*The Photographer takes another flash picture.*)

NEIGHBOR: You stay here and explain everything. I'll be back in a moment. (*She goes off.*)

ANOTHER POLICEMAN: Is that woman your mother?

LÓPEZ VÉLEZS No.

POLICEMAN: No?

LÓPEZ VÉLEZ: Neither is this one. (*There is a whistle. The boy continues talking*). That one was looking for a little old lady and this one was escaping from the lions.

POLICEMAN: Where are the lions?

LÓPEZ VÉLEZ: Over there, on the island.

(*More whistles. Silence and running footsteps. The policemen run on. There are lights in all directions.*)

LIEUTENANT (*through the loudspeaker*): Attention. Attention. Prepare to attack the island. On your guard, check your weapons. The lions are on the island.

(*The Photographer takes several pictures of López Vélez.*)

SCENE THREE

The island. The leaves fall. Ana and the Man are poking the fire.

MAN: Aren't you sleepy?

ANA: No. I often suffer from insomnia, and then I just count the hours or say my rosary. Sometimes I just sit there and remember things and cry.

MAN: I have always slept very well. The dawn is cold.

ANA: I'm usually getting up at this hour.

MAN: I want to improvise a poem for you. You see . . . Do you like poetry?

ANA: I don't know poetry. Oh, maybe one or two poems. But I like it.

MAN: Poetry! A poem forces us to see how beautiful everything is, by comparing things, and with rhyme and meter one describes everything and shows it off . . . you'll see:

> The sky pales into remoteness
> and the dew is of crystalline pearl.

ANA: Remoteness, does that mean "far"?

MAN: I guess so. It's a word . . . rather . . . well, that's the way I say it.

ANA: Oh.

MAN: The sky blanches in the distance.

ANA: Blanches?

MAN: Yes.

ANA: I thought you said "pales" before.

MAN: Blanches is better!

ANA: Oh.

MAN: The sky pales . . . the sky . . . well, it doesn't matter. Pales or blanches, it's going to be dawn anyway. It smells of ducks and lions. On the edge of the lake it smells of rotting leaves. I listen to the trees and a leaf falls against my face, it's yellow and covered with cold sweat, like a dying man. The lake splashes all by itself against the island, on the shore. It stirs up the vapors of the night, and puffs them about quietly. It gives off a sad mist, very sad, as though it were full of drowned men. And the sky is faded at the edges like an old shell. The air seems to hang there and oscillate, white and cold, like a new-washed sheet. And that's dawn for those of us who wander without windows or doors. I'd like to make a nice poem for you, but I'm not in the mood—I can't think of anything.

ANA: What a pity. Let's make some tea.

MAN: That's a good idea.

ANA: How are we going to get off the island?

MAN: Later on, the students come to row on the lake. They'll take us off.

ANA: The fire's going out again. (*She revives it.*) What time do the students get here?

MAN: When the sun's up. I hope that's not too late.

ANA: What's the hurry?

MAN: I don't know. I've a feeling we should get off as soon as possible. Is this a eucalyptus?

ANA: No, it's a pine. (*She starts fixing the tea.*) It won't be long now before they start calling for mass. At home I can hear the bells very clearly—and then my aunt begins screaming for her tea.

MAN: There'll be no one to make tea for her now.

ANA: No. (*She laughs.*) Nor breakfast! (*She laughs, and then is silent.*) You know what, I don't think she ever liked me.

MAN: That's possible.

ANA: I think she just wanted to boss me, and use me. And I believed her—while thousands, millions of people, the whole world, were going around doing what they wanted, at every moment, without waiting for permission, or thinking about their future.

MAN: That's what you think. There are millions of men and women who sacrifice everything, and carefully construct the future of mankind, which others will enjoy two hundred years from now.

ANA: But, in the meantime, what have *they* got?

MAN: Very little, but something. They eat; they work; they wait—and they're afraid.

ANA: But who guarantees them what's to come after?

MAN: Oh, the leaders do that.

ANA: And do they let them travel and read?

MAN: If they find it convenient.

ANA: I can't imagine so many people living that way.

MAN: Neither can they, but don't knock it. I got my freedom, only to be alone, to suffer and go hungry.

ANA: I'm hungry too, but it's an old hunger, the hunger of wanting to know things I never could. The hunger not to be watched . . . of reading whatever I want to read, knowing what I should know. The hunger to wear indecent clothes and to paint my wrinkles with rouge. A hunger for so many other things. Above all, the things which I don't know about.

MAN: My hunger comes from the gut. My guts have been dry, full of wind and noise—and I have cried because my feet hurt so.

ANA: But, that's what you wanted.

MAN: I suppose.

ANA: I didn't want my aunt.

MAN: You're right. In spite of what they say, we're all of us responsible for our parents, our relatives, and our leaders. *We're* to blame for them.

ANA: Perhaps. It seems so to me now. Right now I feel responsible for everything.

MAN: The tea's boiling over.

ANA: Well, take it off the fire!

(*The Man takes it off the fire and pours it.*)

MAN: There's still some sugar left in the basket.

ANA: See how easy it is! Now why didn't I talk to her that way? Why?

MAN: It's hard to say no. When you say no, you're being disobedient, and you may lose something: your candy allowance, your life, a certain percentage, a job . . .

ANA: But I lost so much always saying yes.

MAN: Was your aunt spiritual, idealistic, and catholic?

ANA: Yes.

MAN: Then she made you lose your body and part of your soul! There are some people who lose the opposite, they've got a stomach, they do sports in the fresh air and they proclaim that man is a physical being, all matter, et cetera, et cetera. They don't bother with questions of sex, of course, much less questions of the spirit, complicated things. Others, my kind, believe that being a man or woman is really a question of sex; that it gives us appetites and that we are creatures of division and duality, labyrinths of thought, inspiration, spirit . . . But oh, my stomach! And that's how it goes for everyone: we are all surgeons and butchers, always amputating some limb, or mental plane, or gesture.

ANA: All of us? What do you mean?

MAN: Aunts, governments, leaders, theories—some do it because they're idiots, others do it for profit.

ANA: Profit?

MAN: It's easier to master half men. Complete men are not submissive.
(*The lions wake up and roar.*)

ANA: Sh, sh, sh. Don't roar, my dears, don't roar.
(*The lions are restless. They go to the Man and smell him and lick him. They place a paw on his shoulder and push him over.*)

MAN: Hey, now! Wait a minute! What do you want? Your pets are getting too friendly there! Sh . . . hey, go away, you'd better get back.

ANA: What are you doing? Back with you! Back with you! And you, too!
(*The lions roar, and they obey reluctantly.*)

ANA: They're hungry.

MAN: Hungry! (*He moves back.*) We've got to get out of here in a hurry.

ANA: Don't be afraid.

MAN: Look at them. They're angry.

ANA: Down, down, down! (*She pats them.*)

MAN: Look at the way they look at me!

ANA: They're very gentle.

MAN: So was I when I was working, until the day came when I stole two typewriters because I couldn't stand it any longer without inviting my friends to supper. And so were you with your aunt. Look at those eyes!
(*The lions roar. They begin to sniff at Ana.*)

ANA: Now, why are you smelling me like that? You be careful now, down, down . . .
(*A lion raises a paw toward her.*)
Now, you be good, you understand?
(*The lions roar. Ana takes a stick and hits them. They roar and retreat. Then they lie down, docilely.*)
I hit them! (*A pause.*) You're right. We've got to get out of here.

SCENE FOUR

Edge of the lake. Day is breaking. The policeman is asleep, leaning against the tower of loudspeakers; he holds a microphone in his hand. We hear the sounds of static. The Woman is wrapped in a

policeman's overcoat; López Vélez is also wrapped in a policeman's
overcoat.

WOMAN: Pretty soon now they'll be bringing your father and mother
—and my boys too.

LÓPEZ VÉLEZ: Yes.

WOMAN: I'm so happy they're going to give you a medal.

LÓPEZ VÉLEZ: They award them in front of the whole school! And
the principal makes a speech.

WOMAN: Was it very difficult to save me?

LOPÉZ VÉLEZ: Not really, you were screaming a lot, but you were
walking on the bottom.

WOMAN: I was? But the water was over my head!

LÓPEZ VÉLEZ: Only when you fell down.

(The Woman's sons enter.)

SONS: Mama! Mama!

WOMAN: My boys! My boys!

(The three of them sob.)

THE THREE OF THEM: Mama, Mama!—My boys! My boys!

ONE SON: Mama, you're going to be a grandmother.

OTHER SON: My wife is going to have a baby, too!

FIRST SON: But mine was first!

WOMAN: My sons! My boys!

(The three of them leave.)

LÓPEZ VÉLEZ: I hope my father and mother get here soon.

SCENE FIVE

The center of the lake. Music: "The Prelude to the Nautical Battle."
The sun is coming up. The rowboats of the police rock in the water.

LOUDSPEAKER *(offstage)*: Attention, attention, we continue to wait
for orders from the chief. Be ready to attack at any moment.

(The policemen pay no attention. Some of them take off their
helmets. Others splash their neighbors with the oars. They laugh
and play; some of them race each other, and others applaud the
racers and whistle. There is silence. Then calm. The rowboats rock
back and forth, while the policeman whistles a song. Some of them
undo their neckties and loosen their collars. They row about in

circles, enjoying themselves. The battle begins suddenly with the entrance of the lions, who come on roaring as they swim and bound about. Ana clings to the neck of one of the lions and the Man clings to the other one. Shots are fired. One of the rowboats turns over. The lions roar and overturn another one. Two rowboats try to block the way of the lions, Ana, and the Man—the lions sink them. There are screams and splashings. The lions, Ana, and the Man emerge from the other side of the lake. Confusion. Some of the policemen are drowning, others are trying to rescue them.)

LOUDSPEAKER *(offstage)*: Attention. Make ready to capture the lions. Orders have just come from headquarters. We are about to invade the island!

SCENE SIX

Avenue of the Poets. Dance of the chase. The lions enter, dragging the Man and Ana.

ANA *(screaming)*: I can't run anymore, I just can't! *(She sits on a bench.)* I can't.

(Bullets are fired offstage. The policemen appear cautiously, they move on. The Man runs from one poet's bust to another, hiding. The policemen chase the Man and the lions. They come and go, in hot pursuit and rapid flight. In the meantime, Ana sits in the foreground, arranging her hair and squeezing the water out of her skirts.)

A POLICEMAN *(entering)*: Careful, now, there are lions about.

ANOTHER POLICEMAN: Didn't you hear them roar?

(Ana nods and points offstage. Whistles blow. All of them run in that direction. The Man and the lions return and they drag Ana off.)

ANA: No, no. Where are we going?

MAN: I don't know. Into the streets!

ANA: It's impossible. We would never make it! And anyway, what would we do in the streets?

MAN: Roar! We'd roar until the end!

(The lions roar.)

ANA: We don't have to do anything. I want to go on living and I want the lions to go on living.

MAN: There's no other way. All the roads are blocked.

ANA: Then let's go to the cages!

(*They run off. The policemen come back, firing into the air. They hunt around and then go off after the lions.*)

SCENE SEVEN

The cages. The animals are screaming and very excited. The policemen run out everywhere.

A POLICEMAN (*screaming*): They're coming this way. Get ready! Aim to kill!

(*The lions come on. The policemen fire and kill each other. Ana comes on; she is barely able to keep up with the lions.*)

ANA: To the cage! To the cage!

(*The lions enter the cage. Ana follows them and closes the cage door after her. The Man comes on, trying to arrange his clothing. He must have fallen somewhere.*)

LIEUTENANT: Now we've got them. Surround them! All of you, fire!

ANA: I dare you, you cowards! Sissies! We're in the cage. What more do you want? Go ahead, shoot to kill!

MAN (*beating at the door of the cage*): Let me in! You've locked me out! Let me in!

ANA: Go on, shoot! But you're going to have to kill me first.

POLICEMAN: Shall we shoot?

ANA: What's wrong—are you afraid? Go on! Why don't you shoot? (*The Photographer comes on and takes a picture.*)

POLICEMAN: And you? What are you doing at the door?

MAN: Closing it. I captured the lions. I did! I captured them!

ANA: Why do they look at us that way? They're afraid of us, aren't they?

POLICEMAN: Here's the man who captured them. (*The Photographer takes pictures of him.*)

ANA: One of these days you'll all be in cages while we lions run around loose, roaring through the streets. One of these days you'll see!

*(All of the animals roar and shout and throw things. The Pho-
tographer takes another picture. The policemen are uncertain
whether to shoot or not. Closing music: "March of the Captured
Lions." We see on a drop either painted or projected the pages of
a newspaper with enormous headlines: "The escaped lions are
captured." A photograph of Ana, roaring and clutching to the bars
of the cage: "The old woman who became a lion." A photograph
of López Vélez: "Boy hero." A photograph of the Man: "Winner
of large reward for capturing the lions." The newspaper disappears and we see the title: EPILOGUE.)*

SCENE EIGHT

*The cages. Ana is sitting on the floor of the lion cage, knitting.
There are several bones strewn about the cage. She is somewhat
disheveled. Standing outside the cage is the Neighbor. The lions
look at her with disapproval.*

NEIGHBOR *(drying her eyes)*: The poor thing died talking of you. I
kept promising her that you would come. She lived on in the hope
that you'd come to her.

ANA: Whatever for? So she could hit me?

NEIGHBOR: You're right—she always was quick-tempered. "Ana,"
she'd say, "she'll come." But you didn't.

ANA: I don't go out very much.

NEIGHBOR: I became very fond of her, the poor dear. I brought her
all her meals and stayed with her at night. And I arranged for the
burial. When all is said and done, how insignificant we are! *(She
weeps.)*

ANA: What did you do with your children while you were taking care
of my aunt?

NEIGHBOR: I tied them up. You know how it is, with me they have to
stay on the straight and narrow. But you don't have to thank me.
I know what it means to be a good neighbor. Your poor aunt. Well,
anyway, you got the house. She left me this shawl. Oh, you don't
know how much I miss her. We understood each other so well!

ANA: Don't just stand there. Why don't you come in and sit down?

NEIGHBOR: You're not serious.

(*Ana laughs.*)

Sometimes I think you haven't any feelings at all. Good-bye, Anita.
(*She cries.*) Oh, what would your aunt say if she saw you with
those lions? (*She goes off.*)

ANA: Good-bye, you old bitch. What right does she have to cry for my
aunt? When I think that I spent my whole life with that old woman
. . . I suppose it's only natural that she missed me. On the other
hand, *I* feel a large emptiness. Something frightening has happened to me. I wish I could cry and say, "Oh, my aunt, my little
aunt." But the neighbor cried for her already. It doesn't matter
any more—and I have you.

(*The Man approaches the cage. He is wearing a uniform and wields
a broom.*)

MAN: Well said.

ANA: Have they given you your reward yet?

MAN: No. I have all kinds of forms to fill out, signatures, and then I
have to go and have my picture taken again.

ANA: Do they pay you well?

MAN: They gave me an advance, but I believe they're going to give
me my first check soon. I've eaten well and it's warm in my little
booth. I'm not young any longer.

ANA: Beware of typewriters.

MAN: There aren't any here.

(*The Woman comes on and nods to them from a distance. She's
pushing a double stroller.*)

WOMAN (*softly to the children*): Look over there, children. I spent
a whole day with those lions. Do you see them? Wave, wave to
them, that's right! (*She goes off pushing the double stroller.*)

MAN: Are you comfortable?

ANA: I'm always comfortable. How's the mother bear?

MAN: Quite well.

ANA: And the baby bear?

MAN: Big and fat.

ANA: I'm knitting this sweater for him, look.

MAN: The ostrich is nesting, and the orangutang is pregnant. You know, I used to feel the seasons change in my veins—but not any longer. I do like to see them, though, the animals—they feel the earth turn, they seem to be part of the seasons . . .

ANA: I saw a bit of newspaper the other day that said they're expecting a comet.

MAN: When?

ANA: It was only part of a newspaper. It didn't have a date or anything. And it didn't say when.

(*The boys enter marching. They are led by another teacher. The animals start to scream and throw things. Ana joins them. The lions roar.*)

ANA: Hup, two, three, four! Hup, two, three, four! Stupid children! Idiot boys! (*She throws things at them and roars. One of the boys throws something at her. She hurls a bone at the boy and hits him.*)

TEACHER: Attention, halt!

MAN: You hate those boys.

ANA: Oh, no! They're wonderful! I love them very much. I'd like to play with them. But I scream and roar at them so they'll learn. Do you think they know why I roar at them?

MAN: Not now. Perhaps later.

ANA: Good. You beasts! You worms! You idiots! (*Her voice is drowned out by the animals. The drop comes down with the words* THE END *written on it. And we hear the last bars of "March of the Captured Lions."*)

The Camp

A PLAY IN TWO ACTS AND FIVE SCENES

BY GRISELDA GAMBARO

Griselda Gambaro of Argentina is both a playwright and a prize-winning novelist. She has traveled extensively in the United States and in Europe. Miss Gambaro is without doubt one of the most exciting surprises that I encountered in my search for viable Latin American plays and playwrights. When I met her the first time I was impressed by her gentleness and intelligence. Her gentle disposition in no way prepared me for the quality of her plays. Upon reading them for the first time I was stunned by their brutality and vigor, their economy of means, and their cruel, almost Strindbergian assessment of life. Miss Gambaro shows promise of becoming one of the most powerful playwrights in Latin America. Her plays tend to be free of folkloric limitations. She is certainly as strong a writer as many of the best young playwrights in current European theater. Another of Miss Gambaro's plays, *The Siamese Twins*, is, like *The Camp*, a relentless investigation of aggression and submission, of love and hatred, of dependence and independence. Some indication of the international focus that Miss Gambaro gives to her plays is to be discerned in her amusing suggestions that the song heard in *The Camp* be altered to suit the audience for which it is translated. "What is needed is something utterly corny. I recommend that you use 'Oh Susanna.' " *The Camp* was produced in Buenos Aires in 1967. Miss Gambaro's works have been translated into Portuguese, French, and Italian.

CHARACTERS:

Martin
Frank
Emma
The Piano Tuner
A Group of Gestapo Officers
A Group of Prisoners
An Official
Three Male Nurses

ACT ONE

SCENE ONE

A room with shiny white walls. All furniture is on stage left: a desk, an armchair, and a chair. There is a wastebasket. Two doors: the one left leads to the outside, the one right leads to the interior. There is a window upstage. After a moment the door left opens and we hear someone speaking politely.

VOICE OF SERVANT: Please step in. You can leave your bags here. He will be with you immediately.
(Martin enters. He wears an overcoat, gloves, and a scarf. He removes the gloves and scarf and puts them on top of the desk. He sits in the chair. His movements are deliberate and calm. He reaches into his pocket, takes out a pack of gum, and puts some in his mouth. We hear the gabble of children, mixed strangely with harsh

and authoritative orders. All we understand of these orders is the vague counting: "One, two! One, two!" Beneath this sound there seems to exist a kind of groan that drags itself out subterraneously. It almost seems an illusion. Martin gets to his feet and listens, still chewing his gum. He then looks at the bare surface of the desk, which is broken only by an intercom device. He pushes one of the buttons and we hear a bit of soporific, well-scrubbed music. He smiles and pushes the button once again. The music stops and so does the sound outside. He sits down. We hear someone running down the corridor outside and a voice somewhere between fury and laughter screams: "Run! But not that way, not that way!" We hear, very close, the barking and growling of fierce dogs, as though they were attacking someone. The door opens for a second and is slammed shut. Silence. Martin crosses to the door and opens it. He looks outside. He sees nothing, shrugs, and closes the door once more. He picks up his scarf and gloves from the desk and puts them into the pocket of his overcoat. He is about to remove his overcoat when the door right opens and Frank enters. He wears a splendid Gestapo uniform and carries a whip that is fixed to his wrist. It is a long braided leather whip of the sort the Gestapo used. In spite of this, there seems to be nothing threatening about his demeanor. He is a young man and his face is almost kind. He enters with a busy and troubled air. His arms are so full of papers and files that he has difficulty holding on to them. Some of them fall to the floor.)

FRANK (*grumbling good-humoredly as he picks up the papers*): These kids, these kids! Absolutely wild! (*He puts the papers and files on top of the desk. Quite naturally, he takes the whip from his wrist and pushes it with his foot underneath the desk. He extends his hand to Martin.*) Well, here I am at last. How have you been? Did I keep you waiting?

MARTIN (*looking at him in amazement*): No.

FRANK (*kneeling down to pick up some more papers from the floor*): Take off your overcoat. (*Martin gets down to help him.*) Oh, no, that's all right. I'm used to it. . . dropping things all the time. I'm so clumsy. (*He unbuttons the collar of his jacket*). Oh, it's hot!

MARTIN (*stooping down to pick up a paper beneath the desk*): Here's another.

FRANK (*pushing the whip away with his foot so that Martin cannot touch it, and speaking dryly*): No, let me.

MARTIN (*irritated*): I'm sorry, I just thought . . .

FRANK (*indicating the papers and grumbling*): It's all like that! A fucking mess! (*He sits in the big chair and indicates that Martin should sit in the small chair on the other side of the desk. Then, very friendly*) Sit down! How are you? Take off your overcoat!

MARTIN (*sitting down*): I'm well, thank you.

FRANK (*without listening to him*): We have marvelous weather. A little cold once in a while. Not too much heat, but the rest of it is ideal! An ideal climate! (*Once more we hear the gabble of children, the orders, and the half-choked groans. Frank pushes a button on the intercom. He speaks in a measured, authoritative, but threatening way.*) I want those kids to shut up. (*The noise stops. He smiles and puts his hands on top of the mountain of papers that has accumulated on the desk.*) Well, this is it, all of it . . . Well, not quite all of it. The books are in the office. (*Then, in a very friendly way to Martin, who has been looking at him half amused and half irritated*) What is it?

MARTIN: Nothing.

FRANK: No, no, no, speak up!

MARTIN: The uniform.

FRANK (*amazed*): They all say the same thing! What a half-assed time we live in.

MARTIN: But why that uniform?

FRANK: What other uniform is there?

MARTIN: I don't follow.

FRANK: I like it. And you damn well better indulge your tastes while you're alive! I don't harm anybody with it. I'm not armed. (*Suddenly, and gruffly*) Jew?

MARTIN (*smiling*): No.

FRANK: Communist?

MARTIN: No. (*He chews his gum; a pause; then he leans toward Frank.*) Tell me, does it matter?

FRANK (*bemused*): What are you doing? Chewing gum? (*Then, to himself, with a shudder of disgust*) What an ugly habit!

MARTIN (*undisturbed*): I smoke less.

FRANK: I chew licorice. (*He opens a drawer in the desk.*) You want some?

MARTIN: No. No, I can't stand it.

FRANK: I can't stand gum.

MARTIN (*still calm*): Is that so? Well, it's not that important. (*He points to the papers on the desk.*) Shall we give these a once-over?

FRANK (*politely*): But you've just come! I'm no slave driver. (*He indicates his jacket.*) This may give you the wrong impression. But really, I'm no slave driver.

MARTIN (*smiles*): Of course not. But having brought the papers, I'd like to give them a look-over.

FRANK (*timidly*): Do you mean it? I mean, you're not just being polite?

MARTIN: No. I'm perfectly all right. The trip wasn't that hard.

FRANK: Fine! (*Then, curtly*) But we can't work if you're going to chew gum. No, I don't think we can. (*Martin spits the gum into the waste basket with an insulting air.*) Thank you, thank you! (*We hear the voices and laughter of children, this time without orders and groans. Frank listens and smiles.*) Listen to those kids! They won't obey. They're playing in the yard. (*Then, with a strange smile*) One of them tried to come in here. (*He laughs, and then, abruptly*) What do you think of Vietnam? You don't mind my asking, do you? I don't give a damn about it.

MARTIN: Neither do I. (*He is fed up.*) Shall we look at the papers?

FRANK: Right. It's a pretty sick mess as far as I'm concerned. (*He sits back in his chair.*) Is it right or wrong? The Americans are strong. They're a great nation. As for the others, well, I don't know anything about them. Do you?

MARTIN (*controlling himself*): No. (*He takes out another piece of gum and puts it in his mouth.*)

FRANK (*looking at Martin and with increasing repugnance*): No one knows anything about them, and that makes it hard to form a clear impression. Now the whole *world* knows the Jews. We know less about the Communists. But there are ways of trapping *them*. It's not so hard. We've read the works of Russian Communists. I've read Gorki! *The Mother.* Now there's a book! O . . . we've read . . . (*He breaks off, having lost his train of thought, because he has been obsessed by Martin's chewing.*) . . . we've read many. (*Unable to stand it any longer, he begs*) Please, don't. (*Martin stops chewing for a moment. Frank resumes his conversation animatedly.*) Now you take the Vietnamese and North Vietnamese. It's all one to me. Who knows them? Who's read anything they've written? What language do they talk? The whole thing's a mess! (*Then, gently*) Could you stop chewing that gum?

MARTIN: It takes my mind off of things.

FRANK (*humble*): Like my conversation?

MARTIN: Oh, no. No!

FRANK: What, then?

MARTIN: I like to get to the heart of things. (*A pause.*) Forgive me. I didn't mean to be rude.

FRANK: Oh, no, no. You're not rude. (*He slams his fist on the desk.*) Right to the point. Straightforward.

MARTIN (*pointing at the papers*): Just what *is* all this? Why hasn't it been compiled?

FRANK (*amused*): Compiled? Screwed up! Royally!

MARTIN: Well, we've got to make a start somewhere. (*He gets up with the intention of examining the papers.*)

FRANK (*stopping him with a gesture*): You just sit there and I'll pass them to you. That's an order. You sit there. (*Martin sits down chewing his gum. Frank walks back to his chair, aimlessly.*) Damn heat! I'm burning up! (*He undoes almost all of the buttons on his jacket.*) Here's a list of the staff . . . personnel, dating from . . . (*He begins to hand a sheet of paper to Martin, but stops and speaks brusquely.*) OK! Spit out that gum!

MARTIN (*reaching for the papers*): If you'll allow me.

FRANK: The accounting is all mixed up. You've got your work cut out for you.

MARTIN: That's why I was hired.

FRANK (*rolling his eyes with envy*): Oh, that's nice of you. (*He puts *the paper back on top of the pile, then speaks slowly and threateningly.*) All right. Spit it out.

MARTIN: What?

FRANK (*pointing to his mouth, and speaking with irritation and authority*): Spit it out! (*Martin is furious, but he spits out the gum. Frank continues brusquely.*) Do you call them Yankees?

MARTIN: No.

FRANK: The North Americans are good writers. I know lots of them. The beatniks, Ferlinghetti, people with guts, lots of courage. But then . . . how many of us can be like that? You're timid, aren't you?

MARTIN (*fed up*): No.

FRANK: All right. But you've got no guts. Take your coat off.

MARTIN: I'm all right as I am.

FRANK (*pleased*): Well, you're not a shit-head. That's good.

(*Martin gets to his feet, and almost as an act of provocation, takes off his overcoat, folds it, and puts it on the free corner of the desk. Without rising, Frank stretches and, as his arm extends, very gently pushes the coat to the floor.*)

MARTIN: What are you doing? (*He picks it up and puts it back on the desk. The minute he drops his guard, Frank pushes it on to the floor again. We hear a peasant song, but it is not a traditional peasant song. It is a song that attempts to be a folk tune. "God, oh God, the work we suffer," et cetera.*)

FRANK: You hear that? We still have peasants! Like in the old days.

MARTIN: May I see?

FRANK (*suspiciously*): What for?

MARTIN: I'm curious.

FRANK (*relenting*): Help yourself. If that's all, I've no objection. (*Martin goes to the window and looks out. Frank questions him as though he already knew his answer.*) What do you see?

MARTIN: Nothing.

FRANK: Judging by their song, they should be underneath our window. There's a road beneath the window. When they sing (*and he sings a portion of the song*) that means they're always underneath the window.

MARTIN (*opening the window wide, so that we hear the portion of the song that Frank has just finished, and looking out*): There's no one there. (*He suppresses his irritation and returns to the desk, pointing to the papers.*) Let's give them a once-over.

FRANK: Of course! (*He pushes a button on the intercom and the song ceases suddenly. He gets up, almost pushes Martin behind the desk, and speaks coldly.*) Now that's your place. Sit down and stay there. (*Then, very politely*) Have I been rude?

MARTIN (*maintaining his self-control*): No.

FRANK (*handing him a file of papers and speaking officially*): These are the taxes we've paid for . . . (*He cannot remember or doesn't know.*) Damn heat! I'm burning up! (*Then reproachfully, to Martin*) You left the window open.

MARTIN (*starting to get up*): I'll close it.

FRANK: No, no. You tend to *your* business . . . The peasants are coming back. (*He looks at his watch.*) They come back in five minutes.

MARTIN: So soon?

FRANK: What do you expect? With all the machines nowadays, working is as easy as farting. (*He makes the gesture and sound of a fart.*) Ppft! and it's all done. They go out into the country, into the fields, out of tradition, just to sing. I can't stand this heat. (*He takes off his jacket and throws it on the desk. Only after he has done so does he turn to Martin and ask with exaggerated politeness*) You don't mind, do you?

MARTIN: No. What have you given me here? It's a pile of children's homework.

FRANK (*amazed*): Children's homework? (*He brings his hand to his mouth.*) I got them mixed up! (*He leans over the desk and, almost violently, snatches away the paper.*) Give it here! (*He stirs about the papers on the desk and laughs.*) My god, what a mess! Just look what things have come to! Children's homework . . . drawings! (*To himself, with a faint smile*) They mixed them up with the homework (*To Martin*) Look at this one. (*He shows him a drawing.*) Nice, isn't it? (*Surprised.*)

MARTIN: Yes, but what's it doing there?

FRANK: Why ask me?

MARTIN (*speaking gently, and slowly, as though his mind were wandering*): I saw a photograph once . . . of children . . . being led to a . . .

FRANK: Were you actually there?

MARTIN (*lost in thought*): I? I saw photographs. Marching children. Their school bags in their hands. Marching as though they were going from class to class.

FRANK (*interrupts him furiously and flings his jacket on the ground*): It's this goddamn rag that put these thoughts in your head! Goddamn shitty rag! (*He kicks it. Then, remorsefully*) Allow yourself a little pleasure like that and half the world starts criticizing. (*He arranges his shirt. Then, dryly*) Well, now I look different. Let's go on. Let's see if we can get to the bottom of this mess. (*And then in reply to a gesture from Martin*) You stay there. (*He searches among the sheets of paper and complains*) Nope . . . nope. That's not right. Nope. Nothing but homework and drawings! (*Then in a friendly tone to Martin*) Just a little patience. A little patience. (*He looks at a sheet of paper.*) Now, this must be a donkey. My God, what heat! Ah! Well, here are some numbers, at least . . . and names. Oh, my boots are killing me. Mind if I take off my boots?

MARTIN: You may do whatever you wish.

FRANK (*offended*): You're being a bit rude, aren't you?

MARTIN: It's just my way. Do as you wish!

FRANK: Oh, no. No, no. Certainly not. It's whatever you say. If it bothers you . . . why, that's it. Forget about it. My feet can go on roasting inside these goddamn boots.

MARTIN: But of course not. It doesn't bother me. Take them off.

FRANK: Good! Well. Now the work. (*He tugs and pushes and pulls at the boots.*) Our discipline is an internal matter . . . but as for appearances, they're rather disordered. Long of hair and short of brain seems to be the order of the day.

MARTIN: Yea, verily. Is this establishment yours? Or are there other owners?

FRANK: You'd like it if there were other owners, wouldn't you?

MARTIN (*shrugging his shoulders*): No. Why?

FRANK: Oh . . . I don't know. In case you didn't find me agreeable.

MARTIN: No. I asked because I wanted to know.

FRANK: Professional curiosity . . . Very well, I'll answer you. A corporation. (*He struggles with his boots.*) I can't get them off! Let me call for . . . (*He raises his hand to push a button on the intercom, but then does not do so.*) No. Damn boots! Oh, don't think they let me do whatever I want. I've always had a quirk about this uniform. I can't hurt anyone . . . disarmed. That's just about it. That's all. (*He manages to take his boots off.*) Oh, my God! You're free, my poor old dogs. That's it . . . pant . . . pant. Enjoy the air. (*He puts his feet on the desk and wiggles them almost under Martin's nose. Martin moves to one side.*) Oh, please don't move. (*He plucks at his stockings, which are made of heavy white wool.*) These stockings are the hottest goddamned things! (*He hands Martin a handful of paper.*) Here! Take these. Find out everything. But don't think I don't realize.

MARTIN (*as he takes the papers*): What?

FRANK: About the uniform. You didn't like it. It's a harmless little quirk.

MARTIN (*looking at the papers*): Why didn't you choose another one?

FRANK: Another one? Why? They're all alike. The only difference is that this one has a history.

MARTIN (*calmly, and without looking up*): And a bloody awful history it was, too!

FRANK (*offended*): Oh, no! Don't tell me you're going to start talking that way too!

MARTIN (*looking at him*): When it's necessary.

FRANK (*stares at Martin; a pause; then suddenly, very pleased*): Quick with the answers! I like that. . . . I'm going to take my socks off. (*He takes them off.*) You don't mind, do you?

MARTIN (*impatiently, and somewhat irritated*): Just what are you doing? Are you going to strip?

FRANK: No. Just my socks. My feet are clean, and I'm not going to wiggle my toes under your nose, if that's what you're afraid of.

MARTIN: I didn't come here to discuss your feet. I came to work.

FRANK (*very pleased*): He talks back! A polemicist! Ve-e-ry good!

(*We hear the song.*) Ah, the song. They're coming back. Go look. Take a look.

MARTIN (*irritated*): I don't feel like it. (*He examines several sheets of paper.*)

FRANK (*going to the window*): What a spectacle! Carrying their hoes and shovels. Ah, tradition . . . it never dies. Come, take a look! (*Martin deposits his papers on the chair and goes to the window.*) They've gone. (*However, we continue to hear the song quite clearly. Martin sniffs the air.*)

FRANK: Smell something? . . . Supper!

MARTIN: Something strange. What is it?

FRANK: Oh, that! There's a garbage dump. Sometimes it catches fire. The children make bonfires. Garbage. Don't ask me why. The dirty things!

MARTIN: Stinks! Why don't you forbid it? Smells of burnt meat.

FRANK: It does. A dead dog in the garbage. . . . a cat . . . children are cruel. Sometimes they're not even dead. (*He closes the window and the song stops. Impatiently*) Well . . . shall we get to work?

MARTIN (*going back to the desk and pointing to the papers*): These papers don't mean a thing. It's a mess!

FRANK (*very happy*): Agreed! You see? What did I tell you! . . . Tell me, how did you come here?

MARTIN: By train.

FRANK: You should have come by car. There are all kinds of lovely drives you could take! The country around here is simply marvelous. Step out of the car and you'll find yourself in another world. You'll be buried in the bucolic . . . pastoral, in the . . . (*The dogs bark fiercely. Frank breaks off and listens intently. Suddenly we hear a noise as of a short circuit of high voltage. Frank runs to the door left. He opens it, looks out, and then closes it, preventing Martin, who has followed him, to see what is going on outside. He laughs.*) It's the children! My! Oh, my! They're shouting again! Look at them climb up the fences! They're hanging by their feet! What shouts!

MARTIN (*reaching for the door*): Let me see!

FRANK: Later! (*A pause. He leans against the door and smiles.*) Later.

SCENE TWO

The desk, the big chair, and the small chair. The papers and files have disappeared. On the opposite side of the stage there is a round table with a white tablecloth at which Martin and Frank sit facing each other. They have just finished eating. Frank is still barefoot and without his jacket. His clothes are where he left them in the previous scene, on the floor. Martin's overcoat is also on the floor.

FRANK: Like I said, we were starved. What are you going to do now?

MARTIN: Oh, I'll take a stroll.

FRANK: Around here? What would you see? And you can't reach the town on foot.

MARTIN (*getting up*): It doesn't matter. I just want to stretch my legs.

FRANK: It's as interesting as a garbage pail. (*He leans forward, confidentially.*) Sit down. I've got a better idea.

MARTIN (*distrustful*): You do?

FRANK: You don't trust me, do you? ... Shit!

MARTIN: I don't understand you.

FRANK: Never mind. Give yourself time. You've had a hard day. God, what a mess! We just let things go, I suppose. We were making money. What did we care about keeping records? (*He laughs.*)

MARTIN: Your staff is absolutely ignorant ... absolutely! One of them couldn't even write. He trembled and made crosses. That's all he could write, crosses.

FRANK (*astounded*): You don't say! You see how incompetent they are? Idiots. But let's not talk about work now. Let me ask you a question. (*He hesitates.*) Are you married?

MARTIN: No.

FRANK: There's some lovely boys around here. (*He laughs.*) Oh, no, no, no ... I didn't mean for that! ... And some beautiful women. (*A pause.*) They won't come near me.

MARTIN: Why?

FRANK: Uniform, I suppose. But now you? That's another matter. You're a handsome man. (*Martin laughs. Frank is disturbed.*) I'm no queer, you understand?

MARTIN: I know.

FRANK: People have such dirty minds. I knock myself out to be agreeable and it's no use. We're having company.

MARTIN: Today? Tonight?

FRANK: You seem surprised. I'm going to go change. (*He picks up his boots, socks, and jacket from the floor. Then with his free hand he picks up Martin's overcoat.*) I'll take your overcoat. (*He drags it across the floor.*)

MARTIN: Don't drag it on the floor!

FRANK: Aren't you the neat one! Enchanting! (*He pauses, and then as if playing a game, he drags it across the floor some more, steps on it, and rubs it into the ground as if he were polishing the floor.*)

MARTIN (*crossing to him*): Pick it up!

FRANK (*stopping after a moment and picking up the overcoat*): Now don't get upset. I'll shake it out for you. (*He shakes out the overcoat and attempts to fold it with his free hand, but all he manages to do is to wrinkle it into a great wad.*) How clumsy of me!

MARTIN (*yanking it away from him*): Let go. I'm going to take a walk.

FRANK: No, no. No walks. I don't want you to get lost. Then I'd have no choice but to go looking for you with the dogs. And besides, I want you to meet the lady. I invited her just for you. We can't stand her up, now, can we?

MARTIN: Who is she? Why don't you let me do what I want?

FRANK: I am just trying to be pleasant. I thought that after a hard day's work, among unfamiliar people, far from home, a woman, Venus, a frivolous element...

MARTIN (*folding his overcoat and placing it on the chair*): On with it.

FRANK (*very politely*): Of course. Immediately. (*Then, solicitously*) Be nice to her. I'll be dressed in a minute.

MARTIN: Who is she?

FRANK: My only friend. We've known each other since childhood, so ... don't think anything of it. I hope you like each other. (*Con-*

spiratorially) Good luck. (*He leaves by the door right, and as he goes, almost by accident, he knocks Martin's overcoat to the floor. Martin is furious. He picks up the overcoat and once more puts it on the chair. Almost immediately the door left opens and Emma lurches in as though she had been pushed in. She stands by the door, frightened and defensive. She is a young woman. Her head is shaved. She wears a prison smock of rough gray cloth. The palm of her right hand is marked by a livid wound. And her face bears the ravages of long suffering. She is barefoot. When Martin turns and looks at her, she straightens up and smiles. She makes a terrible effort, as though she were about to act a role. She advances like a hostess welcoming a guest. Her gestures in no way agree with her appearance. They are the gestures and attitudes of a lady dressed in a party gown. She speaks in a sophisticated and worldly manner. Only upon occasion does her real voice break through, expressing the anguish and desperation of her appearance.*)

EMMA: Oh, please be seated! You are eating! Don't trouble about me. Frank told me the new administrator had come, and I did so want to meet you. How *are* you? (*She extends her hand. Martin is stunned, and does not take her hand. Emma continues, still extending her hand.*) Why don't you greet me? (*Then angrily*) Say hello! (*He takes her hand. Emma continues humbly*) But please don't squeeze. (*She grasps Martin's hand and does not let go of it. Looking at his hand*) What lovely fingers! I'm a pianist, you know. That's why I always look at the fingers. (*She makes a frightened gesture of flirtation.*) I don't please you? (*She laughs and lets go of his hand.*) Sit down! (*She sits down and crosses her legs with an elegant air. There is a painful silence. Martin looks at her. She sits still with ever-increasing tension, as though something were driving her to distraction. She rubs her hands, surreptitiously at first, and then with increasing desperation she begins to scratch her hands, her arms, her whole body. All the while she continues smiling and talking with artificial and mannered high spirits.*) It's not lice, you know. Oh, no, that's not it at all. They've been exterminated from the whole area. (*A pause.*) I just itch all over my body.

I did lie down in the grass to rest. That might be it. The grass is full of little bugs of all kinds. Bugs. Fireflies. Fireflies don't bite, though. They've got a little light on their bodies. Have you seen them? (*Then in a sad voice, and without guile*) The light goes on and off, as though they were calling for help. What help? No one knows. The night goes on, dark and silent, and we look on.

MARTIN (*leaning forward, speaking confidentially and with difficulty*): What help?

EMMA (*returning to her social tone, and continuing to scratch herself*): It's such a nuisance. You see? (*She holds out her arm.*) No lice. And it's such a bore. Just think, when I'm playing the piano at a concert and I can't scratch. (*Then, with a faint smile*) But somehow I seem to play better that way. It increases the tension. I achieve better things. Do you want me to play for you? (*Her scratching becomes more frenzied.*) Why don't you talk to me? I'm not that disagreeable!

MARTIN: You ... you're the friend of ...

EMMA (*hastily*): Frank's friend. Yes. Did he tell you about me? (*She smiles.*) What a dear! What *did* he say?

MARTIN (*as though he were chewing the words*): That you were childhood friends. That's what he said.

EMMA: Exactly!

MARTIN: But who are you?

EMMA (*making a great effort to answer him, trying to remember, but in vain; then saying, easily and rapidly*): You wouldn't have a mirror, would you? I forgot my purse, my comb, everything. I can't even touch up my make-up. Do I need to?

MARTIN: No.

EMMA: A handkerchief. You wouldn't happen to have a handkerchief, would you? (*She looks at her wounded hand.*)

MARTIN (*taking out his handkerchief and offering it to her*): Yes. Here.

EMMA: Thanks. (*But she does not reach for it.*) Is it clean? (*Martin nods. Only then does she take the handkerchief and bring it to her wounded hand. But then she gives up the attempt. She does not know what to do with the handkerchief. She wipes her face, and then forgets the handkerchief on the table. She continues scratching.*)

MARTIN (*leaning over and picking up the handkerchief*): What's wrong with you?

(*Emma pays no attention to him. She raises her skirt a bit and looks at her leg. She leans over so far that she seems to be trying to hide her face. She stays in this position for a moment. Martin gets up and leans over her. He is about to touch her in a gesture of pity when unexpectedly she raises her head and smiles seductively.*)

EMMA: What were you up to, you naughty man!

MARTIN (*backing off*): Nothing.

EMMA (*smiling*): They all say that, but the minute a girl drops her guard, there they are. (*She looks at her leg once more.*) They used to chase me down the street. Uh. Here's one. I've got a little scab. (*She pulls it off.*) That's the sign of something, at any rate. But when you look at your skin, smooth and white, and there's nothing, where does the itching come from? From within? (*She laughs. A silence. She continues scratching, her mannered smile set painfully on her face. Martin looks at her tensely. Emma gets up, holding her head up, and walks in the manner of a movie star.*) Why don't you talk to me a little? I need to be amused. I was told you wanted to see me. Was it for this? Oh, I wanted to meet you, too. I thought I was going to spend a good evening in the company of a fervent admirer. At least that's what my secretary led me to believe. The new administrator admires you fervently, he said. Do you admire me?

MARTIN: Yes.

EMMA: I don't grant many interviews. I'm frightfully busy. (*She halts, and seems to sink into herself.*) Frightfully. (*Silence.*)

MARTIN (*coming up to her and speaking in a low voice*): What's wrong with you? I have not seen a secretary. I have spoken to no one about you. (*She begins scratching.*) Don't scratch yourself!

EMMA: I'm not scratching myself. (*She continues scratching herself, smiling all the while.*) And anyway, that was a very rude thing for you to say to me. Who would have thought? (*She touches her shaved head as though she were arranging a full head of hair.*) You look like such a gentleman! (*She raises her skirt.*) Lovely legs, aren't they?

MARTIN (*pulling her skirt down*): What are you doing? Now, stop it! Here you are showing me your legs and you look like someone who's escaped from a . . . (*He halts, surprised, as though he had not realized until that moment that she appears to be an inmate of a concentration camp.*)

EMMA (*smiling*): Escaped? (*Peevishly*) From where? Oh, don't be idiotic. (*She laughs.*) Escaped from a ball. Don't you see the lovely dress I'm wearing? (*She touches her smock.*) I came back yesterday at dawn. We danced . . . we danced on the lawn. In the fields. There's proof for you . . . the itching, the bugs. And I lost my purse. (*She scratches.*) Oh, I made myself bleed!

MARTIN (*extending his handkerchief to her*): Here. And stop scratching. You're going to hurt yourself.

EMMA: No, it's just that my nails are a bit too long, that's all. (*She dries the blood, and is once more tempted to put the handkerchief onto the wound in her hand. She cannot seem to make up her mind to do this, or does not dare to. She then returns it to Martin.*) I give it back.

MARTIN: Keep it.

EMMA: No, no. Never take gifts from strangers. (*Martin takes her arm and twists it so that he can see the inside of her forearm. She laughs.*) Oh, aren't you the curious one!

MARTIN: You're marked!

EMMA: My father. He was afraid I'd get lost. I was always wandering off after umbrellas. If someone came by with an umbrella, I would just wander off and follow them. Rainy days were awful. They had to go calling for me through the streets. They were so afraid they'd lose me, a little child, something that should grow, a hand that grows . . . an understanding that grows! They had all this to to look forward to. Why wouldn't they be afraid?

MARTIN (*rubs her arm, sadly*): You're marked.

EMMA: I am not! I told you! It's for good luck. Four sevens and one

three. But you can touch me if you like. (*Once more she offers her
arm to Martin. He does not touch her. She is amazed.*) Don't you
want to?

MARTIN: No.

EMMA: It was my father. He was eccentric. There really was no need.

MARTIN: Did it hurt?

EMMA (*dryly*): Not a bit. I was so little. (*Then, almost in a fury*)
And it's not a tattoo! It's ink, indelible ink!

MARTIN: Do they beat you? Does that son of a bitch beat you? It
would go with the uniform. Wouldn't surprise me at all!

EMMA (*tense*): Shut up! (*Then, talkative again*) My public adores
me. My last concert was a great success. My fans went wild . . . asking me for my autograph! Ripped my shawl to ribbons . . . they
wanted a little souvenir, you know, all of them! (*Then, serious and
pensive*) They almost destroyed me. (*Then, looking him in the
face*) Utterly.

MARTIN: They have destroyed you. But why? Who shaved your head?
(*She does not seem to understand him.*) Answer me!

EMMA (*fiercely*): I wear it short because of the wigs. I have to change
my coiffure for every concert. It's more practical this way. Put a
wig on, and there you are.

MARTIN: And this? (*He touches her dress.*) And your shoes? And
those teeth?

EMMA (*covering her mouth with her hand, but then immediately putting on airs*): Oh, you awful man, you.

MARTIN: It hurts just to look at you. You remind me of . . .

EMMA (*almost singing it*): For each man hurts the thing he loves.
Don't I please you? (*She sidles up to him suggestively. With a
seductive smile*) It would be so nice if I could please you. (*She
rubs against his body.*)

MARTIN (*unable to control his disgust*): Get away from me!

EMMA (*confused*): But why? Don't I please you? My short hair?
(*She touches her head.*) My itching? Oh, you'll get used to that.
And you'll see . . . when Frank's around I try my best not to scratch.
But just now the itching is driving me crazy. It must be because
I'm excited, and the blood flows more rapidly. I do so want to

please you. They told me your name. (*She tries to remember it.*)
But I'll call you . . . (*She searches for a name, but cannot seem to
hit on one.*) Well, it doesn't matter.

MARTIN (*gently*): I'm called Martin.

EMMA (*gay once more*): Oh, yes! A name! (*Then, excusing herself
with a timid smile*) I don't remember names. There's Frank and
. . . what was your name?

MARTIN: Martin.

EMMA: Oh!

MARTIN (*taking her arm, almost tenderly*): Who branded you? Was
it long ago?

EMMA (*about to touch his face, then stopping*): Don't worry. (*Then,
suddenly distrustful*) What did you ask me?

MARTIN: Who branded you?

EMMA: No. They didn't use fire.

MARTIN (*almost screaming*): Who?

EMMA (*frightened*): Don't scream. I'll give you a name, and then
you'll be satisfied. Any name! It was, um . . . (*She tries to think
of a name and cannot. She smiles artificially.*) Oh, but why don't
you relax, dearie? I'm the mistress of the house. How excitable
you are! I'll sign a photograph for you.

MARTIN (*as though he were testing her*): What kind of picture do
you take?

EMMA (*laughing*): Oh, marvelous! With a little retouching, of course.

MARTIN: I want one.

EMMA: When Frank comes . . . he keeps them. He's my guardian. No.
My, uh . . . (*She forgets. Then, pensively*) Maybe it was the dog.
Maybe I picked up some kind of eczema from the dog. Or the grass.
(*To Martin*) There's no mud, you know. As far as you can see it's
all grass. A green lawn, beautifully kept. I'm sure you thought it
was all mud. I'm sure you had visions of yourself wading through
a mudhole. We live in the camp, but times are so different now.

MARTIN (*almost surprised, and looking at his well-polished shoes*):
You . . . you used to pick up the buckets of shit (*she pretends to be
shocked and brings her hand to her mouth*) to use as fertilizer in
the fields. You did it all day long, buried in snow and mud.

EMMA: Snow? It never snows here.

MARTIN: I can't stand this. That stupid fool and . . . you. No mud. No snow. I'm getting out of here. I'm going to pack my bags and get out. Right now.

EMMA: What are you saying? What's wrong? You're the new administrator. We pay you well. You never dreamed of making so much money.

MARTIN (*somewhat taken aback*): You're right.

EMMA: Well, then, what's bothering you, darling? What's bothering you . . . ? (*She cannot remember his name.*) Well, you've only just begun.

(*Frank enters, once more impeccably dressed in his Gestapo uniform. He goes to Emma and kisses her hand. The scene acquires a tone of mannered and high society.*)

FRANK: Madam!

EMMA: My dear Frank, how are you!

FRANK: Very well, thank you. And you? You're perfect! . . . impeccable as always.

EMMA: You've met my friend. . . .? (*She cannot remember his name.*)

FRANK: Yes, we work together. (*He shakes hands with Martin, and lowers his voice as he refers to Emma.*) What do you think of her?

MARTIN: How can you ask?

FRANK: Why not?

EMMA (*going to Frank and talking to him with an obsequious and servile worry, as though Martin were not present*): He wants to go. I'm not to blame. I didn't offend him. I swear. He's just . . . hard to get along with. There we were, talking pleasantly, and all of a sudden he burst out with that! I . . . I tried to be polite and nice with him, but he's so strange . . . (*Trying really to convince him*) Frank, he's so strange . . .

FRANK (*smiling*): Oh, now that can't be. He wouldn't think of going.

EMMA: Yes. He would. He told me so.

FRANK (*hard*): Then change his mind.

MARTIN: Excuse me, but . . . (*Frank silences him with a gesture and points at Emma.*)

(*Emma is scratching herself. There is a silence. It is evident that Frank's words have taken time to sink in. She smiles artificially, then speaks to Martin.*)

EMMA: I'm giving a concert tomorrow for a very small, select group of friends. You must stay. (*She tries to hold his attention by grabbing his coat sleeve and tugging it toward her in a very strange way. All the time she continues pleading with mannered propriety.*) Oh, stay darling. Please stay. (*She starts to pronounce his name, but cannot remember it. Then, with a faint smile, as though she had learned the whole thing from memory*) The language of music is the language of . . . the soul!

FRANK: Perfect! (*To Martin*) Don't you like her?

MARTIN: No.

FRANK: Goddamn! I paid her in advance, too! (*He grabs his head.*) What a stupid bastard I am! (*He walks back and forth, pounding his head.*)

MARTIN (*taken aback*): No, no. It was just a whim.

FRANK (*stops instantly and smiles*): About going away?

MARTIN: Yes.

FRANK (*jumping in the air*): Hurrah! (*Then he catches himself. To Martin*) You would have had to give me back my money. I'm not that dumb.

MARTIN: I know. (*He is quite nervous. Frank nods his head with every phrase that Martin speaks, for all the world like a mechanical doll.*) But I warn you. We've got to put everything in order. I need facts. I can't do anything without them. I can't tell where to start. What did I come here for anyway? (*He is almost screaming.*) The job is the only thing that means anything to me.

FRANK (*without conviction*): We'll begin tomorrow. Tomorrow.

EMMA (*like a good little pupil*): And after all, work doesn't preclude pleasure.

FRANK: That's what I say.

EMMA: Work simply engenders freedom.

FRANK: That's enough.

EMMA: Frank, give him the afternoon off. (*To Martin*) I'll play for you. And for a very select group. Charming people. (*She puts her hand beneath her dress and scratches furiously.*)

FRANK (*having paid no attention to what she said*): Why are you squirming so?

EMMA (*the question seems to freeze her*): I?

FRANK: Yes, you. What's the matter?

EMMA: The matter? (*She looks at Frank with mounting fear. She speaks flatly, her body absolutely still.*) Why, nothing. Nothing. I'm in perfect health.

FRANK: What's the matter with your hand? It's wounded!

EMMA (*hiding the hand*): No!

FRANK: I saw blood. Show it to me.

EMMA (*staring forward, rigidly, and extending her left hand*): You see? No wound.

FRANK (*hard*): The other one.

(*After a moment, Emma extends the other hand. Frank, some distance away, leans forward and examines the other hand without touching it. Emma stands as though at attention, terrified.*)

EMMA: No wound. Absolutely healthy. I'm in perfect health. (*Her voice trembles.*) The gentlemen'll confirm that. I'm fit for any kind of work. I can carry stones, buckets, clean toilets, dig . . .

FRANK (*looking at her for a moment, and then standing up straight and breaking the tension*): What are you saying, my dear . . . (*he pauses out of amusement*) marquise? What kind of work would your hands perform, your precious hands, other than the work they do? (*He takes her hands and kisses them. But the gesture gradually loses its amiable air and acquires the character of a struggle. He looks at her fixedly.*) Is something itching?

EMMA: No, nothing. (*She manages to pull her hands free, and folds them across her breasts. She is desperate.*) It's this damn itching! What have they put on me?

FRANK: Who?

EMMA: It was . . . (*She stops herself and laughs.*) It was the dog. (*She screams at Frank with double meaning*) Mangy dog! (*To Martin*) And you, my poor darling, why so quiet? (*She laughs *hysterically.*) Why don't you scratch me? Here, let's sit down. (*She pushes him down on one of the chairs and sits on his lap and puts her arms around him.*)

MARTIN: Get off! (*He pushes her away and stands up. To Frank*) What's the meaning of this? I came here to work. What do you think you're doing? You must be crazy. And where did she come from? (*To Emma*) Leave me alone. I want to work and nothing else.

FRANK (*as though he did not understand*): But now, now! My, how impatient!

EMMA (*to Frank, in a paroxysm of fear*): Don't listen to him. Don't listen to him! (*She turns to Martin. She makes a hesitant gesture, and then covers Martin's mouth with her good hand. Martin pushes her aside.*) Don't say a word. Tomorrow you'll think better of it. In fact, you'll like it. I'm very much in demand.

FRANK (*gently*): What harm has this woman done to you? Where were you brought up? You're being rude.

EMMA (*sadly*): That's true enough.

MARTIN: Forgive me.

EMMA (*resuming her artificial smile*): You're forgiven. (*She clings to his arm.*) You like me, don't you?

MARTIN (*pushing her away gently*): No.

EMMA (*confused*): But how can that be? You told me that you found me very . . . seductive. Why do you push me away? There's no reason to keep secrets from Frank.

MARTIN: I have no secrets to keep from anyone. I'm going out for a stroll.

FRANK: Stay where you are.

EMMA: Frank, warn him.

FRANK: Of what?

EMMA: Didn't he tell you anything? (*She searches his eyes anxiously and then turns to Martin.*) You shouldn't push me away. Come, now, sit down here. I'm not going to bother you. (*She points to the chair, begging sweetly.*) Over here, please. Come here. (*Martin sits down. Emma moves behind the chair. She hesitates in the choice of hands and then, with her good hand, begins to caress Martin's face and hair, all the while scratching herself with the other hand.*) Darling, you're a dream!

FRANK (*interrupting her, for all the world like a theater director*): Not like that. That's too crude.

EMMA (*meekly*): I'll improve. (*She starts once more.*) When the music starts . . .

FRANK: I vomit! (*Martin gets up and starts in the direction of the door. Frank cuts in front of him and says with authority*) You stay here! (*They stare at each other and then Martin moves to the supper table. He moves the dishes and glasses aside with a sweep of his arm and sits down, his elbows on the table and his head resting in his hands.*)

EMMA (*looks at Martin and then turns to Frank*): Frank. Frank, make him understand. It's very difficult.

FRANK: You want everything done for you. Well, you've got to assert yourself. (*Emma doesn't move.*) Your hand? (*On hearing Frank's question, Emma moves toward Martin again, tries to touch him, hesitates, and touches instead the back of the chair. Frank screams*) Not the chair! (*Then deliberately*) Lower down. (*Martin raises his head, absolutely stupified. A silence.*)

EMMA (*in anguish, to Martin*): Please don't push me away. No matter how much you want to, please don't push me away.

FRANK: Stop begging! The most desirable woman in the world! Why do you resort to methods like that?

EMMA (*straightens up with a great effort, raises her head, and again addresses Martin, with the falseness of a movie star*): Kiss me!

FRANK (*softly*): Disgusting. (*Then, changing his manner altogether*) You're nerves are frayed, my dear. (*As though he had no idea of it*) Your concert?

EMMA: Yes, tomorrow. I practiced all afternoon. Very select people.

FRANK (*tenderly*): That hand. Will it be in condition to play? Let me look at it again.

EMMA (*making a fist*): There's nothing the matter with my hand! (*Frank reaches for the hand, but she hides it behind her as she leans against Martin's back.*)

FRANK (*finally getting the hand and forcing it open, and almost happy at what he sees*): It's covered with little bugs.

MARTIN: Leave her alone.

FRANK (*agreeably*): But of course. I wouldn't think of intruding upon you. My dear, do you want me to leave?

EMMA: No. (*She presses closer to Martin, who sits tensely in his chair. She crawls around and once more sits in his lap.*)

MARTIN: Please, leave me alone!

EMMA: No. No, I won't leave you. I must make you happy. Don't you want to . . . don't you want to with me?

FRANK (*who has moved away*): Make sure that it happens well in advance of the concert, my dear.

EMMA: Do you want to?

MARTIN: No.

FRANK (*getting down on all fours and looking under the desk*): Where is it?

EMMA: I've got good teeth. (*She covers her mouth.*) No, no. I've got . . . (*Thinking desperately*) good, ah . . . (*She pulls back the neck of her uniform clumsily to show her breasts.*)

FRANK (*still looking*): Entertain him, my dear. I'm always gladdened by other people's joy, isn't that strange? (*He shouts with joy.*) Ah, I got you! (*He gets up, whip in hand, but his gestures are totally free of any threatening quality.*)

EMMA (*softly, begging piteously*): Please say yes. It's only for a moment. And I'm not sick. As for my hand, it . . . (*She tries to hide it.*) Why, they just look at me and they . . . (*She smiles.*) They . . .

MARTIN (*grabs her face and twists it up to his, then barks at her*): Who?

EMMA: That's it. Squeeze harder. Don't be afraid. That's it.

FRANK (*very happy*): Can I announce it? (*He screams*) It's begun!

EMMA: No, my dear Frank, wait . . . Not yet. Wait. (*To Martin.*) Squeeze me harder! You're hurting me. (*Martin lets go of her face. Frank, who has been playing with the whip, cracks it loudly against the floor. He is at the other end of the room. When the whip cracks, Emma screams horribly, as if she had been hit herself. Her scream makes Martin jump to his feet. Emma falls to the floor.*)

MARTIN (*leaning over her with sympathy*): Did I hurt you? I'm sorry. Did I hurt you? (*He tries to pick her up. Emma clings to him and buries her face in his chest.*)

FRANK: What happened, darling? Did I frighten you?

EMMA (*looking up after a moment, forcing her face once more to wear that conventional smile*): No, dear Frank. I know your little tricks.

FRANK: I like the noise. May I? There is lots of time for the other. (*Emma goes pale and bites her lips. Frank repeats the question tenderly.*) May I?

EMMA: Of course.

MARTIN: What?

FRANK: I was talking to her. You wouldn't be frightened by the noise of a whip. Is the itching gone?

EMMA: Yes.

FRANK (*approaching her and running one finger along the contour of her face*): Your skin is absolutely covered with goose pimples. You were frightened, but it's over. You're sure I'm not bothering you? I like the noise, but I wouldn't frighten you, my dear. Not for the world.

EMMA: You're not bothering me.

FRANK: I've never hit anyone. Not even in self-defense. You know that very well, my dear. (*He moves away and picks up the whip. He makes ready to use it.*) Well?

EMMA (*reciting as if from memory, while Frank beats rhythmically on the floor with his whip*): He . . . has never hit anyone. I know very well. We've been friends since childhood. (*She can speak no more.*)

FRANK (*begging her*): Please, a little more.

EMMA (*continuing in the same tone*): He's never hit anyone. The children would chase me and he would defend me, one against four, one against five, one . . . (*Frank beats with the whip. Emma shudders and is about to faint.*) I can't stand it.

MARTIN: Then it's true?

FRANK (*continuing to beat the whip against the floor, but in a conversational tone*): Of course, how could you doubt it?

MARTIN (*screaming at Emma*): Is it true?

EMMA: What? (*She's not listening to him. All of her concentration is devoted to the noise of the whip on the floor.*)

MARTIN: That you are locked up? That they have beaten you? (*Emma tries to laugh, but the laughter will not come. She covers her ears.*)

FRANK (*stops cracking the whip and looks at them, then bursts out laughing*): Answer him, dear. Answer him, my darling! (*He laughs while Emma's hands slide across her face, her eyes closed. When she opens her eyes, she stares fixedly, straight ahead. Martin looks at her. Frank's laughter dies down. There is a brief silence. No one moves.*)

SCENE THREE

Some large benches, like church benches, or the sort one finds in school auditoriums. In front of the benches, a piano on a platform. Martin sits erectly on one of the benches; his hands rest on his thighs. Frank stands at his side with a large bouquet of flowers in his hand. There is a piano tuner listlessly tuning the piano. Suddenly Frank slaps himself on the forehead.

FRANK (*with concern*): The programs! I knew I'd forgotten something! (*To Martin*) Shall we call it off?

MARTIN: Does it matter?

FRANK: You don't mind? (*He smiles.*) Very well. I don't know what she's going to play. (*Then jokingly*) "The Great Scratch," in four movements.

MARTIN: Why don't you have a doctor look at her?

FRANK (*with a threatening gesture*): Ah, no, no! You . . . mind your own business! (*Seriously*) You think I don't take care of her? That she has no doctors? Vaccinated! She's vaccinated against all diseases and all plagues of this world!

MARTIN: Her hand is . . .

FRANK (*cutting him off, and speaking innocently*): Perfectly all right. She said so herself. (*To the Tuner*) Are you through?

TUNER (*without moving*): In a bit. (*Listlessly he plays a note.*) (*Emma enters. She is wearing a ridiculous wig on her shaved head and drags a satin train that has been sewn on clumsily to her gray prison frock. She rubs her hands together and exaggerates the tension of a performer just prior to a concert.*)

EMMA (*smiles*): Oh, my nerves! I've got butterflies in my stomach. Don't pay any attention to me.

FRANK (*goes to Emma and gives her the bouquet of flowers, sincerely*): Good luck.

EMMA: Thanks, darling Frank, how sweet of you. You shouldn't have bothered. (*She takes the bouquet of flowers, but she holds them stiffly away from her body.*)

FRANK: Smell them.

EMMA (*as though she had forgotten something she was expected to do*): Oh, yes! (*She smells them.*) They are so sweet!

FRANK: They have no odor. They are artificial.

EMMA: Oh? I didn't notice ... Perfect!

FRANK: Is the piano placed the way you want? Is it all right?

EMMA (*looking at the piano*): Yes, it is. Thanks for all you've done. (*She looks at the floor with amazement.*) Why ... they've swept it!

FRANK (*very politely*): Not one scrap of garbage left. It's the least I could do. I'm so happy to be able to contribute to your success. (*A row of Gestapo officers enters in impeccable uniforms and gleaming boots. Behind them a group of prisoners, skin and bone, real inmates of a concentration camp. They wear the characteristic uniforms and old, worn-out shoes. The officers seat themselves in the front rows and the prisoners sit in the last.*)
(*Quite normally*) The people are coming. Now don't be nervous. Just remember that I'll be in the audience. Think that you're playing just for me. (*Then he turns to Martin.*) And for the administrator too, of course. (*To Martin*) You haven't greeted her.

MARTIN (*very tense*): You told me not to move.

FRANK: You're much too literal. Now, go ... and pay your respects. (*Martin rises and goes to Emma, who waits for him with a false smile. They look at each other in silence. The smile vanishes slowly from Emma's face, and is replaced by a look of enormous sadness.*

Martin moves closer to Emma and finally kisses her on the cheek.)
(*Approvingly*) Very good! Polite and delicate. Very nice. (*Then brusquely to Martin*) That's enough. Sit down. (*Martin obeys. Then Frank turns to Emma, affably.*) The hall is filling up. Now, don't be nervous. You're not depressed, are you?

EMMA (*animated instantly*): No, no! Just a fit of nerves. (*She paces from one side to the other with a smile of false excitement.*) It's just that when I get ready to . . . to offer myself . . . my art being judged, criticized . . . opening my heart to . . .
(*Quite naturally and without her noticing, Frank steps on the train of her prison uniform. Emma walks past and the train is ripped off.*)

FRANK: I understand. You're all excited. (*Then, with the faintest hint of irony*) And . . . um . . . your itching?
(*Emma notices the train on the floor and picks it up. She does not know what to do with it. Frank snatches it from her, wads it into a ball, and throws it into a corner. All this is done as she speaks.*)

EMMA: Oh . . . completely gone! It must have been the little bugs in the grass. I have a sensitive skin . . . but the itching's completely gone. Although . . . (*She hesitates.*) When I have to play, it always seems to come back and I have an irresistible desire to . . . it's a veritable ants' nest and then . . . (*She looks at her hands, starts to scratch, but stops herself.*) Then I . . . (*She presses her hands against her face. In an uncontrollable gesture she laughs briefly.*) Forgive me.

FRANK: It's just a little tension, that's all. The hall is full, the cream and flower of our society. Are you happy?

EMMA: Be sure to applaud me.

FRANK: With pleasure. (*He kisses her hand courteously, then turns it over roughly and looks at the wound in her palm and inquires tenderly*) How's this?

EMMA: Better. It dried up. It healed over. (*The Piano Tuner plays some notes apathetically.*) Aren't you through yet? Oh, this is intolerable! Why haven't you finished?! (*Almost screaming at him*) But how could this be? Why?

FRANK: Problems of organization. I'm to blame. I mailed the invitations, got the flowers, had the hall cleaned out, but I forgot the most essential thing.

EMMA (*very nervously*): I know, I know. And I don't want to make them wait, there's so many important people.

FRANK: No, no. Today you're the important one. Remember that! (*To the Piano Tuner, brutally*) All right, knock off that goddamn noise! I've had it! (*To Emma, agreeably*) Once more, I wish you the best of luck. (*He moves off and sits down on an empty bench in the middle.*)

(*The Piano Tuner picks up his tools and moves off, imperturbably. Emma pretends to make an entrance. She bows with the bouquet of flowers in her arms. The Gestapo officers rise and greet her with a click of their heels, and then sit down again. The prisoners remain seated in a cowed attitude. The officer at the end of the row looks back at the prisoners and gives them a warning look. Instantly, the prisoners seem to wake up, and one of them begins to stomp on the floor. Then there follows a silence. Emma puts the flowers on the table, and sits on the piano stool. The prisoner resumes his stomping, and is joined by other prisoners one at a time. Their stomping stops and starts in such a way as to build in intensity.*)

MARTIN (*stands up and screams*): Shut up!

(*Two Gestapo officers rise quietly and come to his side. They put their arms on his shoulders in a friendly gesture. Martin tries to free himself, but he cannot do so. They put their hands over his mouth and force him to sit down. The stomping becomes louder. When it reaches its climax, it stops suddenly. Only then does the Gestapo officer at the end of the bench rise and face the prisoners.*)

GESTAPO OFFICER (*screaming*): You uneducated pigs, quiet!

(*At this moment the two officers who have been holding Martin let go of him and smile in a friendly way. But they stay beside him on the bench.*)

MARTIN (*jumping up furiously*): I'll break your heads in two!

(*The officers laugh good-naturedly. There are shushes for silence. Martin takes out his handkerchief and wipes his mouth. When Emma begins to speak, he moves forward and sits on one of the empty benches. Gradually the two officers will drift toward him surreptitiously, the way people do who try to move from one place to another in a full theater. As they do, they will be joined by two more officers and finally they will surround Martin once more.)*

EMMA *(squeezing her hands nervously and suppressing her intense desire to scratch, announces)*: I will play . . .

FRANK *(warning her with a smile)*: No. No announcements!

(Excusing herself with a smile, Emma sits down at the piano and arranges herself, but she can stand it no longer and begins to scratch.)

ONE OF THE PRISONERS *(hooting from the back)*: Now that's what I call playing!

(The prisoners burst out laughing. The officers turn and shush them feebly. Frank rises and takes a bottle of dark liquid from underneath one of the benches. He has a piece of cotton in his hand. He goes toward Emma, and as he passes Martin he growls between his teeth.)

FRANK: I don't take care of her, huh? You say I don't take care of her? You bastard! *(He goes to Emma, wets the cotton with the liquid in the bottle, and rubs it over her skin, while she, without rising from the piano stool, tries to avoid the treatment.)*

EMMA: Thank you very much, but I'm perfectly all right!

FRANK: Sit still! This will soothe you. I'm always taking care of you, but this son of a bitch says I don't. What the hell did you tell him?

EMMA *(frightened)*: Nothing! What did he say? He's a liar!

FRANK: That's better. Now try to be dignified. I arranged this concert for you. Don't make a fool out of me.

EMMA: I'll play marvelously, just for you, Frank. I'm a great concert pianist.

(Her itching appears to be worse. The prisoners imitate her, squirming and scratching grotesquely on their benches. They scratch themselves and each other. One prisoner takes the shoes off another and scratches the soles of his feet. The other prisoner does not try to pull his foot away but rather grabs on to the bench and endures it, laughing hysterically. The Gestapo officers approach Martin. One of them scratches his cheek with a finger. Martin brushes his hand away, but then the other three surround him as

as well. The fourth officer approaches Martin with both hands extended and scratches his face. When we see Martin's face again, it is all bloody. All this is executed almost tenderly and without violence.)

FRANK (*putting the cork back in the bottle and squeezing out the cotton*): I'll save the cotton. There's a shortage. (*He puts the bottle and the cotton on the floor and then pulls Emma's hands away from her body and forces them on to the keyboard. Instantly the prisoners stop scratching and put their hands in their laps. The only sound we hear is a hiccupping sigh from the prisoner who was laughing so.*) Now start playing! The public is becoming impatient. It has paid to hear you play. Is the public becoming impatient or no?

(*Only then do we hear the grumbling of the prisoners. Frank returns to his bench, making signs for silence. The grumbling ceases immediately. Martin is wiping blood from his face with a handkerchief and the officers who have surrounded him place their hands on his shoulders and force him to sit down. There is an expectant silence. Emma is not yet through adjusting herself on the piano bench and scratching and arranging her clothes. There are coarse clearings of the throat and again, silence. Putting her hand on the keyboard, Emma begins to play. We hear two or three notes, but when she presses the remaining keys there is no sound at all, except for one or two times when we hear the strange sound of a broken toy piano.*)

ONE OF THE PRISONERS (*calling from the back*): Let her play with her ass! Let her play with my . . . (*The other prisoners join in.*) Let her play with her . . .

GESTAPO OFFICER (*jumps to his feet and screams*): Silence! (*There is a brief silence and then the prisoners begin stomping on the floor again.*) Why don't you obey? (*He says this with a faint smile that becomes a giggle.*) How dare you disobey?

FRANK (*approaching Emma.*): Play!

EMMA (*pounding on the keys, then shakes her head, raises her hands, and turns imploringly to Frank*): It . . . it won't sound.

FRANK: What do you mean, it won't sound? We had it tuned! . . . Sing it! Pretend. What a debacle! I'll get even with you . . . And stop scratching!

EMMA: I . . . I can't! What did you put on me?

FRANK: Water. Does it sting?

EMMA: I . . . I can't stand it!

FRANK: You will stand it or else! You hear me? You wouldn't deprive our new administrator of his concert, would you? He's never heard you play. Martin, have you ever heard the young lady play? (*He looks toward Martin.*) *Where is he?* (*The officers who surround Martin force him to stand up. One of them raises his arm.*) Oh, there you are. Have you ever heard her play?
(*Martin makes no reply. One of the officers grabs his head and shakes it negatively.*

MARTIN (*to the Gestapo*): Leave me alone! (*All of them laugh and nod their heads affirmatively. They step back. Then to Frank*) What's going on here?

FRANK (*to Martin*): Sit down. (*Then, more forcefully*) Sit down! (*Martin sits down, then Frank addresses the rest of them, the way one speaks to unruly students.*) Now, the first one to create a disturbance will leave the hall. (*Pointing to the group of officers around Martin*) And you, you're making the gentleman uncomfortable. You must have more respect. Martin, do you wish to hear the young lady?

MARTIN (*exploding as he moves forward*): Leave her alone, damn you!
(*Immediately, the officers surround him and force him back to his bench, brutally.*)

FRANK (*as though he had not seen or understood any of it*): No. I ask if you wish to hear her.

GESTAPO OFFICER (*gently, to Martin*): Calm yourself.

MARTIN: Don't lay your hands on me again. (*The officers raise their hands and step back.*)

GESTAPO OFFICER (*excusing himself*): We wouldn't think of it. (*But immediately the four of them fall on Martin, pin him down, and force him once more to sit on the bench. At the same time the prisoners begin screaming.*)

PRISONERS: We want to hear her! We want to hear her!

FRANK (*to Emma*): You see? A logical reaction. They bought their tickets. You musn't disappoint your public. If you do, nothing will satisfy them. They might become *very* demanding. You must please your public.

PRISONERS (*in a chorus*): Let her play! Stop the scratching! Stop the scratching! Let her play!

FRANK: Play. I won't tell you again. (*He smiles.*) Take courage, my dear. After all, art is your business.

(*Emma sits once more on the piano stool and presses on the keys. No sound. She runs her hands across the keys until she comes to the last one. And only this one emits a hollow tinkle. The prisoners make obscene noises. The whole scene has the air of a collegiate joke.*)

(*Frank claps his hands until he has obtained silence.*) And now the distinguished concert pianist here will delight us with a piece from her repertoire. (*Sotto voce to Emma*) What'll it be, my dear? Well, it doesn't matter. Anything will do.

(*Emma gets up and tries to move away. Frank forces her to sit down and pats her head in a friendly way that makes her lose her wig. He holds the wig up in the air and looks at it, amused, and deposits it on the piano.*)

PRISONERS (*screaming, like children*): Hi, baldy! Look at the billiard ball!

MARTIN (*frees himself from the officers, moves forward a few steps, and screams*): Leave her in peace!

EMMA: Why is that gentleman making such a fuss? Throw him out! The liar!

(*The officers grab Martin and drag him back to his seat with fierce brutality.*)

GESTAPO OFFICER (*to Martin, with offended courtesy*): We'll have to eject you from the theater. You should know how to behave . . . at a concert. (*They hold Martin down and cover his mouth.*)

FRANK: Silence! (*To Emma*) Now play. A minor interruption like this shouldn't upset you so. After all, I was your teacher. (*He gets off the platform and returns to one of the benches and sits.*)

(*Emma puts her hands on the keyboard and begins to imitate the sounds of a piano with her voice, but they seem to be no more than random notes, not intoned in any particular pattern. Her itching becomes worse as this goes on and she scratches herself violently, trying to keep from being noticed.*)

PRISONERS: We want our money back!

(*The officer at the end of the aisle turns about and looks at the prisoners, but he does not get up this time.*)

GESTAPO OFFICER (*screaming*): Silence! (*Then he gets up once more.*) Silence, you dogs! (*The prisoners seem to be somewhat disconcerted. They look at each other fearfully. Then the officer adds in a friendly tone*) That's the way I like it.

FRANK (*gets up and shrugs his shoulders*): Lamentable. (*He goes to Emma and whispers something in her ear. She looks at him, frightened. He smiles happily and returns to his seat. Emma returns to the piano, playing with grand gestures while she imitates with her voice Chopin's "Polonaise." He rises and applauds.*) Bravo!

PRISONERS: More! More! More! Encore, encore, encore!

(*Emma bows hesitantly before her public, then looks at Frank for instructions.*)

FRANK (*quite naturally*): Give them another.

(*Emma sits once more at the piano and plays as she did before. At a given sign from the Gestapo officer at the head of the bench, the prisoners begin to sing, or rather to hum, softly at first, and then louder, with the obvious intent of drowning out Emma's voice. Emma becomes louder, but in spite of her efforts, which are ever more desperate, the chorus of prisoners drowns her out. At another sign from the Gestapo officer, the prisoners cease suddenly. Emma continues with her performance, but even though her mouth is wide open, all we hear is the frayed thread of her hoarse voice. Frank begins to applaud.*)

PRISONERS (*mechanically*): More! More! Encore! Encore!

FRANK: No, that's enough. Stop. (*He goes to Emma, and then changes his tone.*) Charming, my dear, marvelous interpretation. You've surpassed yourself. My congratulations. (*He kisses her hand. Confidentially*) My dear, you must take your bow.

PRISONERS: With flowers! We want her to throw flowers!

FRANK: Make them happy, my dear.

(*He places a bouquet of flowers in her arms. She arranges the bouquet and throws several flowers toward the audience, but the prisoners remain absolutely impassive, as though they had just finished playing their role. At another sign from the Gestapo officer, they rise and leave in a file, in an orderly fashion, though dragging their feet, as always. The officers, including the force around Martin, follow them out, guarding them.*)

(*Frank turns to Martin.*) You haven't congratulated our concert pianist. It would make her very happy. Go on, don't be shy. (*Martin rises and goes toward the platform.*) Go on, congratulate her. Tell her she was marvelous. (*To Emma*) And you, give him your hand. (*To Martin*) Or would you prefer her cheek? (*He smiles.*) It's more intimate. (*And then coldly*) There's less danger of contamination, perhaps. (*Neither Emma nor Martin moves.*) Come on! Didn't you enjoy her interpretation? Or are you hypercritical? (*To Emma*) And you. Stop scratching, my dear. (*He laughs.*) Do you want me to swab you with water again?

EMMA (*terrified*): No! No, I'm not scratching! It's . . . um, all over now. Absolutely. Just nerves. (*Hesitantly she extends her hand toward Martin.*)

FRANK (*brutally*): Not that filthy, rotten paw! (*Emma closes her hand and pulls it back. She extends her good hand. Frank turns to Martin and commands*) Congratulate her!

MARTIN: I . . . I . . . (*He tries to speak out but cannot.*)

FRANK: What's happened? Cat got your tongue? (*He grabs Martin's face and pushes it back. Martin swats aside Frank's hand. Frank continues gently.*) Now, now, be careful. Think before you act. Why such rudeness? Do you want to lose your job? (*He sniffs the air. What he smells gives him pleasure.*) What an odor! The odor is coming back! They are starting to burn again! (*Martin covers his mouth, strangling a scream, and falls to the floor.*) What's wrong? Do you feel sick? Is it the odor? Get up. (*He tries to pull him to his feet.*) It's just the children burning dogs again . . . dead dogs. But what timing they have! (*Softly and kindly*) The little savages. (*Martin crams his fists into his mouth to prevent his scream, and then tries to put his arms around Emma's legs.*)

EMMA (*terrified, breaking loose*): Why are you crying? (*To Frank*) Pull him off!

FRANK (*aloofly and across a great distance*): You had to be entertained. (*Then, with a threatening sadness*) We organized all of this to entertain you. Why did we fail? How?

EMMA: We didn't fail! He's an idiot. (*She bends down to Martin and raises his face. Anxiously*) Please say you enjoyed it. It was all a joke to amuse you. I don't itch at all. And I shave my own head. I like to be bald because of the wigs. Say you enjoyed it. Oh, *I* enjoyed the joke very much . . . If it weren't for this damned itching! (*She scratches herself savagely.*)

FRANK (*with an ingenuous hope*): Really? Did you have fun?

EMMA (*screaming*): Yes! And you say yes too! Oh! I can't stand it. I can't stand it any longer. (*She twists and turns, scratching, and finally, not being able to stand the itching any longer, throws herself on the ground and rolls about, scratching furiously. Martin looks at her. Emma finally cowers in a corner, crying now like a little girl.*)

FRANK (*leaning towards Martin and putting his hand on his shoulder*): Did you enjoy yourself? (*Silence*).

MARTIN (*still on his knees, straightens up, looking at Emma, who sobs on*): I enjoyed myself very much. Very much. Very much . . .

CURTAIN

ACT TWO

SCENE ONE

The only furniture on stage is a large embroidery frame and its high stool. The high stool, however, appears to be much too high. It is painted black. It does not seem to go with the embroidery frame. It seems to be more a painter's stool.

Martin and Emma. Martin is seated on the ground surrounded by a great quantity of paper and portfolios. He writes on a small tablet that he supports on his knees. Emma is embroidering, sitting very erect. She is plying her needle with her left hand. Her right hand is covered with a dirty bandage. She scratches, but less frequently than before. We hear some military music. Silence.

EMMA: How clumsy I am with my left hand!

MARTIN: How's it going?

EMMA: Better. Frank put some salve on it. Real salve.

MARTIN: And that made your hand all better?

EMMA: Yes, Yes, It's a bit swollen, but . . . um . . . well, there's nothing wrong with it. Do you want to see it?

MARTIN: No! Who hurt you?

EMMA (*suspiciously*): What are you insinuating? Do you think I'd allow someone to cut my hand with a knife?

MARTIN: I thought they had hurt you.

EMMA (*insulted*): Do you think I'm a fool (*And then, mannered*) With the way I take care of my hands? (*She caresses them.*) Golden fingers, that's what they are! (*Then, brusquely*) Frank *told* me to be on guard.

MARTIN: Against whom?

EMMA: You! You told him all kinds of lies . . . and to him too! . . . when all he does is take care of me. Why, I'm the apple of his eye! (*Sadly*) Why did you do that?

MARTIN (*meekly*): I didn't.

EMMA: Yes, that's right. Squirm out of it. But remember the concert, right there before all those people! Such an elegant and genteel audience, too. (*As if she were dreaming*) A sweet kindness to temper cruelty.

MARTIN: They scratched me.

EMMA (*disconcerted*): Where?

MARTIN: On my face. They gagged me.

EMMA: Well, you must have done something to deserve it. You were screaming. I heard you.

MARTIN: The piano didn't play.

EMMA: And what of it? An accident. I'm not going to criticize anyone.

MARTIN (*leaving the tablet on the floor*): How did you come here?

EMMA (*frightened*): Go on working.

MARTIN: I want to know.

EMMA: I'm not going to answer any questions. (*Anxiously*) They left you here to work. Now you go on working, or I won't say another word. If you don't, they'll accuse me later on of distracting you and . . . and . . . (*she does not know what to say*) of bothering everyone.

MARTIN (*once more picking up the tablet and his pencil*): Very well. Go ahead.

EMMA: I was working in the garden cutting roses and I cut myself with the pruning shears. The cut became infected. Frank took it very well. Never a question. He's so understanding. A real love. My itching is almost gone. Have you noticed? I don't scratch much any more.

MARTIN: Yes.

EMMA: I took some cold baths. Showers at uh . . . in . . . (*She forgets, then suddenly she is terrified.*) No! No showers! They go into the showers and . . . (*she smiles and continues confusedly*) and they forget to . . . (*She ends with a vague gesture.*)

(*Suddenly we hear a fierce barking of dogs and the sound of machine guns.*)

MARTIN: What's that?

EMMA (*quickly*): They're fox hunting. Weren't you invited? I always rode to the hunt, but now with this itching, and this useless hand of mine . . . No! Not useless. I can work. I love the hunt. Don't you?

MARTIN (*stops working and listens anxiously*): No.

EMMA (*urgently*): No, no. Don't stop working. It's absolutely necessary to keep up. Don't let them accuse me. You see, I embroider. I'm embroidering a little goat! Come look (*Then, changing her mind suddenly*) No, no. Stay there.

MARTIN (*dropping his pencil case*): What's wrong?

EMMA (*going to him, picking up the pencil case, and putting it in his hand*): Don't tremble. Here.

MARTIN: I'm not trembling. Who are they hunting?

EMMA: Please go back to work. There's nothing wrong! Frank told me about a movie. The horses, the gentlemen, the hunting jackets, the shining boots . . .

MARTIN: Who are they hunting?

EMMA: The whips . . .

MARTIN: Those are machine guns. They left the gates open. They thought they were free. It couldn't be true, but there it was. The gates were open, the smiles that invited them to leave . . .

EMMA: Of course, they enjoy hunting so . . . You go on with your work. I have to finish my embroidery. Here, take your pencil case!

MARTIN: They'd go out. And the others would be watching. And then they'd turn on their searchlights. Plentiful game. It was perfect.

EMMA: No, no. That's the way you hunt rabbits. They are fox hunting now. It's more distinguished.

MARTIN: Fox? (*He laughs painfully.*)

EMMA: I'm finally beginning to understand. Well, just think, there can't be a hunt without a fox. The poor beast, panting, its lungs bursting. (*Sadly*) I wonder how the fox feels? We'll never know. (*We hear fierce barking and brutal orders.*) There's the pack. Do you hear them? Listen to them bay! Oh, they're wild. It's such a passionate sport! (*Nervously*) And Frank's such an avid sportsman. He's good at everything, swimming, rowing, big game hunting, boars in the south . . . (*Martin lets his tablet and pencil box fall. She places the tablet on his knee and tries to make him hold his pencil. He listens to the sounds of the hunt. He trembles and the pencil falls from between his fingers. Emma continues trying to guide his hand. As she does this, she goes on speaking in a tone of faint superficiality.*) He's such a talented boy. A veritable prodigy. Didn't you ever go to one?

MARTIN: No.

EMMA (*going on with the game*): The dogs with their ears pricked up, smelling the scent. And the fox, running and running and running. The minute one moves in line, the dogs attack. The fox, that is, climbs up the rock and can go no further. If he falls, that would be the end of him. Oh, it's thrilling! It's absolutely thrilling!

MARTIN: Do they eat the . . . ?

EMMA: Yes. Why on earth would they go on a hunt if they didn't?

MARTIN: They have to beat them off to keep them from eating the warm flesh off the miserable corpses.

EMMA: Who? The boys? Oh, yes. They're full of the devil here too. But it's delicious, the flesh. (*With an exasperated smile*) Oh, me! How they bay! They're in the woods and . . . Oh, it's too much! What a way to enjoy oneself! They really do get out of hand.

MARTIN (*getting to his feet, desperate*): I can't stand any more. I'm going to see.

EMMA: Don't be a fool. Do your work. It's a dark night, and they hunt by night. The fools! Afterward, they burn.

MARTIN (*embracing her in anguish*): Please shut up!

EMMA: Oh, you've got your arms around me! If Frank were to see us now! He's not my sweetheart. He's my childhood friend. But we should tell him about it. (*She giggles.*) He'll be so happy!

MARTIN: Stop your crazy talk!

(*We hear the machine guns, at a greater distance. And then they stop.*)

EMMA: Don't push me away! It was so nice!

(*Frank enters, wearing the same uniform, except for the fact that his Gestapo jacket has been replaced by a hunting jacket. He carries a rifle under his arm.*)

FRANK (*laughing*): Aha! Leave you alone and what do you do? (*Jokingly, to Martin*) You, there! (*Pointing to the pile of papers on the floor*) When are you going to put everything in order? (*Looking around him*) No chairs? Oh, I'm exhausted! I couldn't stand any more! How they run! (*He sits on a stool. It is quite evident that he is not exhausted. A pause.*) And? No questions? You heard nothing?

EMMA (*trying to speak, but not being able to find her voice*): Were you hu . . . hunting?

FRANK: Yes. (*A pause. Then, brusquely*) Go take a look.

EMMA (*looking toward Martin and pointing toward him uncertainly*): Did you mean him?

FRANK (*cuttingly*): No. You.

EMMA: No. Thank you, Frank. The poor beasts, bleeding and . . . white. They turn white immediately. I can't stand it. (*She begins to scratch.*)

FRANK: Oh, not again! I thought we'd agreed that you'd been cured.

EMMA (*holding her hands away from her body, tense and anxious because of her desire to scratch*): I am! Our friend . . . (*She screams*) what is his name?

MARTIN: Martin.

EMMA: He can tell you. We talked and I never . . . (*Her hand moves toward her body.*)

FRANK (*smiling*): You're dying to scratch. It's not very feminine or attractive, but go right ahead, my dear, scratch. As far as I'm concerned, scratch all you want.

EMMA (*relieved*): Do you mean it?

FRANK: Enjoy yourself! Come on! (*Emma scratches fiercely for a moment or two. Then Frank goes on coldly*) Now go out and look.

EMMA: No. Later. I have to finish my, uh . . . (*She points to the embroidery.*)

FRANK (*without severity*): You should have thought of that before you spent all your time talking. (*He jokes with her.*) I'll finish it myself.

EMMA (*laughing*): You? Why, the embroidery's so fine it's almost invisible. You've got to have a hand as steady as . . . (*She moves toward the embroidery frame. As she passes Frank, he grabs her without letting her finish her sentence and forces her to turn toward the door.*)

FRANK: Don't you understand me? Go out and look!

EMMA: Why?

FRANK: There's a mountain of animals in front of the door. If you want one, you can take it. We don't waste anything: hair, nails, skin, hide, all. Go.

EMMA: No, no. Please, Frank. Sincerely, I really don't need anything.

FRANK (*fiercely*): Go!

MARTIN (*taking Emma by the hand*): Come, I'll go with you.

FRANK: Not you!

EMMA (*disconsolately*): No, please, uh . . . it's just me. He told me to go. One at a time.

FRANK (*laughing*): No, my dear, what are you thinking of? Martin has so much work to do, and he doesn't seem to be getting on with it. There'll be plenty of time for him tomorrow morning. We've caught enough game for everyone. Oof! I've never seen so much game! Martin can have his pick of the catch tomorrow morning. He can have it prepared for him and he can eat it if he wants. We'll let it age . . . hang overnight in the dew, *faisander*, you know, to season it. (*He laughs, opens the door, and then speaks in a friendly way.*) Now, darling, if you please . . .

EMMA (*without moving*): I'm coming.

FRANK (*as though playing a game, raises his gun and points it at her*): Then come.

EMMA (*to Martin*): Uh . . . good-bye.

MARTIN: Where are you going?

FRANK: But my darling, why so solemn? We're not condemning you to death. I just thought you'd like to see it. And don't think that we were just lucky. It's nothing but small game. Abundant, but small game. Dull, dark pelts. Short hair. Half of them ruined with the mange, but good bones. They're perfectly evident. Some teeth recoverable. My dear, you're letting in the cold. (*There is an expectant pause, then Emma goes out. Frank rubs his hands together and laughs conspiratorily.*) So you finally got chummy, eh? And how I had to work to accomplish it! Strait-laced, that's what you are, and proud. But she's a lovely girl. Swallowed your tongue?

MARTIN: No.

FRANK (*pointing at the papers on the ground*): Well, now, show me. How's all this coming along?

MARTIN: How do you think?

FRANK: God, what a disappointment! And you seemed so efficient, too. Well, show me your progress.

MARTIN: You must be joking.

FRANK (*sincerely*): May I burst in two if . . . You must have organized something!

MARTIN: What? They're nothing but old papers torn out of heaven only knows what account book. Ledgers from different companies. What do you expect me to do? You know very well nothing can be organized out of this mess. (*Desperately*) And whatever for?

FRANK: What for? What do you mean? We need order. Or do you think I'm paying you for the privilege of throwing my money away? (*He looks at the papers without any interest and then throws them and scatters them about. Then indifferently*) I believe that you're quite lost.

MARTIN: I am. (*Then, screaming*) What was going on outside?

FRANK: Very well. It was to be expected. No one seems to last long at this job. Shall we rescind the contract? You asked me what was going on. A hunt. From time to time we go hunting.

MARTIN: Whom?

FRANK: They all leave us. I'm not refering to the employees, the staff. They don't mind the chaos. But as for the management, that's another matter. Administrators can't endure the disorder. (*He continues stirring the papers about.*) And the children's drawings?

MARTIN: I save them.

FRANK: For what?

MARTIN (*sadly*): For myself.

FRANK: How sentimental! Isn't that nice! Well, I'll break the contract. There, I've made up my mind.

MARTIN: What does that mean?

FRANK: When do you want to leave?

MARTIN (*stunned*): Today.

FRANK: Pity! I took a liking to you. You stopped chewing gum. Disgusting habit. (*He pats him on the back.*) Yes, I've taken a liking to you. And you'd come to like me, isn't that so? In spite of this shitty uniform! I'll pay you the rest of your salary.

MARTIN (*distrustfully*): You owe me nothing.

FRANK: Oh, I do. I do! You behaved very well. Most efficiently. It's not your fault you failed. We let ourselves go and before we knew it we were in a tangle worse than a whore's bed. (*He hands Martin an envelope.*) For you. (*After a moment's hesitation Martin takes the envelope, but does not open it. He plays with it nervously.*) Open it!

MARTIN (*opening the envelope and looking at the contents distrust-fully*): It's too much. I don't want . . .

FRANK: Don't bother. We have more money than we know what to do with. (*Brusquely*) But you'll take her, won't you?

MARTIN: Whom?

FRANK (*rudely*): Her! You got stuck on each other, um? So. Then. (*He changes his tone.*) I can't stand it any more. Let someone else take care of her. She came for a day and . . . (*He scratches him-self.*) It's contagious. I'm afraid the kids will catch it. You can leave her anywhere you want along the road. Some hotel. But be sure she's well taken care of. Don't leave her in any old hole. Do you have any money of your own?

MARTIN: Yes.

FRANK: I can't stand her. Always scratching herself. And those airs she has. Like a prima donna. Who does she think she is? And then every time I see her she wants me to kiss those rotten hands of hers. And she's rotting me, that's what she's doing! Rotting me!

MARTIN (*somewhat upset*): You?

FRANK: Yes. Suprised you, didn't I? You thought it was the other way around. No, no. I'm the victim.

MARTIN: You mean, she can . . . leave?

FRANK: I keep telling you I want to get rid of her. Don't you see? (*He starts scratching.*) The minute I talk about her I'm beset with fleas. Mangy bitch. (*He has second thoughts.*) No, not a mangy bitch. That's putting it too hard. I don't know what's wrong with her. Always scratching. But with that one exception she's not a bad girl. Very useful. Very obliging. Please, do me the favor, would you?

MARTIN (*with a faint smile that is only slightly hopeful*): All right, I'll take her with me. You say we can go. Very well, I'll take her.

FRANK (*in a burst of gratitude*): Thank you! (*He takes his hands and kisses them.*)

MARTIN (*pulling his hands away*): What are you doing?

FRANK (*overjoyed*): To be free of fleas! There's, um, a soap. (*He tries to remember the name, snapping his fingers.*) A medicated soap. For the mange. You must get some. And then, once you've won her over, you can make her play the piano. Her playing is beastly, but it's amusing.

(*The door opens and Emma is pushed in once more. She wears a long dark overcoat above her prison dress. It is out of style. She is still barefoot. She carries a small black bag in her hand.*)

My dear, ready so soon? And in such a hurry to leave us! (*He goes to her and kisses her hands. Then, with his eyes closed*) How I'm going to miss your music! We've had such good times together. Say something. Console me. (*Then, humbly*) Touch me, just once.

(*Emma fearfully extends her hand, as though fighting an invincible disgust. She moves the hand toward Frank's head. He stays with his head bent. She brings her hand close to his head, then moves it slowly away without touching him.*)

(*As though he had received the caress*) Thank you. (*He smiles quite naturally.*) Did you see our catch? What did you think?

EMMA: Yes, I saw them. (*She steps away from him slowly and begins laughing as though the question had amused her. The laughter mounts until it becomes hysterical. She cannot stop.*)

SCENE TWO

A room in Martin's home. It is a simple room with a table and several chairs, one of which is turned over. On the tablecloth are several cups and saucers and at one end some school books and tablets and utensils. There are two doors, one to the outside, the other to the inside. The interior door leads to the kitchen and the other doors of the house. One window. Martin and Emma enter from the street. Martin is no longer wearing his overcoat, gloves, and scarf. He puts his two suitcases on the ground. Emma holds on to her little black bag. She is wearing a pair of Martin's old shoes.

MARTIN: There's no one home. One moment, let me see. (*He goes into the house.*)

EMMA (*sits down still clinging to her little black bag, mumbling*): The beasts. The least they could have done was to give me a pair of shoes. (*She takes off the shoes. Then, abstractedly*) They have whole mountains of shoes . . . and hair. (*She touches her head and then stands up suddenly.*)

MARTIN (*coming back*): They're not here. (*He touches one of the cups on the table. Then, slowly*) The cup's warm.

EMMA (*terrified*): Have they disappeared?

MARTIN (*laughing*): No! They must have stepped out for a moment. (*He picks up the fallen chair, then holds out his hand toward Emma's bag.*) Here, let me have that.

EMMA (*clutching it*): No! No. To each his own. Here, you take your shoes. (*She pushes them toward Martin.*) I'll take care of my bag.

MARTIN: As you wish. Please sit down. (*He offers her a chair. Emma sits down.*) Do you feel better?

EMMA: Yes. I'll be able to play the piano. A little practice, some re-hearsals, and then once more . . . (*She raises her hand over the table as though she were going to play the piano but the gesture makes her sad. Her hand remains in the air. Then she scratches her cheek, gently, slowly.*)

MARTIN (*begging her*): Please don't start.

EMMA (*realizing that this time it is actually true*): Isn't that strange! It doesn't itch anymore! (*She scratches mechanically with one hand while clutching the bag to her breasts with the wounded hand.*)

MARTIN: I'll go get some salve.

EMMA: Don't bother. Stay here, I'm all right. (*Making an effort, she stops scratching. We hear the same noise of children that we heard at the beginning of the play, but without commands and groans.*)

MARTIN (*going to the window and looking out*): There's no one. (*A pause.*) Oh, yes. Kids. But I can't see my brothers. (*He turns to Emma.*) I have lots of brothers, a whole tribe, all of them younger than I am, like this. (*He indicates the steps of the stairway. Then he goes to the table.*) They left their homework. Half finished. (*Almost as though he hated to do it, he pushes their work onto the floor and does not pick it up.*) They've run off to play. The cup is warm. What's your name?

EMMA: Mine?

MARTIN: Yes.

EMMA: You're Frank, aren't you?

MARTIN: No. Martin!

EMMA: Oh, that's right, that's right. (*She crosses her legs and looks about her with a critical air.*) Your house is, um, how shall I put it ... modest?

MARTIN: I'm sorry.

EMMA (*abstractly*): That's what they always say.

MARTIN: You can leave after a while.

EMMA: Yes, of course, when I go on tour. You won't be able to see my hair any more. (*She touches her head.*) Do you think it'll grow in a hurry?

MARTIN: Yes.

EMMA (*bursting forth*): How those children scream! (*A pause.*) Could you make them be quiet?

MARTIN: Why?

EMMA: Nothing. It's just difficult getting used to it.

MARTIN: Do you want to eat? Do you need a rest?

EMMA: Well, I don't really want anything to eat. (*Then, as though she were asking for something impossible*) But I would like ... a cup of tea. (*She points to the cups.*) It just came over me. (*Then, distrustfully*) Do you think I might?

MARTIN: I'll fix it for you.

EMMA: Wait. I should unpack first. Help me, won't you? (*Once more very mannered*) I just can't do for myself alone. And you're not my maid, after all ... I know. My secretary used to take charge of my baggage. It's been ages since I've had a bag in my hands. (*She caresses the suitcase.*) Perhaps he mixed it all up, the rags ... and the bottles of perfume ... the scores and ... (*We hear barking from the streets. Emma is frightened.*) They're dogs! Frank, there are dogs here too!

MARTIN: Street dogs ... that's all. Martin. Call me Martin.

EMMA (*without listening to him, anxiously*): I hoped I would never run into another dog, anywhere, not on any street, not even the graves ...

MARTIN (*exasperated, in a kind of fury*): These dogs don't bite, they're dumb dogs. They don't know how to take orders. They play all day, they don't even know how to obey commands, and from the time they're puppies they do nothing but make a mess. They chew up socks, gnaw at the mattresses, bury bones in the flower pots, they dig holes and expose the roots to the air! (*Screaming*) They're just stupid dogs!

EMMA: No, no!

MARTIN (*controlling himself*): Of course they are. Look. (*He goes to the window.*) It's just an old hairless dog.

EMMA: Hairless? What do you mean?

MARTIN: Nothing. It's just an ordinary dog. (*Presently, before the noise of the children fades out, we hear a scream of pain.*) What was that? Did you hear it?

EMMA (*definitely*): No. I wonder where your family could be. You told them you were coming, didn't you.

MARTIN: Yes. That's why I can't understand . . . they left the house empty! But sometimes the kids run away.

EMMA (*not believing, softly*): Is that possible?

MARTIN (*correcting her sadly*): They've run away to the street, to the park, chasing a ball. (*He smiles.*) I've gone after them many times. I'd bring 'em home, dragging 'em by the ears.

EMMA (*acidly*): And now? Why didn't you go for them now? A fine welcome. I have no intention of living here alone with you. Rumors spread like wildfire. But anyway, this house is too plain, too simple for me. I'm not used to this sort of thing. I want you to make a reservation for me at the hotel.

MARTIN: Rest a little first.

EMMA (*nervously*): But of course. What do you think I've been doing all of this time except resting?

MARTIN: I'll get you some fresh clothes.

EMMA (*pounding on her suitcase*): I have clothes here!

MARTIN (*going to the kitchen*): I'll get your tea.

EMMA: Don't bother. I asked for it because I didn't want to offend you. (*Then, fearfully*) Frank, I didn't want to offend you.

MARTIN (*coming to the door of the kitchen*): My name isn't Frank. My name is Martin. (*Then, gently*) Martin.

EMMA (*meekly*): Yes. I always forget names. Don't let it bother you.

MARTIN (*returning to the kitchen*): It doesn't.

EMMA (*nervously but animatedly*): Once the dogs chased me so far I thought I was going to die. I got off the train. It was so dark and there were so many people. Some of them were hungry, or thirsty, or they were trying to relieve themselves . . . and the children, the children, all squeezed together like sardines in a can. And I got off the train. I literally flew up the stairs. (*She laughs.*) I didn't even see them. I ran blindly, like someone blind from birth who suddenly sees the light. But then an enormous dog jumped on me and bit me. Guess where? It was bad luck. Then . . . I had no more flesh on me than the others, so it hurt, awfully. And in such an important part of my body. (*She laughs, hysterically.*)
    (*Martin enters with the tea. He places it on the table and stands by Emma's side. Gently, tenderly he places his hand on her shoulder.*) (*Her laughter dies out.*) You're very kind. (*Then, looking suspiciously at the hand on her shoulder*) What does that mean?

MARTIN (*moving his hand away*): Drink your tea.

EMMA (*drinking*): It's delicious. It's hot. Delicious. I'd forgotten the taste. (*Then, disgustedly*) But it's not English tea.

MARTIN: No.

EMMA: That's the only tea I can bear. (*Miserable*) Why did I drink it?

MARTIN (*looking once more out of the window*): The children are gone. All of them. (*With a kind of relief*) But now there are people. At last. A couple. Men going to work. (*He sees something that makes him laugh.*) A fat man slipped and took a tumble. Everyone's laughing. Come, look. Look at them laugh. Oh, this is rich. (*He rubs his fists into his eyes.*) No, what am I saying? (*He moves away from the window. A brief pause.*) Do you want more tea?

EMMA (m*oved, and speaking with a timid spontaneity that she has never before expressed*): No, thank you. (*Martin looks at her, smiles. Emma continues in the same tone.*) You threw the notebooks on the floor. (*She picks one of them up. Martin picks the rest of them up and arranges them once more on the table. Emma* *continues.*) He stained the cover with ink. The teacher's going to scold him. (*She smiles briefly.*) What's your name?

MARTIN: Martin.

EMMA (*touches Martin's hand tenderly; then, sadly*): I don't know anyone. That's why I can't remember names. It's very difficult for me.

MARTIN: Call me by my name.

EMMA (*making an effort*): Mar . . .

MARTIN (*helping her*): Martin.

EMMA: Yes. Now I can. Martin! Do you think my hair will grow in soon?

MARTIN (*smiling*): In a month.

EMMA: That long?

MARTIN: Fifteen days. A week.

EMMA: Oh, that's too long!

MARTIN: Tomorrow.

EMMA: Tomorrow?

MARTIN: Now. It's growing.

EMMA (*touching her head and smiling*): Not right now. I'm not that foolish. *Now* is for silly fools. Nothing good happens *now*.

MARTIN: Yes, but it's all over.

EMMA: For everyone?

MARTIN: I don't know.

EMMA (*sadly*): And if you don't know . . .?

MARTIN (*squeezing her shoulder*): It is all over, I tell you.

EMMA: Very well. I'm going to open my suitcase. I want to change. Do you have a spare room? Is the house quiet? Is it possible to believe that everything is . . . all right . . .?

MARTIN (*pointing*): There's a bedroom in there.

EMMA: I want to change. I want to take this off. Always the same dress. I need to change color . . . wear shoes. I . . . I had a red dress. (*She places her suitcase on the table, opens it, starts to put her hand inside, and then pulls it back. Her face changes.*)

MARTIN (*coming to her*): What's the matter?

EMMA (*closing the suitcase; suddenly, in a mannered way*): Didn't I

tell you? Who packed my suitcase? Don't you know? My secretary? My maid? No, my secretary, there's nothing like a man to
do something like that. (*Martin comes to her and opens the suitcase. Emma pushes him away.*) Let me be. Only one dress and
that's a party gown! What are they thinking of? That I don't have
any private life? That I don't need petticoats? Bathrobes? Night-
gowns? Suits? Other shoes? This is a fine mess! Look! (*She pulls
from the suitcase a gray smock exactly like the one she is wearing
and holds it out in front of her.*)

MARTIN: That's a stupid joke.

EMMA: What do you mean, joke? I'm the one to blame. Always
willing to give concerts, playing for charity, entertaining . . . and
. . .

(*While she has been talking, the outside door has opened silently.
Standing in the doorway is a man with the face of a happy pig. He
tries to get their attention by going "psst". He rubs his hands and
smiles almost abjectly, trying to excuse his presence. But somehow
the smile also expresses a kind of self-satisfaction.*)

(*Emma continues exasperatedly.*) Rehearsals! Practice! Trips
from one end of the world to another. No rest, ever. Tours. Interviews. A beastly exhaustion. And I'm to blame, I suppose. (*Then,
as though she had seen the figure standing in the doorway and were
trying to ignore him*) You think I have no private life? That I
can't fall in love? Or be alone, by myself, like anyone else? . . .
There are many, many people out there. You said it, Fran . . .
(*She tries to remember the name but cannot.*) Children! Kids . . .
and a fat man fell down. You were laughing.

MARTIN (*who noticed the entrance of the man the minute he came
in*): Be quiet. (*To the man*) What do you want?

(*Emma faces the man slowly and looks at him in fear.*)

OFFICIAL: Pardon me, but the door was open.

MARTIN (*louder*): What do you want!

OFFICIAL (*excusing himself*): Nothing.

MARTIN: If you don't want anything, then get out.

OFFICIAL: Why did you leave the door open? If it had been closed
I wouldn't have come in. What I mean is, who knows?

MARTIN: Who are you? What do you want?

OFFICIAL (*abjectly*): Nothing. I'm not trying to see anything. Look. (*He shows him his palms, but starts rubbing his hands again.*) It's nice in here. Nice and warm.

EMMA (*laughing half-hysterically*): Frank sent him! With a face like that ... Frank sent him!

OFFICIAL (*sincerely and definitely*): No. No, I don't know him. You came in just now. I saw you go by. (*To Martin*) I know you by sight. You know me, don't you?

MARTIN: No. And I don't want to!

OFFICIAL (*excusing himself unctuously*): But here I am ... there's no changing that.

MARTIN: Get out! This is my house.

OFFICIAL (*excusing himself; at the same time we hear sounds in the hall, as though someone pushing a hospital tray or bed with metal wheels*): Precisely. I'm in your home. And it's a very nice house. Now, if you'd locked the door completely ...

MARTIN (*taking two steps toward him and stopping, as though he were tied to a rope; furiously*): If you'll get out, I'll lock the door!

OFFICIAL (*smiling, gently*): There's no point. All I wanted was confirmation. (*He looks about the room.*) Very nice. As you see, I'm not leaving, but I'm not entering, either. (*Obviously wanting some*) Were you drinking tea?

EMMA: Offer him a cup of tea so he'll go away!

OFFICIAL (*quite docile*): Of course, we'll go whenever you wish! But just a cup ... I'd love ...

EMMA (*laughing almost madly*): He wants a cup of tea!

OFFICIAL: Yes, but after.

MARTIN: After what?

OFFICIAL: Just a formality. Believe me, I'm such a kind person ... such a good person ... I wouldn't harm a flea. If only everyone were like me ... and (*he shakes his head, remaining always on the threshold*) and, to tell the truth, if everyone were happy ... (*The sounds approach. He looks over his shoulder.*) In a little bit. (*Then, begging their pardon*) My ... um ... boys are out here. (*To Martin*) Your brothers? My, how they've grown! Yesterday they were no more than this. (*He indicates a height.*) And now, today, they've got a beard. (*He laughs. Then, with friendly interest*) Jew?

MARTIN: No!

OFFICIAL: Communist?

MARTIN: No! I told Frank No!

OFFICIAL (*as though trying to console him*): Well, it must be something else. We're all of us something or other. It's hard to choose. (*He laughs.*)

(*Three other men enter. They look like burly male nurses. They drag in a metal table on wheels on which rest several instruments, which are not seen by the audience, and a lit burner. Emma rises and moves off gradually, dragging her open suitcase and her gray smock, and ends up cowering in the corner. She scratches her cheeks and then later tries to fold up her gray dress and put it in the suitcase. One of the men takes a branding iron and holds it to the flame as if it were the most natural of gestures. The other approaches Martin slowly. Martin pretends to be gathering up the cups and saucers from the table. A cup falls from his hand and breaks. He freezes, looking stupidly at the floor. The men halt. Emma begins laughing softly. Little by little her laughter transforms itself and becomes sobbing.*)

(*The Official looks at the cup.*) Oh, what a pity! I could wait for the tea. (*Softly*) Have you been immunized?

MARTIN (*his head jerks up and he speaks with terrified assurance*): Is that it? Why, yes! I'm vaccinated! Vaccinated against all kinds of diseases. All of them!

OFFICIAL: All but one. (*A pause.*) It'll all be over in a second, and we won't bother you any more.

MARTIN (*with the same terrified assurance*): Get out of here!

OFFICIAL (*excusing himself*): That's what they all say . . . but it's so hard to go. And it's so nice and warm here. (*At a sign from the Official, the two men move toward Martin slowly.*)

EMMA (*without looking at what is going on, her attention on the task of folding and arranging the gray dress in the suitcase*): I used to get lost. I'd follow the umbrellas and then . . . I *had* to have some kind of mark. I couldn't go through life . . . through the world escaping like a smile that vanishes from a face. I had to have a mark. (*She laughs.*) In order to know who we are, a little mark . . . (*She wails desperately.*) Martin!

(*The Official seems to approve, and continues smiling. Meanwhile, one of the men has prepared an injection and places it on the table. During this process, the needle falls to the ground. He picks it up and screws it into the syringe. He whistles softly, rocking back and forth. Martin is frozen. We hear only his deep breathing, like an animal about to be caught. The two male nurses reach him and, with almost feminine care, remove his jacket and roll up his sleeves.*)

MALE NURSE (*quite naturally*): You're wearing an undershirt, too. Now that's what I call keeping warm. (*He smiles in a friendly way. His smile in no way has any relationship to what is going on.*) (*Suddenly Martin breaks loose and fights with savage energy until they give him the injection. He screams and then subsides into a kind of lethargy, conquered. The two nurses hold him up with a kind of solicitude. One of them takes a handkerchief from his pocket and wipes Martin's brow. When the branding iron is hot, the Official leaves his place in the door, takes it, and goes to Martin. We hear only the groan from Emma, who clutches and squeezes her suitcase.*)

CURTAIN

The Library

BY CARLOS MAGGI

Carlos Maggi has written for film, radio and stage. One of his television pieces, *La raya amarilla*, won first prize at the Brussels International Festival in 1962. He is without doubt Uruguay's most prolific and successful dramatist. *The Library* was first produced in 1959. It is a comic assault on the bureaucratic life and the regimented mind of the Latin American middle class. It laments the absence of a work ethic and it attacks intellectual dilletantism, crass materialism, and the tendency to emasculate the social influence of intellectual endeavor—all of these cultural millstones are pulling the old order down and under. These problems are acidly and delightfully brought into focus by the milieu of the library— one of the most ignored and difficult-to-use facilities in Latin American life.

Sr. Maggi has written other fine plays, of course, and in our correspondence concerning the nature of this anthology he suggested to me that perhaps *El Patio de la Torcaza* might be a more suitable piece. Although I agree with him about the excellence of *El Patio de la Torcaza,* I do not find it as accessible to "nordic" audiences as *The Library*. Finally, I admit that my own childhood experiences in Latin American libraries endear the humor of this play to me. I find that, although *The Library* can be directed toward easy farce, if one produces it with a bite of realistic irony and thematic depth one can make this play twice as funny and important as one would by a lowbrow comedic technique. The haunting and absurd way in which the characters are trapped in their setting, that implosive library, can render this play as macabre as it is amusing.

CHARACTERS:

Martínez	*Handyman*
The Subdirector	*Marcuciano Perluchino*
The Secretary	*José Luis*
Monteiro	*The Scholar*
The Janitor	*Ema*
The Director	*The Friend of the Director*
María Zulema	*The Critic*
The Spanish Reader	*The Engineer*
Estela	*First Workman*
The Tailor	*Second Workman*
First Employe	*The Orator's Voice*
Second Employe	

ACT ONE

Midsummer of 1917 or 1918. The office of the Director of the library.

There is a double door upstage and a small door at right and a brightly lit window at left. There are the Director's desk, the small table for the Secretary, various chairs and other office appointments.

Before the curtain we hear the strains of a military march. The curtains open and we are confronted with the indolence that characterizes government offices. When the military march is over, Martínez goes behind the Director's desk, assumes a pompous stance, and begins a parody of an orator. He is encouraged by the Subdirector, the Secretary, Monteiro, and the Janitor, who laugh and exclaim such things as "Bravo," "Hear, hear," "Good," "That's it."

MARTÍNEZ: My dear Director Don Schopenhauer Pérez, and my dear Subdirector Don Esteban Fattori (*the Subdirector acknowledges this with a bow*), fondly known to us as the old goat (*the Subdirector makes a gesture of disapproval*), ladies and gentlemen! (*Martínez' audience expresses approval of his imitation.*) We are gathered here today to place the cornerstone for the new wing of the library. Now . . . what exactly is the cornerstone? A cornerstone is a stone which, having been placed, in no way indicates that the building will be constructed around it or because of it! And if later, by chance, it should be removed, it will have no effect upon the building whatsoever. Gentlemen, let me say that a cornerstone is the only stone that cannot be considered crucial. (*Exclamations of approval from the audience. The Janitor takes a flag that has been leaning in the corner of the room, unfurls it, and places it in its standard next to the orator by the desk.*) Thank you, thank you, thank you! And now, ladies and gentlemen (*he begins to look through his pockets*), and now, ladies and gentlemen, ah, here we have it! (*He holds up something minuscule between his index finger and thumb and shows it to them.*) Upon this stone, I will build my library. (*There are cheers of approval.*) Ours is a nation of justice, democracy, and freedom and so: this stone, this stone of freedom, this free stone upon which we construct our library! (*He flicks the imaginary stone into the air.*) Whoops! Where did it go? I see it! Behind the old goat's beard. (*He makes as though to pluck the Subdirector's beard. The Subdirector makes a gesture of disapproval.*) Very well then, keep it as a charm against the young goat.

JANITOR: Watch it! Here comes the young goat himself! (*There is a brief pause.*)

DIRECTOR (*entering*): Good afternoon! (*He is an efficient man, aggressive and authoritative.*)

ALL: Good afternoon.

SUBDIRECTOR: And how are you, sir?

DIRECTOR: Very well, thank you. I could hear you outside the door. I suppose you're preparing for a ceremony?

SUBDIRECTOR: Oh, yes, sir! We're preparing . . . ah . . . the band . . . ah . . .

JANITOR: See, I've already set up the flag.

DIRECTOR: It's hard to believe a little flag like that could make so much noise. Martínez, go and borrow the carpet from the Society of Progress, you know, the red one they loaned to us at the time of Menéndez' donation. Then see that it's placed in the vestibule, and close the main doors until we're ready for the ceremony. I don't want any footprints on it when we receive the Secretary General.

MARTÍNEZ: It will be virginal, sir. (*He goes.*)

DIRECTOR: Monteiro, you go make sure that the band posts a lookout at the corner so that the moment that the Secretary General's car stops, the music starts. Not one instant sooner, not one instant later, but precisely at that moment! We must achieve the greatest psychological impact. (*Monteiro goes. Then, to the Subdirector*) Don Esteban, it would be nice if you, ah . . .

JANITOR: If you'll permit me, sir.

DIRECTOR: Yes . . .

JANITOR: We've got a problem. There's no spittoon.

DIRECTOR: Oh, now, really!

JANITOR: I bring it up because the Secretary General is a great spitter. I've seen him. He talks a little bit and then . . . poohie . . .

DIRECTOR: Well, what became of the ones we had?

JANITOR: We never had any. No one spits around here.

SUBDIRECTOR: Of course not! These are halls of culture, sir!

DIRECTOR: Señora de Luppi, do me a favor. Send someone to buy one of those . . . receptacles. And be quick about it. I have my speech to prepare and still, I think . . . well, it seems to me that . . .

SUBDIRECTOR: I hope you'll pardon me, sir, but I don't believe it's possible to buy a receptacle of that sort. There just are no funds for that purpose.

DIRECTOR: Very well, it's not important. Let it be.

JANITOR: I warn you, the Secretary General is a great spitter and that's no lie. He's going to make a regular mess of the rug!

DIRECTOR: This is all quite immaterial! We must attend to the fundamental things! The rest doesn't matter.

SUBDIRECTOR (*almost to himself*): I would't go as far as that, sir.

DIRECTOR (*becoming disturbed*): Don Esteban, do you really think
. . .

SUBDIRECTOR: Well, it *would* be convenient to have one. It's somewhat essential and it's the custom, courtesy and all that.

JANITOR: If you want me to, I'll take the screen off the lamp, turn it upside down, and put it on the floor. It looks almost like a spittoon.

DIRECTOR: Oh, no, man, that wouldn't do! It would be, oh, well, indecorous. And the shade has a hole in the center of it! (*To the Secretary*) Really, Madam, you mean to say that the cashbox is empty?

SECRETARY: Oh, no, there's some. We have about a hundred pesos.

DIRECTOR: Then have someone go and buy a spittoon.

SUBDIRECTOR: But there are no regulations to cover such a purchase.

DIRECTOR: We need a certain object. And objects are purchased with money. We have money. All we need to do is pay for it and that's that!

SUBDIRECTOR: But if there's no regulation, there's no regulation! And after all, regulations have their function, don't they?

DIRECTOR: This is ridiculous!

SUBDIRECTOR: It may well be ridiculous, but it also constitutes a misappropriation of funds. I will not be an accomplice to such a maneuver. This is a very grave matter.

DIRECTOR: Well, what do you propose? Shall we make the Secretary General choke on his own spit or shall we let him make a mess of our rug?

SUBDIRECTOR: We must find a solution that does not infringe upon the regulations. Infraction of regulations is strictly forbidden in article 96, paragraph 9 of the law covering financial ordinance. This is a typical case of misappropriation. If there is no regulation, there is no regulation. And after all, there must be some reason for regulations.

(*Small pause.*)

DIRECTOR: Achilles, go buy it. Madam, give him four or five pesos from the box, please. It shouldn't cost more than that.

(*The Secretary and the Janitor go out.*)

SUBDIRECTOR: If you allow me, sir, I would like to go home. I'm not feeling very well today. I . . . ah . . .

DIRECTOR: Señor Fattori, you began as a stack boy and today you are the Subdirector. Your thirty-four years of service have acquainted you with everything.

SUBDIRECTOR: Yes, but I . . . I . . .

DIRECTOR: How would you like to go to the main office and wait for the Secretary General and then usher him in here by the arm, accompanying him, as it were? That's what I was going to ask you to do. Would you be so kind as to help me out with this little amenity? Today's visit means so much to all of us!

SUBDIRECTOR: Director, please don't distract me. I swear to you it is a misappropriation! One of these days that youth of yours is going to lead you astray!

DIRECTOR: I'm far more likely to lose my youth before it leads me astray! . . . Now, now, Don Esteban, calm down and go wait for the Secretary General . . . and then lead him in here. But don't let this little purchase upset you. When the issue is crucial and fundamental, the problem is to act! Yes, crucial, like our cornerstone. (*The Subdirector goes out and the Director sits down at his desk, takes out the handwritten copy of his speech, and starts to go over it. He reads softly but makes large gestures.*)

SECRETARY (*coming in*): Oh, sir. There's . . .

DIRECTOR: Shhhhhh! (*He indicates his speech.*) What's better, "at this crucial moment" or "at this transcendental moment"?

SECRETARY: Crucial. It's shorter.

DIRECTOR (*correcting*): You're right. (*Once more the orator*) At this crucial moment . . .

SECRETARY: But sir, there's . . . there's . . .

DIRECTOR: I can't see anyone, look at the time. The ceremony begins at six, and I have to correct this speech and make a clean copy.

SECRETARY: But it's the editor of that journal. If I tell her you're busy, it won't make a bit of difference to her. She'll come in just the same.

DIRECTOR: Who?

SECRETARY (*indicating the ample proportions of María Zulema*): Señora María Zulema Alcanfor de Strauch.

DIRECTOR: Oh, her. Well, tell her to come in.

SECRETARY (*from the door*): Come in, please.

(*From this point on the rhythm of the act picks up until it becomes positively vertiginous.*)

MARÍA ZULEMA: My dear director. (*Then suddenly very familiar*) How are you, sweets?

DIRECTOR: And how are things with *The Blue Calling*?

MARÍA: Marvelous. We're almost ready with volume fourteen. The unpublished collaborations of two young French poets. Unfortunately, one of them lives in Buenos Aires (*the telephone begins to ring*) but he writes French most happily. Of course, it's beautifully translated. And then we have an epic poem of lower Normandy that is simply heavenly, all laid in Modernist hendecasyllables, patent proof of Rubén's* influence in France because . . .

DIRECTOR: Pardon me. (*He goes to answer the telephone.*) Yes, Schopenhauer Pérez here. Oh, yes, Isabel . . . yes . . . (*Pause.*) Why yes, of course, of course. (*Pause.*) Yes, with the lace border on the inside. Yes, my thoughts exactly. (*Pause.*) Yes, dear, of course, a tiny lace border. Perfect, yes, yes, good. What time is it? Well, it's almost five-thirty. Shall we say seven o'clock? (*Pause.*) Because of the ceremony, rem . . . Yes, Isabel. Yes, yes, yes. (*Pause.*) Seven o'clock sharp. As soon as the secretary is gone, eh? Until later, dear. Until . . . yes, well, we'll talk about that later. I have a speech to, to . . . (*Pause.*) Until later. Of course, you silly thing, very much. Until later. (*And he kisses into the telephone.*)

MARÍA ZULEMA (reciting dramatically):

---

* Rubén Darío (1867–1916), Nicaraguan poet, leader of the Modernist movement in Spanish.

Love. If it answer not,
Let no one call it love.

DIRECTOR (*picking up the photograph that rests on his desk*): It was Isabel. We're getting married this coming Saturday. She's an angel.

MARÍA: Love. If it answer not,
Let no one call it love.
For not matter, form,
Or shape can resist . . .

DIRECTOR: You know, those verses don't seem even to me.

MARÍA: But sweets, they're by Calderón.

DIRECTOR: Calderón?

MARÍA: Well, or by Lope . . . Do you suppose they're by Gracián?

DIRECTOR: The syllables, ah . . . Oh, if I weren't so stupidly busy . . .

SECRETARY (*from the door*): Sir, if you give me the original of your speech, I could copy it for you.

DIRECTOR: Not yet. It needs a few corrections. I'll give it to you as soon as I'm finished. (*The Secretary goes out.*)

MARÍA: Oh, darling, you're busy. I'll come back some other day. I had no idea you'd be busy today.

DIRECTOR: Well, as a matter of fact, today is . . .

MARÍA: I just came by to pick up your poem. It's a precious poem, so lovely, so moving, so . . .

DIRECTOR: Yes, my dear, but today. I really don't know if you know about it but . . .

MARÍA: As far as I'm concerned . . . well . . . that poem is unforgettable! It was some sort of homage to the Belgian people and their invasion . . . wasn't it? Oh, I remember perfectly! The Belgian invasion never affected me half as much as it did when I read your poem. Now, what was it called? "The Song of the Gong" or "The Chill of the Cello"? What was it, sweets? It was so musical, so . . . so . . . I had it on the tip of my tongue. "The Harpy of the Harp"? "The Peach of the Piano"? "The Case of the Bass"? What was it? Oh, I've got it right before me! "The Storm of the Horn," "The Matin of the Baton."

DIRECTOR: I called it "The Low Blow of the Oboe." (*And then wax-*

ing to the subject) "A modern and impressionist vision. A moon-struck meditation on the ruins of Belgium."

MARÍA: Oh, that's lovely, sweets. Just lovely.

DIRECTOR: Do you remember in the portico? Two years ago when I recited the first verses to you?

> The vision from the lesion,
> Charnel and sidereal butcher shop,
> Symphonizing . . .

JANITOR (*bringing in and brandishing a package as though it were a trophy*): Here's the spittoon, sir.

DIRECTOR (*startled, alarmed*): Achilles!

JANITOR: What?

DIRECTOR: What have you got there?

JANITOR: The spittoon!

DIRECTOR (*losing his temper*): That's enough! Put it there and leave me alone.

JANITOR (*mumbling to himself*): First he tells me to buy it and I buy it. Then she tells me to come in and I come in. What's all the shouting about? Be damned if I can make any sense in any of them.

DIRECTOR (*in a conciliatory tone*): Achilles, you did a fine job. Now, just leave the package over there, that's all. Yes, yes, up there.

SECRETARY (*from the door*): Sir, you've got less than half an hour before six o'clock.

DIRECTOR: Oh, yes, my speech, of course. Um, really, I must hurry, ah . . .

MARÍA: Sweets, you're so busy. I *should* go, I know, but your poems are so lovely they simply transport me! I swear to you they transport me! They're so . . . so . . . what should I say? They're so lovely, so . . . so . . .

DIRECTOR (*to the Secretary*): We'll tend to the speech in a moment. Achilles, is the band ready?

JANITOR: Been ready for hours. And they've posted a lookout on the corner like you told them. And I bought the, ah . . . well . . . everything's ready.

DIRECTOR: Well, as you see, María Zulema . . . well, you can see for yourself, really . . . now . . . today I . . . I . . .

MARÍA: I understand. You're busy. But give me your poem? Hum?
I want it for this issue of *The Blue Calling* because it's so . . .
well, it's so . . .

JANITOR (*leaving*): It's so! so! so! so! so! Sounds like a bell.
(*The telephone rings.*)

DIRECTOR (*as he goes to answer it*): Well, to be perfectly frank with
you, María Zulema, I'm, well, I'm not quite satisfied with it yet. It's
not really what I call finished. (*Into the telephone*) Hello? Yes,
yes, it's me, dear. I can't hear you very clearly, speak up. Yes, yes,
Isabel, yes. (*Little pause.*) Yes, with the lace border toward the
inside. But darling . . . (*pause.*) Why? Why do I say I want it toward the inside? Is that what you think? Yes? (*Then to María
Zulema*) I've got to polish it up a bit. There are some stanzas
which . . . ah . . . (*Then into the telephone*) Yes, Isabel, of course.
(*Then to María Zulema*) I don't know, but I don't seem to feel
some of those verses. (*Then to the telephone*) Of course, of course,
darling, surely. On the outside. (*Small pause.*) Very well, call her.
Yes, of course, I'll speak to your mother. (*Then to María Zulema*)
Some of the verses just don't scan right. (*Then to the Secretary,
who has stepped into the door and is waving some blank sheets
of paper at him*) Yes, Madam, there's still time, there's still time!
It'll only take me a minute and I'm doing it right now! (*Then to
the Janitor, who has started to open the box he had brought in
before*) Achilles, don't open that now! (*Then to the telephone*)
Ah, yes, yes, yes, Ma'am. Very well, and you? I said, "Very well,
and you?" I asked how you felt!! Ah, I'm glad, yes, yes. Hello,
hello, hello? Miss, Miss, please don't cut us off, don't cut us off!
Yes, we're, we're talking, yes. Don't cut us off, Miss. Yes, hello?
Hello? Oh, it's you. Yes, yes, yes, yes, yes, yes. Of course (*Pause.*)
Yes, yes, yes, Ma'am. (*Pause.*) I agree completely, the little lace
border on the outside. (*Pause.*) Big? Big lace border? Oh, I agree.
Of course. (*Pause.*) Yes. (*In the meantime, the Janitor has un-
packed the spittoon, which is made of blue glass, and has cleaned it
off. María Zulema, who has moved toward the desk, now picks up
the spittoon as though it were a flower vase. Then to María Zulema*)

Oh, but María Zulema! Achilles, Achilles, take that . . . that away, please!

MARÍA ZULEMA: Oh, it's lovely, sweets. Simply lovely! A blue vase. Only an Amado Nervo would think of something like that!

DIRECTOR: Yes, yes, a blue vase for . . . for roses. (*Into the telephone*) What? No, no, no, I mean yes! . . . I said, ah, she would look lovely. (*Pause.*) Of course. With a large little lace border on the outside. Yes, yes, of course, of course, yes, yes. (*Pause.*) Very well, agreed! . . . When the Secretary General is gone. Well, naturally. The cornerstone . . . (*Pause.*) Yes, because I have already . . . (*Pause.*) Today at six o'clock. No, I'm coming at seven. Yes, yes, until later, until later, b . . . bye-bye, Mom-mom, bye-bye!

SECRETARY (*standing in the door again*): There is a certain Dr. José Carlos de Guiñazul, Marquis of Cierraceño, to see you, sir. He has been waiting for quite some time and he's becoming very impatient. And Monteiro wants to talk to you about something urgent. And a young lady just came in who says she'll wait. I've already told her that you've got to finish your speech! (*She looks pointedly at María Zulema.*) And the ceremony is about to begin! But she insists. She's one of those pushy types.

DIRECTOR: And, ah . . . ah . . . well, what time is it?

SECRETARY: It's well after five-thirty.

DIRECTOR: I really must hurry now. Would you mind closing those blinds? The glare in here really hurts my eyes.

MARÍA ZULEMA: Oh, you're so busy!

DIRECTOR: No, no, that's not it. It's just that I'm busy.

MARÍA ZULEMA: Ho, ho, ho. Well, I'll be going, then.

SECRETARY: This way, Ma'am.

MARÍA ZULEMA: Well, what about the rough copy? Just give me the poem in that form. Please, sweets, please?

DIRECTOR: Señora Luppi, would you please ask all of those people to come in. All, please. I'll close the blinds myself.

SECRETARY: All of them?

DIRECTOR: Yes, all of them! At once! It will be faster that way. If it weren't so hot! What time is it? (*He closes the blinds. The Secre-*

*tary enters with the Spanish Reader, Monteiro, and Estela. They
are followed by the Janitor, who is carrying a large container of
water. During the following scene, he will fill the spittoon with
water and remove it from the table where María Zulema had put
it, placing it on the floor.*) It's a pleasure, sir.

SPANISH READER (*correcting him*): Doctor, Doctor José Carlos de
Guiñazul, Marquis of Cierraceño. Spanish, of course.

DIRECTOR: Charmed. Won't you be seated. (*Aside*) And what's your
problem, Monteiro?

MONTEIRO: It's the finals. They're played on Saturday.

DIRECTOR: What finals?

MONTEIRO: We're playing finals for admission into the second class.

DIRECTOR: The second what?

MONTEIRO: Team! Team! There's practice today and I've got to go!
Think of the responsibility we'll have on Saturday.

DIRECTOR: You've got your gall, to stand there, bald-faced . . . I'm
getting married on Saturday!

MONTEIRO: And you're not practicing? Training . . . I mean, ah . . .
you're not making preparations?

DIRECTOR: I'm up to here with preparations.

MONTEIRO: You see, even you've got to prepare. Can't I go? We'll be
moving up in the league.

DIRECTOR: And who will take care of the reading room when the
Secretary General arrives?

MONTEIRO: Why don't we close the reading room for the afternoon.
Who's going to be reading . . . with the band playing out there!
And anyway, I don't think there's going to be any readers. There
haven't been any for three or four days now. If you called this
place an oven, even the books would agree and melt. And, Mr.
Director, if the Secretary General sees how empty it is, he's going
to realize that this . . . ah . . . well, it won't look so well!

DIRECTOR: Oh, very well, very well, go on, go on! But be sure to lock
the reading room before you leave.

MONTEIRO: Thanks! I'm in great shape! Just wait till I start slipping
in through those backs . . . (*He goes dancing out with an imaginary ball.*)

DIRECTOR: Please excuse the interruption. I don't believe I greeted you, Miss. Please forgive me.

ESTELA: Estela Grisel. I've got a little card here for you.

DIRECTOR (*bowing to her*): My pleasure, Miss . . . ah . . . (*He becomes conscious of the mumblings between the Janitor and María Zulema, who have for some moments been arguing about the purpose of the spittoon, he insisting it should be on the floor, she continuing to place it on the desk. The Director interrupts his greeting of the Young Lady and makes some sort of negative gesture towards the Janitor.*)

JANITOR (*giving up his efforts to place the spittoon on the floor*): But, Director, if we leave it there the Secretary General is going to have to stand up every time he wants to spit! And if he misses, with the spittoon here on the table . . .

MARÍA ZULEMA (*arranging the spittoon on the table*): Here, isn't that so? To set off that wonderful talent that flows like a fountain of inspiration onto the pages of *The Blue Calling.*

SECRETARY (*with considerable venom*): Be sure to put it next to the picture.

DIRECTOR: It doesn't matter! Anywhere will do! I'm so busy today and it's so hot! (*The Janitor goes out grumbling.*) Yes, now you gave me this card, didn't you, sir? (*To the Secretary*) What time is it? (*To Estela*) No, no, *you* gave me the card, didn't you? (*He reads it.*) Mmm. Mmm, mmm . . . Very pleased to meet you, Señorita Grisel.

MARTÍNEZ (*from the door*): There is a man here who has brought something for you, Mr. Director, and he wants to see you.

DIRECTOR: Ask him to leave it. I'm . . . much, much too busy. (*Martínez goes out. To Estela*) And so you are . . . ah . . . ah . . .

ESTELA (*a little brashly*): A childhood friend of the sister of the ambassador from Costa Rica.

MARTÍNEZ (*from the door*): The man says it's the frock coat that you rented for Saturday. He says that you've got to try it on and sign the receipt.

DIRECTOR (*to the Secretary*): Madam, will you please take care of that. (*To Estela*) And so you are, ah . . .

SECRETARY: She is a childhood friend of the sister of the ambassador from Costa Rica. (*She goes out.*)

SPANISH READER: If you would be so kind . . . but I am in something of a hurry . . . and it is going to . . .

DIRECTOR (*to the Reader*) : Pleasure, pleasure. Very good. Pleasure, sir!

SPANISH READER: Doctor. Doctor José Carlos de Guiñazul, Marquis of Cierraceño, at your service.

DIRECTOR: Charmed, charmed. Won't you be seated?

SPANISH READER: I came to speak to you, my dear Director, if you permit me to address you in that fashion. I came to speak to you because, here in this repository, there rests without any question a very rare and wonderful collection of engravings of one of the master craftsman of his art, not to mention . . .

MARÍA ZULEMA: Sweets! Sweets! You look so busy. I ought to be running along, shouldn't I?

DIRECTOR (*running to her*): Yes, my dear. Why don't you come some other day. Tomorrow. Whenever you want. As you can see, well, I'm . . . I'm swamped.

MARÍA ZULEMA: But what about your poem? I absolutely refuse to go away without that marvelous "Trump of the Trumpet."

DIRECTOR: "Low Blow of the Oboe." (*Leading her out*) Tomorrow, María Zulema, come back tomorrow. As you can see, I'm in a terrible rush.

MARÍA ZULEMA (*to the visitors*): Oh, he's a marvelous poet, a great poet! Even though he *is* getting married on Saturday. Well, until tomorrow, sweets. Oh, but seriously, sweets, can't you get me the poem now? (*The Director shakes his head.*) Oh, you bad boy! (*And she goes out.*)

SECRETARY (*taking the Director to one side*): Sir, the man with the frock coat insists. He just can't leave it here without trying it on first.

DIRECTOR: Well, ask him to wait! That's all I needed!

SECRETARY: His shop closes at six and he has to be back before then. He says either you try it on today or they can't promise to have it ready by Saturday.

DIRECTOR: Well, ask him to wait a few minute s. . . at least! What time is it? I'm sweating so it squirts out! (*As he moves toward Estela, he wipes his face and neck with his handkerchief.*) And so you are . . . ah . . . ah . . .

SPANISH READER (*simultaneously with Estela*): Doctor José Carlos de Guiñazul, Marquis of Cierraceño, at your service.

ESTELA (*simultaneously with the Spanish Reader*): The childhood friend of a sister of the ambassador from Costa Rica.

SPANISH READER: After you, Miss. For although courtesy doesn't overcome exigency . . . I . . . I bow to beauty!

ESTELA: Ah, after you, please. I'm really not in a hurry. In fact, I have a sneaky suspicion I'm going to be here for years and years.

DIRECTOR: Well, ah, Marquis, I mean, Doctor, ah . . . ah . . .

SPANISH READER: Well, as I was explaining, here in this repository you possess an admirable collection of engravings by the great Piranesi, the greatest of all draftsmen, if one *can* say such a thing . . . and, ah, as you must know, the inventor of special perspective. Juan Bautista Piranesi, Venice, 1720–1778.

DIRECTOR: Yes, I'm well aware of that. Now, ah, you wanted to . . . ah . . .

SPANISH READER: I'm coming to that. It's simply fascinating! Your spendid collection embraces, among other examples of great artistry, one engraving of positively singular merits in and of itself, but especially for me . . . although even more for me, for my title, my house . . . by my house I mean family. Let me be more precise . . . important for my clan, as it were, genealogically speaking, that is to say, all those who share my name and blood!

DIRECTOR: I, ah . . . of course, I understand. But you wanted, ah . . .

SPANISH READER: It's really quite fascinating, although I'll have to indulge in a little bit of history, if you don't mind. In or around the year 1653, in a little hidden village of Sienna, a young girl of about some seventeen years married a young captain of the infantry. She was vivacious, charming, utterly delightful. He was a strapping young man, well-built and, ah . . .

DIRECTOR: Forgive the interruption, but I am really so rushed! That is to say, I'm so pressed for time! I don't know whether you are aware, but today within a few minutes we are laying the corner-stone of the new ... (*He goes to the door.*) If you'll forgive me ... (*Calling out*) Madam, what time is it?

SPANISH READER: Well, really, it's only twenty minutes of six.

DIRECTOR: Well, sir ... I mean, Marquis, if you could be a bit more to the point ... I beg your pardon, *Doctor!*

SPANISH READER: Well, now, really, Mr. Director, I came to see you at four-thirty. That's more than an hour ago. After keeping me waiting for such a length of time, the least you could do is hear me out. Especially in view of the fact that I do not really demand that you grant me my request!

DIRECTOR: Believe me, I want nothing more than to be able to satisfy you, but at this moment ...

SPANISH READER: Oh, I'm pleased to find you so cooperative and I'm very grateful. As I was saying, it was in Sienna about the year 1653. She was fresh, and gentle, and charming, and he ...

DIRECTOR: Please, will you tell me simply and clearly what it is you want?!

SPANISH READER: But you won't listen to me! Whenever I start to weave my thoughts, you interrupt!

DIRECTOR: To the point, please. To the point!

SPANISH READER: And I beg you please to follow my thoughts.

DIRECTOR: You want to examine the Piranesi engravings, am I right?

SPANISH READER: In a certain way, yes, and in another way, no! And don't you forget I have witnesses to the fact that I have informed you of this! Even though you refuse to allow me to explain the whys and wherefores, I ...

DIRECTOR (*to the Secretary*): Señora de Luppi!

SECRETARY (*entering*): Sir?

DIRECTOR: Tell Monteiro ... no, ah, I gave Monteiro the afternoon off! Tell Martínez to come here. And quickly, please.

SECRETARY: What am I going to do with the man from the tailor shop? He's going to leave.

DIRECTOR: Ask him to wait two minutes. Entertain him.

SECRETARY (*calling offstage*): Martínez. The Director.

(*Martínez enters.*)

DIRECTOR: Martínez, this gentleman wishes to examine the Piranesi engravings. Do me a favor.

MARTÍNEZ: But the reading room's closed.

DIRECTOR: Then open it.

MARTÍNEZ: But the engravings are in the basement . . . and the man in charge of that collection is Monteiro. And you gave him the afternoon off, didn't you?

DIRECTOR: Please, take care of it yourself. Please!

MARTÍNEZ: I don't know that it's worth the trouble. What I mean is that I don't know if I will be able to find them.

DIRECTOR: If you try, Martínez! If you try!

MARTÍNEZ: What's the use?

DIRECTOR: Because I tell you to!

MARTÍNEZ: That depends. I don't have to do everything you tell me.

DIRECTOR: And just what do you think you're going to get by that attitude?

MARTÍNEZ: And what will I get if I agree? A raise in pay? Not likely! You don't draw up the budget and there's no hope of a promotion because there's no vacancy. Bonuses are forbidden. The most I can get is thanks from you, and a dirty suit from wandering around in the dust of the basement. That's all I'd get! So?

DIRECTOR: Will you go or not!

MARTÍNEZ: All right, I'll give it a try . . . if it isn't too much work. Tell the old man to come along, too . . .

DIRECTOR: If you would be so kind, Doctor. This . . . functionary will make the selection available to you.

SPANISH READER: But if you will permit me, I insist upon explaining that I . . .

DIRECTOR (*conclusively*): Examine the engravings and we will talk about it tomorrow! (*Martínez goes out, accompanied by the Spanish Reader.*) Oooph! I thought I'd never get rid of him! You'll have to forgive me, Miss.

ESTELA: Oh, it's been my pleasure!

DIRECTOR: What possible pleasure could you derive from observing that encounter?

ESTELA: Well, I was looking at all those books. I love books! I've got one at home.

DIRECTOR: Oh, do you?

ESTELA: It's so exciting. It's a love story. Mad love! Burning love!! Illicit love!!! . . . But I like the serials much more, don't you? I follow four of them.

DIRECTOR: The card says that you want to work in the library.

ESTELA: Oh, I'm just mad about catalogues.

DIRECTOR: Catalogues?

ESTELA: Oh, I just love culture! I don't know why but I like you very much. You're so cultured! I'm sure that working by your side would be very exciting.

DIRECTOR (*somewhat disturbed*): Yes? Well, ah . . .

ESTELA: You're so strong and so gentle, both at the same time! I was just fascinated watching you give orders. You're a man of steel, that's what you are! But at the same time, you're so gentle!

DIRECTOR (*flattered*): Well, that's what I'm here for.

ESTELA: Why, if I were working here, I couldn't take my mind off your orders day or night.

DIRECTOR (*again somewhat upset*): Oh, now, you're much too young to devote all your time to the library.

ESTELA (*moving close to him*): And what would I devote myself to if not that?

SECRETARY (*interrupting, abruptly*): What will I do with the fellow from the tailor?

DIRECTOR: Ask the man from the tailor to wait!

SECRETARY: He can't wait. And he's going away. (*Then, getting in her dig*) And you won't be able to get married on Saturday.

DIRECTOR: But, Madam!

SECRETARY (*calling off*): Come in! Yes, you. Come in. (*The Tailor enters and bows obsequiously. During the following scene he will make the Director remove his jacket and will put the frock coat on him. Later he will tear off the two sleeves of the frock coat, tug the lapels in place, and then, with a piece of chalk, mark the alterations and the button holes, very much in the way of a painter standing in front of his canvas. He will raise and lower the Direc-*

tor's arms as though he were manipulating a puppet, forcing him into perfectly absurd positions. He will mince around the Director constantly. Finally he will put a sleeve back on and fix it with pins. While the left sleeve is still off, the Secretary General will enter.)

DIRECTOR (*paying no attention to the Tailor throughout all of this*): Now what were we talking about when we were so rudely interrupted?

ESTELA: I was confessing that I would really like to work with you.

DIRECTOR: And you will, my dear. I suppose you're impressed, because instead of finding me to be a little old man (*he has spoken it in the tone of a little old man*) with a qua . . . quavering voice, you found me to be a young man instead . . .

ESTELA: Oh, I adore you. You're marvelous! (*She laughs and puts her arms around him.*)

SECRETARY (*interrupting*): The Secretary General will be here in five minutes.

DIRECTOR: Please, Madam.

SECRETARY: Five minutes!

DIRECTOR: But Madam . . .

SECRETARY: Miss, the Director is very pressed for time!

ESTELA: I know. Five minutes. You said so twice.

SECRETARY: From another point of view, Miss, he can give you two days. The Director isn't getting married until Saturday.

DIRECTOR: Margarita! You've got no right! Excuse me, I mean, ah, Señora de Luppi.

(*Martínez enters, followed by the Spanish Reader.*)

MARTÍNEZ: Can't find them anywhere. (*He dusts himself off.*) What a mess. Covered with dust!

DIRECTOR: What can't be found anywhere?

MARTÍNEZ: That book!

DIRECTOR: Madam, take into account that . . . Don't go away! Look through the catalogues, Martínez.

MARTÍNEZ: I already did, and it's not in the catalogues nor in the lists of new acquisitions, nor in classified books, nor in the pink cards!

DIRECTOR: So?

MARTÍNEZ: It's in the catalogue invented by the Subdirector.

DIRECTOR: Very well, what's the problem?

MARTÍNEZ: No problem at all. Except he's the only one who understands it and I sometimes wonder if he understands it himself!

DIRECTOR: It's very simple, Martínez.

MARTÍNEZ: It may be simple for you. (*He takes out a paper.*) I looked through the *P*'s from *P* to *Pi*—Piranesi. Very well. Since I do happen to know the alphabet, I found it. Here it is: 23–4–5–7.

DIRECTOR: Very well, Martínez. Room 23, stack 4, shelf 5 . . .

MARTÍNEZ: Room 23 has been flooded for two months.

DIRECTOR: Did the book get wet?

MARTÍNEZ: All the books were moved to room 21 until the next budget comes out and they appropriate money to cover floods. But then at the bottom of the card it said small *a*, then 6A–38–7–7 and then it goes on with NA 6698–P5 G8 and finally it has an *R*.

DIRECTOR: So, Martínez? *R*!

MARTÍNEZ: *R*, Director! *R* for recatalogued, so it's gone back to its place.

DIRECTOR: Very well, there you . . .

MARTÍNEZ: But who knows where the place is? That's what I went to the catalogue for to begin with.

DIRECTOR: Bring me that volume of the index. It just can't be. You'll see how I'll straighten this out.

(*Martínez and the Spanish Reader go out.*)

ESTELA (*smiling and quoting him with admiration*): It just can't be. You'll see how I'll straighten that out. (*They both laugh. She plays with his tie.*) Mr. Director, I wonder. If I were to ask you for a little favor, a little tiny something, you'd do it for me, wouldn't you?

DIRECTOR: What something?

ESTELA: I'd be the happiest girl in the world if you would just read me one of your poems. The one that that old lady was asking for, the one with the funny feather in her hat. Because you see . . . I just love culture! Now, you'll read it to me, won't you?

DIRECTOR: My poem, "The Low Blow of the Oboe"? Well, now, ah . . . well, I suppose I can confess it to *you* . . . I've only written one stanza! It needs, oh, fifteen or twenty more. A great deal. Oh, I've got lots of writing to do on it.

SECRETARY (*from the door*): You've got lots more writing to do on your speech, as well.

DIRECTOR: What time is it? Oh, I know, I know! It's late! But then, he won't come on time. They're always late. (*He is playing nothing less than a love scene, in spite of the fact that his words do not indicate this.*) Now if I read you my poem . . . my stanza, you'll be a good little girl and go away, won't you? (*The Tailor raises the Director's caressing hand from Estela's behind and places it on her shoulder.*)

ESTELA: Of course I'll go. But I'll come back . . . to work here, won't I?

DIRECTOR: Yes. Yes, yes. I'll, I'll, ah, talk to the Secretary General. Now, do you want to hear my poem? (*Estela nods, admiringly.*) Good. It goes like this: (*He declaims amid very large gestures, provoked by the Tailor as he measures and tries things on.*)

> A vision from the lesion,
> Charnal and sidereal butcher shop
> Symphonizing pedestrian acoustics
> Exorcising equestrian mysteries—
> The hero of the oboe presses musically on.

ESTELA: Oh, it's divine! It's absolutely impossible to understand!

DIRECTOR: If I could only make the last line fall right—"The hero of the oboe presses musically on"—then the whole stanza would be finished. But somehow that needs another syllable. I don't know. What does it have? Nine, ten, twelve? Thirteen syllables? It needs something. It seems short to me.

SECRETARY (*coming to the door again*): The only thing we're short of around here is time! The Secretary General will be here in one minute!

(*Martínez and the Spanish Reader enter, carrying between them an unusually large book.*)

MARTÍNEZ: Well, here's your catalogue. (*They drop it with a large thud onto the middle of the floor.*)

SPANISH READER: It weighs more than a coffin . . . and in this heat, too!

DIRECTOR (*stooping down and opening the catalogue.*): Well, now, let's see. *Pe . . . pi . . .* Piranesi . . . yes, here it is. Well, what did I tell you, Martínez: 23–4–5–7!

MARTÍNEZ: Go on.

JANITOR (*bursting in*): There's a big limousine at the door and the lookout from the band has given the signal. It's a big, black car.

SECRETARY: The Secretary General!

JANITOR: And the spittoon is still on the table!

(*The Director runs to the table and takes the spittoon, and, as he is looking for a place to put it on the floor, the band bursts into a lively march. The double doors upstage open, revealing the great hall, brightly lit. The Director runs off in that direction, his arms wide, ready to embrace the Secretary General. The Tailor follows in his wake like a gadfly. The Director's left arm is in shirt sleeves and in his right hand he holds the spittoon.*)

DIRECTOR (*speaking in the direction of the door*): Oh, Mr. Secretary! My dear Mr. Secretary . . .

QUICK CURTAIN

ACT TWO

SCENE ONE

Ten years later. The scene is the same, although there are some details that indicate the passage of time. When the curtain goes up, Martínez and Monteiro are center stage on all fours with their rears facing the audience. They wear long dusters and they are measuring and marking the floor, crawling about with a yardstick in one hand and a piece of chalk in the other. They should give the impression of grunting animals snuffing about the feet of the furniture. They bring their heads together mysteriously in a corner and then crawl underneath various pieces of furniture, et cetera.

MARTÍNEZ: Hum . . . hum . . . hum . . . (*And he draws a line.*)

MONTEIRO (*pause*): Arump! . . . Hrump! . . . Arump! . . .

MARTÍNEZ: Hum! Hum . . .! and . . . hum! hum . . .! (*He draws a line.*)
One . . . one . . . and one . . . (*He puffs.*)

DIRECTOR (*also wearing a duster and indulging in the same game, emerges from beneath his desk, where he had been hidden from the sight of the audience, measuring something while he pushes a chair ahead of him with his head*): One . . . two . . . and three. You're sure the center one is three, also?

MARTÍNEZ: Aha!

DIRECTOR: And the large one is on that side?

MARTÍNEZ: Aha!

MONTEIRO (*standing up*): Oh! My joints! My knees are turning to stone. (*He begins to measure on the walls.*)

DIRECTOR (*standing up*): Well, it looks as though it's going to be all right. Fits perfectly . . . and there's room for expansion upward!

MARTÍNEZ (*from beneath the window*): We better make sure that the window stays closed. If anyone were to open it, the draft would blow through here like a cannon. (*He stands up and puts a lock on the window bolt.*)

DIRECTOR: Well, I suppose we could be more useful if we went and helped bring things down.

MARTÍNEZ: One moment. There'll be a double file here in the center and we haven't marked over here. (*He traces some new lines and looks down at them with satisfaction.*) If you rush me, I might slip up and transfer the fifth stack in here. Well, we've ruined our knees, let's go break our backs.

DIRECTOR: Our backs? Oh! (*He laughs.*)

MARTÍNEZ (*as the three of them leave the stage*): It's going to be hard work, I tell you! Positively Egyptian, like building the pyramids! (*There is a pause.*)

DIRECTOR (*entering again*): With the marks we've made, it'll be very easy. (*He is followed by the Subdirector, Martínez, Monteiro, the Secretary, Estela, the Janitor, Marcuciano Perluchino, and José*

Luis.) Now the shelves are marked here on the floor, you see. So we must carry the books and the packages and place them here in the very same order as they are over there!

JANITOR: Place them here as if they were over there? We bring the whole fourth stack over here and we set it up and . . . but where are the book shelves?

DIRECTOR: We place the books and the packages on the floor and then we place more books and more packages on top of the books and packages. It's only for a few months. The important thing is to maintain the correlative order . . . in order that . . .

SECRETARY: The topography?

DIRECTOR: That's it, precisely! And so, with this correlative order, there will be no change and the catalogue will not have to be altered. As you see, we've left space between the present shelves and the books we're going to move in so that we will be able to have ready access to *all* the books!

SUBDIRECTOR: But what about the window? It's going to be . . .

DIRECTOR: There's no need for fresh air in here. And there'll be more than enough light. Just make up your minds to it! This is your future!! I hope you realize that the Secretary General's idea was nothing less than a stroke of genius. If we place the fourth wing in the third wing and the second wing in the first wing, and so on and so on and so forth with all of them, number 23, number 22, the sixth and the seventh, et cetera, et cetera, the library will then be reduced mathematically in half! It's been ten years, men, since we laid the cornerstone for the new building. But . . . it's taken us ten years to get a young and enterprising Secretary General full of initiative and new ideas! And during all those years, we always felt that it was impossible to have put up the new building. And why? Because none of us knew where we could put the library in the meantime. Just what would we do with the books while they were laying the foundations and putting up the walls? You just can't throw books around. But, by the same token, you can't just move them about, either. Because if there were room for them in some other place, that other place would obviously have to be the new library! You see the problem, don't you? Where to put the books. Ideally, we'd take them to another library. But then this old building is the only library there is. What could the answer be? How to find a solution?

MARCUCIANO: I know. Move *in* rather than moving out.

DIRECTOR: Exactly! Those were the very words of the Secretary General. Move in, that is to say, move *inward*. You're new, aren't you? I don't believe I know you.

MARCUCIANO: I came to help José Luis. He's a friend of mine, and, well, they hired me the day before yesterday.

DIRECTOR (*speaking to José Luis*): Ah! So you're the new one. (*To Marcuciano*) And you, what did you say your name was?

MARCUCIANO: Marcuciano Perluchino, but they call me Tito. I came to give him a hand because he's my friend and because, ah . . . well, he told me he was all fagged out.

(*Everybody laughs.*)

DIRECTOR: Well, Mr. Perluziano, in days like these . . .

MARCUCIANO: Marcuciano Perluchino, but they call me Tito.

DIRECTOR: Well, in days like these, Mr. Marcuchino, we have a particular need of eager young men who wish to work.

MARTÍNEZ: If the two of them manage to carry more books in one day than we do, I'll buy them coffee.

DIRECTOR: Splendid! That's a fine wager. And now, boys, we're off! We have to move a whole wing this afternoon.

(*They all leave. From this moment on they come and go at a dizzying speed, singly or in pairs, carrying books and packages and boxes, all of which they place along the chalk lines on the floor. Everybody works furiously, and so, with the assistance of the extra help, they erect real walls of books that begin to obstruct the main door and cover over the window, turning the Director's office into two compartments surrounded by a narrow aisle. The dialogue is carried on while they come and go but independent of the incessant business of running in and out from either door. As the action mounts, they form a chain very much in the manner of workmen who are transferring bricks. They pass the books and packages from one to the next.*)

MONTEIRO: They say that in 1924 it was really wild. We went and, ah . . . excuse us, let us through, please. But these Olympics are going to be played at home and I've got a right to be worried. I stand a damned good chance of becoming an Olympic star. If only one of them gets hurt, or one of them can't go because of his job, any little thing! Then they'll take me as a substitute. Got my foot in the door, as they say! Know what I mean?

JOSÉ LUIS: I saw you play Sunday.

MONTEIRO: Oh, I can do better than that. Much better. But then I'd have to take care of myself, you know. Smoke less, and, ah . . . go to bed earlier.

SUBDIRECTOR: I'm going to hang little bells all along the sides. And inside there'll be swings and a little fountain.

SECRETARY (*sitting in the big chair behind the desk*): And when do you plan to retire, Don Esteban?

SUBDIRECTOR: In another month and a half. I will have been here forty-four years! I spent sixteen of those years as a porter, too.

SECRETARY: You've earned a rest.

SUBDIRECTOR: When I was a young man I used to go out hunting for wagtails and finches . . . even a cardinal once. And so now . . .

SECRETARY: And have you filed your papers with the accounting office?

SUBDIRECTOR: Of course . . . Well, I told you, didn't I, that I've drawn up plans for the aviary? Oh, it's going to have everything! Little swings and nests, a bird bath, and a tree for them to perch on. And even a little fountain, no matter how small.

MARTÍNEZ: Oh, I tell you this library gets better and better every day.

DIRECTOR: And now we're taking the giant step. This is going to be of extraordinary importance for all of us!

MARTÍNEZ: But let me tell you, if it weren't for those readers who come in every once in a while, this building would do just fine! Get rid of those readers and this library would be perfect.

DIRECTOR: But the new building is going to be marvelous. (*Pause.*) And speaking of marvelous, the real marvel is my daughter. Ana-María. She's nine years old and she plays Chopin on the piano. Oh, she's a phenomenon.

MARTÍNEZ: Well, Mr. Director, let's make another trip. This exercise is good for you, isn't it?

DIRECTOR: They gave her an "excellent" on her examination. And her mother just sat there and wept. Imagine, nine years old, a little tiny thing, no bigger than this, and she just breaks your soul to pieces with Chopin.

JOSÉ LUIS: And it's even going to have suction tubes for messages.

MARCUCIANO: You're kidding me! What about stoves?

JOSÉ LUIS: Central heating, no less!

MARCUCIANO: Hah! That means you're going to have to work in your swimming suits in mid-August.

JOSÉ LUIS: Subterranean passages! Fireproofed! And all the wings are going to be rigged for instant flooding.

MARCUCIANO: What do you want to flood them for?

JOSÉ LUIS: Against thieves. If a thief tries to steal a book, the alarm is set off and automatically water starts squirting from everywhere. The stacks are going to be fifty yards deep, carved out of bedrock.

MARCUCIANO: Now look, José Luis, if it floods, it's going to be good-bye to all your books! They're going to get wet.

JOSÉ LUIS: That's all been taken care of. They tell me that all the shelves are equipped with some kind of clockwork that pull the shelves up into the ceiling, while the thief drowns down below. Well, you saw *Doctor Mabuse*, didn't you? The movie over at the Dore Theatre? Something like that.

MONTEIRO: Next year is going to be hell. You're getting married now in September, aren't you?

ESTELA: No. We had to postpone it.

MONTEIRO: Oh, Estela, not again.

ESTELA: Cacho says that his mother isn't feeling good.

MONTEIRO: But it's March now and the wedding was set for September. Surely she has time to recover by then.

ESTELA: Well, it seemed best to postpone it . . . you know . . . well, till the twenty-ninth of February.

MONTEIRO: The twenty-ninth of February!

ESTELA: Yes. It was Cacho's idea. He thought it would be fun to get married on an unusual day.

MONTEIRO: Well, so you're getting married next year? I told you 1928 was going to be hell. Oh, if only Vasco Cea would get sick, or if Benítez couldn't go, or if García weren't so good! I'd have it made! I'd be a sure thing!!

ESTELA: I'm going to get married in white, with a long dress and a veil and everything . . . everything . . .

SECRETARY: Well, my dear, did you talk to the Secretary General?

DIRECTOR: What was that?

SECRETARY: Old man Fattori told me that he's retiring within the month. Did you mention my promotion?

DIRECTOR: Oh, you can count on my support. I told you I would. Of course the executive and confidential posts are always chosen directly by the commission.

SECRETARY: But did you speak to him?

DIRECTOR: The Secretary General told me that your promotion made sense and that it would be taken care of.

SECRETARY: Oh, thank you. Thank you very much. I knew it would come through.

DIRECTOR: I repeat I have virtually nothing to do with it.

SECRETARY: Oh, when you talk, everyone listens! How is your daughter?

DIRECTOR: Wonderful. They published a picture in the *Voice of Music*. The caption read, "The Little Mozart from Minas Street."

SECRETARY: And the other daughter?

DIRECTOR: The little one? She's got the measles. Her mother spends day and night taking care of her . . . oooph!

SECRETARY: I never dreamed I'd be Subdirectress. You know I feel giddy. I want to laugh and dance. I could fly about like a bird! The first thing I'll do is put a stop to readers who come early . . . and readers who come late! Oh, I'm so happy!

JANITOR: It's going to be a radical change. I'm going to post the orders for the help on the walls: "Porters must report to the maintenance room from one to two and janitors must report from two to three." Signed, Achilles Arrieta, maintenance chief. They say my new uniform will be decorated with three strands of gold braid. What do you think? Do you think there'll really be three?

SUBDIRECTOR: And they say that they're doubling the salaries.

JANITOR: Of course, why not?

SUBDIRECTOR: That's what I'm waiting for, and when they do, I'll retire. Look, when you figure deductions, and the social security, and the rent, and the Cooperative, and the quota for the club, and the advance of the three salaries, I'm left with about fourteen pesos thirty-seven a month.

JANITOR: Oh, that's barbaric.

SUBDIRECTOR: When they double our pay, I'm going to get that aviary on credit. Even if my wife says no, I'm going to get it!

SECRETARY: I've got to make myself a new suit for the day I will receive my appointment. Carmucha's going to turn green when she finds out. She's one of those who believe that women weren't meant to work.

ESTELA: And let me tell you she makes a lot of sense!

SECRETARY: To each his own. If you're efficient, it's all right. But if you can't do a blessed thing, then . . .

ESTELA: I'm getting married in February, did you know that?

SECRETARY: Wasn't it set for August?

ESTELA: Well, we were set for September. Then his mother, you know . . . But now it's definitely going to be February, on the twenty-ninth.

SECRETARY: Definitely? Oh, you're a lucky girl, aren't you?

MARCUCIANO: I think they're beating us. I counted their loads and then I counted ours. I think they're ahead by two boxes and one package.

JOSÉ LUIS: Well, let's hurry. Pretty soon there won't be anything left to bring up. We've got to beat them before that.

MARCUCIANO: There's nothing left.

JOSÉ LUIS: Let's find out. Come on, come on. Hurry.

MARTÍNEZ (*imitating a barker*): Ladies and gentleman, our next number will be a very popular little ditty dedicated to the most solemn commemoration of this little old shack of ours and the people that run it. (*He begins to imitate the sound of a scratched gourd.*) Bbrrrr . . . Chim-pum. (*And he begins to sing.*)

The library, the library
The library is going to move!

(*He repeats this and the others join in little by little.*)

DIRECTOR (*cutting off the song*): Gentlemen! I congratulate you, gentlemen! We have finished the transfer! I'm very happy to see you enjoying yourselves. (*He indicates the walls that have been built out of books, packages, and boxes.*) I think that we can say in a very real way that we have built our library. (*They chime in with expressions of approval.*)

MONTEIRO: The older he gets, the more the young goat likes to hear himself bleat.

JOSÉ LUIS: Who is the young goat?

MONTEIRO: Shhhh . . . the Director.

MARTÍNEZ: Be quiet.

DIRECTOR: In a very special sense, we can say, yes, we can say that this is the new wing of the library. And that in fact it is the best of them all. This building was erected with our own hands and constructed with our own enthusiasm, an enthusiasm capable of moving mountains. (*They applaud and cheer.*) Now, let me finish, let me finish. Tomorrow, gentlemen, or the day after tomorrow at the very latest, the pick-ax will sink its steel tooth into the rotten putrefaction of this ancient building. Therefore, my friends, let us look forward to that day, full of optimism for what the future promises, and let us take leave of each other now, repeating to ourselves the great word of hope and promise: Tomorrow! (*There is much applause. The song about the library, led by Martínez, starts up once more, and all of them sing and dance.*)

FAST CURTAIN

SCENE TWO

Ten years have passed. A catacomb that serves as a reading room. There is a backdrop painted to look like a wall covered with book-shelves, nine to twelve feet high. Above these shelves are two very small windows that admit two thin shafts of light. These pencils of light are the only illumination. A very long table cuts the stage in half; actually it is simply a series of planks thrown over sawhorses. The chairs that line the table are seen in profile and are very plain. There are three or four lamps with green conical shades that hang down from the ceiling and serve to cast light on the table should any-one care to read. At the moment they are not on. At right there is a low door, more like a mouse hole than a door. Because of this door, one can make out the great thickness of the cellar walls, for the read-ing room is now in the cellar. Against the right wall there is a desk of the kind that requires one to stand up in order to write at it. Above it, hanging from a nail, is a little kerosene lamp that makes a small yellow circle on the whitewashed walls. Estela and Martínez are on stage, along with the Janitor and the Subdirector. They surround the Scholar, who is seated at the head of the table on the left side. The Scholar is for the moment invisible because of the closeness with which the employees have surrounded him. As the curtain goes up we hear loud laughter.

MARTÍNEZ (*laughing as he speaks*): What did you say? What was that again?

ESTELA: Oh, really, say it again!

TWO OR THREE OTHERS: Yes, I want to hear it. Yes, what was it?

SCHOLAR (*still unseen, as he speaks up in the voice of a frightened mouse*): ÜBER DIE VIERFACHE WURZEL DES SATZES VOM ZUREICH-ENDEN GRUNDE.

MARTÍNEZ (*trying to imitate him*): Über zurenchender Grunde . . . (*He bursts into laughter.*) Oh, my sides hurt! Don't make me laugh like that.

SUBDIRECTOR: Me too! Oh, you don't know how happy I am I came. It's absolutely unbelievable! What he does with his mouth!

JANITOR: That's good enough for a circus. Isn't that so, Don Esteban?

ESTELA: Oh, please, say it again! What book was it you wanted?

SCHOLAR (*repeating just as before*): ÜBER DIE VIERFACHE WURZEL DES SATZES VOM ZUREICHENDEN GRUNDE.

MARTÍNEZ: You're absolutely sure that noise stands for a book? Sounds as though you were imitating a railroad train!

SCHOLAR: Are there no specialists in philosophy among you?

ESTELA: Oh, now, sir!

MARTÍNEZ: That's a good one! Philosophy!

SCHOLAR: And, ah . . . the German collection. Don't you have one?

JANITOR: The poor man must be crazy.

SUBDIRECTOR: When I see something like this I'm sorry I ever retired. Oh, oh, it was a good thing I came today.

MARTÍNEZ: Now get this straight, my friend, if that noise you've been
making is a joke on me, I'm going to push your face in. (*He threat-
ens him.*)

ESTELAS Oh, now, don't pay any attention to him! He's just playing
tough. Ah, would you explain to me what you want?

SCHOLAR: The original was published in Rudolstadt in 1813.

MARTÍNEZ: Well, what do you know!

SCHOLAR: But, ah, if the first edition isn't available, well, even if you
don't have it in German, I could consult the Spanish translation,
although I would prefer . . .

SUBDIRECTOR: Now, books in Spanish, that's another matter. That's
a lot easier.

MARTÍNEZ: We've got more of them than we know what to do with.
We've got them to burn! (*He laughs.*)

ESTELA: Can you translate, well, whatever it was you said?

SCHOLAR: ÜBER DIE VERFACHE WURZEL . . .? Well, ON THE FOUR-
FOLD ROOT OF THE PRINCIPLE OF SUFFICIENT REASON.

ESTELA (*she is shocked, as though he had uttered some filthy word*):
Of the what?

SCHOLAR: It's Schopenhauer's doctoral dissertation.

MARTÍNEZ: Schopenhauer? (*He bursts into laughter.*) Why didn't
you say so? The minute you said Schopenhauer!

SCHOLAR (*shrinking even further into himself*): Arthur Schopenhauer.

MARTÍNEZ: Well, now, things are beginning to come clear. Now by
Schopenhauer Pérez, for example, we've got the complete works.
And we can offer you a much better book than the one you asked
for. What's it called? Oh, yes, yes. MEMOIRS OF A YOUNG GOAT.

You'll get a whale of a lot more out of this one than from that German one. It's a lot better.

SCHOLAR: Well, that may well be. But if it's at all possible I would like, that is to say, if you have it, a copy of THE FOURFOLD ROOT, that is, of course, if you have it in your collection.

JANITOR: Over here we've got all the works by the Young Goat.

(*There's a knocking at the door.*)

SUBDIRECTOR: That must be the Director. When I told him I was coming down to the cellar to greet you, he said he'd be right down.

(*Martínez opens the door and the Director enters stooped over.*)

MARTÍNEZ: A reader. What do you think of that?

DIRECTOR: No!

MARTÍNEZ: There he is. Look at him.

DIRECTOR: It's just Don Esteban, who has come back for a visit, to talk over old times.

MARTÍNEZ: No. There's an honest-to-God reader. He's insane, though. Keeps asking for a book in Russian.

DIRECTOR (*half way across to the left*): Martínez says there's a reader.

ESTELA: Yes, sir. But he's just a waste of time. He keeps asking for some ridiculous book.

DIRECTOR (*catching sight of the scholar, speaks in a highly approving tone*): And so, you've come to ... ah ... read?

SCHOLAR: Yes, sir. I'm here for a few days. I study in Mendoza.

DIRECTOR: Oh, very good, very good. Someone was bound to come. And just what is it that you are looking for?

SCHOLAR: Apparently the book is very little known. Actually, it's much too little known! And I thought that perhaps here . . . but I suppose not. In fact, I . . . I know not!

DIRECTOR: Well, um, what is it about? We're here to serve you. (*Almost imploring*) Please!

SCHOLAR: Well, I don't wish to offend you. But . . . um . . . to be perfectly frank, I need to consult Schopenhauer's doctoral dissertation. (*He looks ashamed and almost chokes on the title.*) ON THE FOURFOLD ROOT OF THE PRINCIPLE OF SUFFICIENT REASON.

DIRECTOR: Oh, yes, I remember. Unfortunately, I don't believe we have it in German. But I'm sure that we have it in the Spanish edition. Martínez, go and look in those big books on philosophy. Schopenhauer, Martínez.

MARTÍNEZ: If you say so. (*And he goes out.*)

DIRECTOR: Please, sir, be seated. (*The shafts of light from the windows have become more and more faint. The stage is actually crepuscular. The Director lights a candle near the Reader.*) I'm afraid you're going to have to work in the dark. We haven't had any electricity since yesterday. They'll bring the book in a jiffy. Well, so things are going nicely with you, aren't they, Don Esteban?

SUBDIRECTOR: Oh, yes, onward and upward. I went to the occulist yesterday. And he tells me that I can't be operated on yet. I see everything fuzzy, but I can't be operated on yet.

DIRECTOR: But you're just as spry as ever.

SUBDIRECTOR: Oh, yes, I'm perfectly well. But I wanted to talk to you about my son-in-law. That's what I came for. Remember him? The one who married Chiquita, the daughter who took me in. Ah, I'm living with them now. I mentioned him to you some months back. I was wondering if you couldn't make . . . well, a little push to get him nominated for a position. Even as an assistant.

DIRECTOR: Don Esteban, I'm your friend. And what's more (*he is obviously lying*) I've already spoken to the commission. But in any case . . . now what was his name again? (*To the Janitor*) Achilles, have you finished stamping the donations from Daniel Ferrere?

JANITOR: I'm almost finished, sir. But José Luis . . .

DIRECTOR: I want three seals in each book, remember that. (*To the Subdirector*) Now what was your boy's name? (*They go out.*)

JANITOR: You know, Don Esteban is lucky. He's been retired for four years. But I warn you, I've already spoken to the Director. "Next January," I told him, "come hell or high water, I'm retiring."

ESTELA: But Achilles, you've got a perfect right.

JANITOR: You're damn right I do. Now you tell me if you think it's fair for an institution of this size to have only one maintenance man.

ESTELA: No, you're right. Has Margarita called for tea?

JANITOR: They're all bosses in this place. I'm the only one who ever does anything. It's always Achilles this, Achilles that! But what about me? Who do I give orders to? Huh? No one!

ESTELA: Life is unfair.

JANITOR: You can say that again! And I'm not young any longer.

MARTÍNEZ (*entering*): That queer book happens to be right here in this room, what do you think of that? (*To the Scholar*) Well, what do you think of that? Here we are, looking high and low for that damn book of yours, and it's here all the time. Right here on this wall. Achilles, you go up that way and I'll go around the other side. And you, Estela, do me a favor, will you, and hold the lamp. (*Martínez and the Janitor climb up the bookshelves on rope ladders not visible to the public. They go up and down and cling sideways like flies on the wall. Estela goes to the desk and takes the electric lamp. The sunlight that had lit the stage has now disappeared altogether. The circle of light from Estela's lamp alternately picks out Martínez and the Janitor in their various insect-like attitudes. The effect is a series of photographs of the tortured positions adopted by the two men.*)

MARTÍNEZ: Estela, over here! (*She lights him up and he hunts about.*) Oh, my God, you'll never guess what I just found. Volume two of the National History. We've been looking for it for years.

JANITOR (*to Estela*): Please, over here. (*And he hunts about.*) When you're busy working you don't realize just how many books there are. I wonder why the hell anybody writes new ones! No one has the patience to read the ones we've got. Thank you, that's enough. It's not over here.

MARTÍNEZ: We're having a little barbecue out at the ranch on Sunday. There's going to be music and everything. I know they've invited Sosa, the one who plays the guitar. (*He is enthusiastic, makes a gesture, and almost falls from his perch.*) Light, for God's sake! Keep me in the dark! See if I fall down!

ESTELA: What do you think I'm shining on you! Oh, ho, I'm in a fine mood to put up with that temper today. (*She starts to get teary.*)

MARTÍNEZ (*apologetically*): Oh, now, Estela. Estela!

ESTELA (*now openly crying*): Oh, don't pay any attention to me. It's just private matters, that's all! (*She sobs and lowers the lamp.*)

JANITOR: Estela! (*After a pause*) Martínez, Martínez, forgive me but . . . what were we looking for?

MARTÍNEZ: That book by Schopenhauer.

JANITOR: It says here . . . Sha . . . kes . . . peare. That's not the right one, is it?

MARTÍNEZ: No, that's another guy. We're looking for someone whose name begins with *S-h-o-w* . . .

JANITOR: You know this business of providing culture is hard work, dedicated work.

(*We hear the Secretary's voice in the same tone that she will employ in the next scene. This time the voice is edged by the spectral echo of the cellar. However, the voice must be recognizable as the Secretary's.*)

SECRETARY'S VOICE: Estela! Martínez! Come on up now! Tea will be ready any minute! It's time to come up for tea!

(*Martínez and the Janitor climb down.*)

MARTÍNEZ: Come on, Estela.

ESTELA: All right. Good. I could use something hot.

(*They go out. The Scholar continues to sit at the head of the table. The Janitor goes to the other side of the stage and stands guard. He is dimly lit by the little kerosene lamp. There is a pause. The Scholar sneezes in spite of himself. He has made rather painful efforts to prevent the sneeze.*)

JANITOR (*quite normally and softly*): Bless you!

SCHOLAR: Thanks.

CURTAIN

SCENE THREE

Ten more years have passed. The scene is once more in the Director's office, but the walls that were improvised in the earlier scene out of boxes and packages and books have now become permanent aspects of the library. Furthermore, the room has been divided into two stories, thus making four compartments of the two divisions that had been created in the previous scene. The two upper compartments are so low that it is impossible for one to stand up straight in them. And in the lower compartments one is able to touch the ceiling by reaching up. The stage has been divided into six cells, four compartments, and two lateral passageways. The setting produces the claustrophobic effect of the inside of a submarine or the belly of a whale. In compartment A the light should be dimmed to the point of discomfort. Compartments B and E are joined by a ladder. Compartments A and C are connected by a metal pole of the sort one encounters in fire stations. In the downstage side of the second-story partition there is a small opening just large enough to permit one to crawl through. It is the only means of communicating between compartments A and B. Compartments C and D are joined by a very narrow door cut into the upstage side of the partition. In compartment A there is a desk and a high stool that squeezes its occupant against the ceiling. A small table lamp makes it possible for us to see the actor who occupies the desk. This is the only illumination. The rest is darkness. In compartment B there are filing cabinets against the walls and no other furniture. In compartment C we find the director's desk, table, and chairs, so crowded together that it is very difficult to move about. In compartment D, against the upstage wall, there is a small table on which rest a tiny butane burner and the other necessities for preparing and serving tea. Hanging on the wall near the table is a giant oil painting in a massive and splendid gilt frame. The subject of the painting, a proud and severe dignitary in a uniform, stares into the cubicle. Compartments C and D as well as the passageways are dark when the curtain goes up. José Luis is working in compartment A, perched on his high stool like a cockroach. In compartment B, Ema Fontes and Monteiro move from filing cabinet to filing cabinet, their shoulders stooped.

EMA: Papa told him, because they're just like brothers, papa told him here's something to keep my little girl busy. And he was right, because I was bored to death at home. Embroidery bores me to tears! . . . so does sewing! And I wasn't about to start keeping house. Well, imagine it . . . and so . . .

MONTEIRO: P Q 8519 R8 A, 1924, you got that?

EMA: I think so.

MONTEIRO: Did you look?

EMA: I think I did.

MONTEIRO: In what file is it?

EMA: In this one . . . I think.

MONTEIRO: You've got to keep on your toes around here! In this institution, seeing is believing!

EMA: Oh, you're so right! As I was saying, embroidery and sewing and cleaning, all that's so boring! The radio puts me to sleep. And when I want to read a book it puts me to sleep, too. Of course in summertime there's always the beach, but in winter . . . that's why papa told me I had to keep busy and amuse myself. And they're just like brothers, you know. If it hadn't been for that, I woudn't have come to work here at all! (*She takes out a little bottle of fingernail polish and begins to paint her nails.*) Do you mind holding my polish for a second? Look out! Don't spill it. (*Pause.*) Like the color? Mónica Patricia says it's too daring. It's called Bolshevik Revolution. Hold it over . . . I wan'na dip! (*And she dips the brush into the fingernail polish.*)

MONTEIRO: P Q 8519 R8 is simply not here! This filing cabinet is some sort of beast. It devours cards instead of preserving them! It digests them, dissolves them, shreds them to pieces! I'm positive that yesterday I filed P Q 8519! But it's always the same.

(*The Secretary enters and turns the lights on in the passageways. Then she turns the lights on in compartment B. Then she finishes preparing the tea, the water for which was boiling on the stove. She pumps up the butane stove. She hums to herself and moves about like a housewife.*)

SECRETARY (*sticking her head out into the passageway*): Estela! Martínez! Tea's ready! Call Martínez! (*Then coming again to the foot of the ladder*) Monteiro, the tea will be ready any minute now. Tell José Luis and come on down.

MONTEIRO: What did you do with the candle?

EMA: I filed it . . . under *C* for candle.

MONTEIRO (*takes a candle out of the filing cabinet, lights it, and, with candle in hand, crawls through the opening in the partition, but*

stops with his body half in one compartment and half in the other):
José Luis, tea's ready.

JOSÉ LUIS: I'm coming. Do you remember the number for Cutter
Carolina de Invernizio?

MONTEIRO: Y 593, isn't it?

JOSÉ LUIS: Let me finish this and I'll be right there.

*(Monteiro returns to his compartment on all fours, backing up,
and puts the candle away. Martínez and Estela are now in compartment D.)*

EMA *(from above)*: Martínez, don't look up, I'm coming down.
*(Martínez turns his back and Ema comes down, followed by Mon-
teiro. The Secretary hands out the tea and passes a box of cookies.)*

MARTÍNEZ: You know, there's been a fellow coming here for three
days. Over and over. He keeps saying he wants to read a book in
Greek.

ESTELA: Greek? He must be out of his mind.

SECRETARY: Some people have nothing better to do than make trouble.

MARTÍNEZ: When I told him that the library was simply not up to
it, his jaw dropped down to his chest and he began grumbling.
And then I had to face right up to him. I told him that if he went
on that way I was going to have to report him to the Director. That
frightened him and he went away.

MONTEIRO: If he'd known the young goat! *(They all laugh.)*

ESTELA: Thanks, Margarita. I can't eat anything today, I didn't even
have breakfast.

SECRETARY: You've been seeing your husband again!

ESTELA: No, I haven't seen Cacho for months. *(She starts crying.)*
It's because of Rafael!

DIRECTOR *(entering with his friend)*: This way. Well, good afternoon, everybody.

MONTEIRO: Hello.

(The Director and the Friend go on into compartment C.)

MARTÍNEZ: That must be the new Subdirector.

SECRETARY: Must be! Looks dumb enough.

ESTELA: Margarita, would you believe it, it's been three days since he called me or even came to the house. (*She starts crying.*) Rafael isn't even jealous of me!

DIRECTOR (*sitting down at his desk*): Well, sit down, Jorge. Move that table. Yes, make yourself comfortable. (*A little pause.*) I *had* to talk to you in the worst way. Now I don't seem to know how to begin. (*Pause.*) Oh, I'm so tired. I've been exhausted for years but I didn't realize it. I don't know if you'll understand what I'm about to tell you. Well the best thing for me would be to get a good rest. That would really set me up. If I could only go to Europe for a little while, everything would be all right! (*Pause.*) I've wanted to finish that book of mine for years. I've told you about it, remember? The last war, some things about the invasion of Belgium that, in every day and every way, appear more and more certain to me! But that's not what I wanted to talk to you about! Jorge, oh, I can't stand Isabel any longer! I swear I can't stand her! She *and* my daughters! Oh, the headaches and the bills and the Malvarezes and the Gómez Pendolas, the whole thing! You've got to understand me. It's just too much, too much! And for no good reason, no good purpose! My life's become meaningless, bitter. I'm wasting my life, throwing it away on one stupidity after another. I'm forty-seven years old, my boy, and I'm fed up! Fed up! The very thought of going home makes me sick. Gives me indigestion. I hate my daughters. I hate my wife! Yes, I hate her! I'd like to see her . . .

JOSÉ LUIS (*who has just slipped down the pole*): Oh, excuse me, I'm . . . um . . . I'm going to have my tea, Mr. Director. (*He gets caught in the furniture and trips and spins about.*) Oh, excuse me. No, no, I . . . I didn't hear a thing! I swear . . . I . . . I . . . not a thing! (*And he goes into compartment D.*)

MONTEIRO: I remember it was the ninth of March. Here, look at the clippings! They mention me by name. See, here! There where they mention Monteiro . . . that's me! There were three of us up for the team. Practice started on the twelfth . . . and I began sneezing on the ninth! If I hadn't caught the flu I would have gone. When all the Olympic athletes went by in their open trucks, I tell you the tears ran down my face. All I could think of was, if I hadn't caught the flu, if I hadn't had the fever! It was exactly the ninth of March when I began sneezing. It remember it so clear! That flu should have turned to pneumonia. I should have died.

SECRETARY: José Luis, is that man the new Subdirector?

JOSÉ LUIS: I don't thing so. He's just a friend of the Director, judging by what they were saying.

SECRETARY: Well, he appointed him a week ago. You'd think that after the post had been vacant for four years, the least he could do is hurry a bit to get to work. This new goldbrick must have real pull!

JOSÉ LUIS: Yesterday, over at the ministry, they were saying that they were going to start the excavations for the new building. Easy on the sugar.

MARTÍNEZ: Don't tell me you believe that . . . you little cherub!

ESTELA: Rafael told me they were going to start construction.

MARTÍNEZ: Oh, well, then, it's certain! Whatever Rafael says is absolutely correct because he's so handsome, after all, because he's so young! Oh, he's a lively one, that Rafael.

ESTELA: Martínez! (*She starts to cry.*) How could you?

JOSÉ LUIS: A porter told me and those guys know a lot.

MARTÍNEZ: Don't be a goose. Do you see these walls? We constructed them ourselves one afternoon because we had to make room. Or have you forgotten? And that was how many years ago? Eight? It must be eight years.

MONTEIRO: Oh, more than ten! That was before Columbus.

MARTÍNEZ: There, it has been more than ten years since they made us move in and they tore down half of the building. What do you say to that?

SECRETARY: Have another cookie, José Luis. No one's eating! My little María Inés made them for me.

DIRECTOR: Jorge, I'm going out of my mind. You've got to help me out. That's why I had to talk to you. (*Pause.*) I realize that this isn't usual. I can't imagine it happening to anyone else. But if you knew her! (*Pause.*) And furthermore, there's something magical, something between her and me that . . . well, I call it magic! It's one of those coincidences that absolutely stuns you. I start to say something and she takes the words right out of my mouth. No, seriously! You won't believe me, but looking into her eyes I can tell exactly what she's thinking! I swear. It's happened to us a thousand times. Oh, she's such a lovely little thing. She's almost an angel. And a year younger than my daughter. Imagine! Some nights on the way home, all of a sudden I understand my life and I know what I'm here for! I . . . I really . . . I can't explain it to you, but believe me, I have a feeling that somehow, some way, I'm getting closer and closer to something that has real meaning. Something that will bring real order into my life. I feel as though God or something like Him really did exist, as though we could know Him and share in His absolute knowledge. Do you see what I'm talking about. I now feel that everything is easy and true and that things are fine the way they are. I feel the world was born from God and that we should be happy! Here, in this world that God made! I feel that I have to give in to this thing that is dragging me on . . . because it is stronger than I am! Because it's God itself!

MARTÍNEZ: Well, I interrupted him. I said, "Enough." In a country like ours, governed by nothing but red ants, what are we going to do but scratch? (*Everybody laughs.*) What do I care if his brother is chief of police. I told him to his face . . . *ciao*! And if he didn't like it, I told him to go get the book himself! That that's what his legs were for. (*Pause.*)

MONTEIRO: That's right. In order for you to get your promotion, Estela, I would have to get mine first. And in order for me to get mine, Martínez would have to die or retire before two years are out.

MARTÍNEZ: Retire? That'll be the day.

MONTEIRO: Well, then, you'll have to die.

ESTELA: Or . . . *you* could die, Monteiro.

JOSÉ LUIS: I like your daughter's cookies. You can tell she's a great little housekeeper.

SECRETARY: What I can tell is that you've already *seen* her!

JOSÉ LUIS: Well, yes, I did. The other day when she came to fetch you. She's a cute little girl.

SECRETARY: And *very* serious! She's studying engineering.

DIRECTOR: Oh, life is wonderful, believe me. For years now I've been thinking I was an old man, but now, today, I suddenly realize that I am younger than ever. I've only got one life, Jorge. If I don't give it all up, if I don't give in to the demands that life makes upon me, what am I living for? What's the meaning of it all? (*Pause.*) Of course, there's Isabel. But she's *had* her life! She's another matter altogether. And the daughters. They'll get married and they'll have their lives. But what about me? I'm going to write my book. I've got my dreams and I've got . . . I've got this love of mine that's capable of dragging me anywhere. Because . . . I mean this! I'm capable of anything . . . everything! I swear! Anything. At night, in bed, I feel that the sheets are strangling me, tying me to Isabel! There've been nights when I thought the very worst . . . yes, I mean the worst. I'd rather put an end to everything than go on living this way. Life is so wonderful . . . I've thought of killing myself. Calling her and . . .

(*There is a deafening explosion that makes the whole building shake. The Director continues his pathetic monologue as though nothing has happened. His friend continues listening phlegmatically. In compartment D, Martínez, Monteiro, and the rest cover their ears and go out to investigate. They take a turn around the corridor and then look out of the left window. They pantomime their surprise and joy or indifference or disapproval of the new event. Some of them return to compartment D, others go off. Just before the Secretary enters the Director's office, the din stops suddenly and the Director's words boom out.*)

DIRECTOR: That's why I want a revolver, so that I can kill myself and then kill my wife!

SECRETARY: Sir, they've just begun the excavations for the new building. The machine's working out there in the patio.

DIRECTOR: Oh, please! Leave me alone. Get out! I don't want to be interrupted! Get out! (*The Secretary leaves.*) Jorge, I'm so happy! I'm so sure I know perfectly what it is I have to do. I *know* my sacred duty! First . . .

(*The sounds of the machines and the piledriver begin again. The Director continues to mime his monologue as the curtain falls slowly.*)

ACT THREE

Five years later. It is winter, a cloudy day. Again the scene is that of the Director's office, but it is now completely empty. The partitions have been removed and so has the false floor. Not a stick of furniture is left . . . nor rugs nor artifacts. Along with the furniture the doors, the windows, and the roof have also been removed. In this stage of the demolition, we get a certain vertical light pouring down the naked walls. The light is blue-green and gradually it will become more and more chilly, almost miasmal as dusk sets in. There is a white mason's bucket, and strewn about here and there are piles of sand. Someone has improvised a bench out of two boxes and an old white board. José Luis is sitting on the bench, his clarinet between his knees. He is not playing it. One hears the thunderous conclusion of a military march. When the march is over, José Luis begins to practice his scales. He cannot seem to manage to get past the fourth or fifth note.

CRITIC (*entering*): Is this Madungue 1-1-1-0?

JOSÉ LUIS: Umhuh.

CRITIC: Are you sure?

JOSÉ LUIS: This is it.

CRITIC: But there's a band out there.

JOSÉ LUIS: And what has a band got to do with the name of a street or the number of a house?

CRITIC: You're right. That's good! But there's also a speaker's stand and . . . a . . . a podium. It seemed to me that they were getting ready to lay a cornerstone.

JOSÉ LUIS: Right again. But it's not the first cornerstone. Around here, cornerstones are as common as dirt.

CRITIC: And so this is . . .

JOSÉ LUIS: Madungue 1-1-1-0.

CRITIC: Oh. Well, then, I better go around to the front. Thank you. (*He goes out.*)

JOSÉ LUIS (*exclaiming after the critic has gone*): Foof! (*He goes back to his scales, and this time he cannot seem to make it past the seventh note. Ema enters, sits on the plank next to José Luis, and snuggles up to him. After a moment José Luis talks to her without looking at her.*) Honey, I think it'll be enough, I really think we'll make ends meet! (*She does not answer. He turns around and takes her by the chin.*) C'mon. Let me see that pretty little mouth say that we've got enough.

EMA: Ummmm, ummmm.

JOSÉ LUIS: After taxes and charges, I get 123.50. What do you get, honey?

EMA: I've told you, sweety, 300 gross.

JOSÉ LUIS: Net, dear, net. How much money do you take home?

EMA: I think . . . oh, I'm not sure. Oh, honey, I think it's around 180. You like a 180?

JOSÉ LUIS: I like a 180. With your salary and mine, we've got 300, I think it's enough. If we live with your folks, sweet, I'm sure we can.

EMA: Oh, my love.

JOSÉ LUIS: My little pigeon.

(*While they are kissing each other, the Critic returns.*)

CRITIC (*interrupting them*): Should I inquire at the place where they're holding the ceremony or over there by the little shack?

JOSÉ LUIS: Try the little shack.

(*The Critic goes off.*)

EMA: What does he want?

JOSÉ LUIS: How should I know? Who cares, so long as he goes away. Come on, give me another kiss, huh?

(*While they are kissing, Monteiro and Estela come on through the opening that was once the main door. They are half frozen and walk underneath an open umbrella. They do not notice the sweethearts, who in turn pay no attention to them either.*)

ESTELA: They got thirty-two stones out of him. All of them the same size.

MONTEIRO: But a bladder operation nowadays is easier than an appendectomy.

ESTELA: Julia had more than twenty-seven stitches. I mean they just gored the poor child from here to here.

MONTEIRO (*amused and happy*): They do fantastic things nowadays, huh? Juan Carlos' godfather, remember him? The skinny one who used to come to pick me up on Saturdays. Well, they performed a Caesarean on that man!

ESTELA: Oh, wonderful.

MONTEIRO: It was! They took out his stomach, cut out part of his small intestine, and then there were a couple of skin grafts around the colon. And I'm not so sure, but I think they replaced one of his kidneys. Of course, it comes back to me now, they gave him a plastic kidney! They've got to replace it every two years. Seems that the plastic wears out with the ...

ESTELA: Oh, that's incredible! But I'd prefer that to my headaches. You know, there are some days, Monteiro, when ...

MONTEIRO: I feel the same way about my rheumatism. They can't operate for rheumatism. And my legs hurt so I can't stand it any more. The doctor comes and gives me some little pills. Stupid ass! For all the good they do, he might just as well put his hand on my head and mumbo-jumbo some hokem-pokem, tickle-me-ass!

ESTELA: Monteiro! (*They both laugh. Pause.*)

MONTEIRO (*speaking to the sweethearts*): Hey, they've started the ceremony. Going to listen to the speeches?

JOSÉ LUIS: It's stopped raining. The drizzle stopped a long time ago! (*Monteiro holds his hand out and then closes his umbrella.*)

ESTELA: As though you two could tell the difference. You don't even feel the cold.

EMA: Cold. She says it's cold. (*The two of them laugh.*) Come here, I want to tell you something. C'mon closer. (*She whispers in José Luis's ear and the two of them laugh once more.*)

MONTEIRO: You'd have to see it to believe it. And then they talk about man being a reasonable creature. José Luis, look out!

JOSÉ LUIS (*looking around suddenly*): What? What's the matter? What ...

MONTEIRO: You're pushing your luck! You had a double hit, you know. The Subdirector retired in less than fifteen years. And then Martínez died. So you moved up two steps! It's time you took stock.

JOSÉ LUIS: Stock in what, ah?

EMA: Oh, don't pay any attention to him. You know him.

JOSÉ LUIS: Stock in what, come on.

MONTEIRO: You got a forty pesos raise and you're as ripe as ripe can be. You're ready to fall from the tree.

JOSÉ LUIS: What do you mean by that?

MONTEIRO: You're a ripe little plum, man! All she has to do is hold out her hand and you'll *drop* into it. Plop! Head first into matrimony.

EMA: You're a filthy old man! Don't pay any attention to him, José Luis.

JOSÉ LUIS: Wait a minute! You can't just talk to me that way and then. . .

EMA: Don't pay any attention to him! Listen, I've got to tell you something about yesterday. About last night. (*She lowers her voice and they resume their secrets and giggles.*)

(*Monteiro and Estela sit on the other side of the stage. Pause. José Luis tries unsuccessfully to play another scale. He breaks down on the fourth or fifth note.*)

MONTEIRO: It took me twenty-eight years to do what he's done in fifteen years. Two steps and forty pesos.

ESTELA: Some people are lucky. (*Pause.*)

MONTEIRO: Once, a long time ago, my brother's boss offered me a job selling refrigerators, but I told him I thought it was a disgrace to go around selling things from door to door.

ESTELA: You were right! It's horrible. Remember Juan Emilio?

MONTEIRO: Was he a salesman?

ESTELA: Juan Emilio, that young buck with the pretty face that you fought one day out here in the hall.

MONTEIRO: Oh, yes, I remember.

ESTELA: Well, he left me. He was staying at my place. I don't know if you knew. But . . . well, anyway, he left me. Three nights ago. I went looking for him from door to door. First I went to the boarding house where he used to live. And then I went to the cafe and then I hung around the door of the cafe and then I hung around the door of the club until two o'clock in the morning. There I stood in front of the club with one eye on the club and the other on his boarding house. From one door to the other! And then, when he showed up, he dashed up to the third floor and wouldn't let me in. Oh, that was really horrible.

MONTEIRO: To each his own.

ESTELA: I've been waiting for him three nights now and each time it's the same thing. He won't let me in. Makes me bring his clean laundry to the porter. And . . . you want to hear something worse?

MONTEIRO: What would you do if you came to the middle of the month and didn't have a dime for a cup of coffee. Last week I hit bottom, rock bottom!

ESTELA: I know. Yes, but . . .

MONTEIRO: One learns to accept everything. You know, Estela, after I heard about José, you know, the black man? Well, you probably don't even know who he is, but he was really something, that nigger! He was the greatest soccer player I ever saw. He used to run *forward*, you know, with his body leaning forward, understand? And he was the one who invented the cut pass between the backs.

ESTELA: Did he used to play with you?

MONTEIRO: No. When I made the first league he was already a masseur. He was a relic by that time. And he had all his teeth, hah! A smile from one side of his face to the other!

ESTELA: Yes, of course. But you know, Monteiro, if you . . . if you really knew everything, well, I . . . I've been . . .

MONTEIRO: What a strange thing! They used to feel sorry for him in those days. Whenever I saw him I'd feel sorry. But then I'd forget about him the minute he was out of sight. But now, for a week now, I can't get him out of my head. Poor old nigger. He was really something. Well, we're raising a collection to buy him a radio over at the club. (*Pause.*) That José! He probably wants to listen to the games. I guess that's about all he can do. Don't you think?

(*The Director enters, half frozen, his nose red. His head is covered by a black hat with a slouch brim. He is wrapped in a black overcoat and a bulky muffler. He sneezes and continues to sound off at brief intervals for the rest of the act. No one pays attention to it.*)

DIRECTOR (*after a pause*): They haven't finished down at the wharf and they're already laying the cornerstone up here! (*Pause.*) Well, at least it's stopped raining. (*Pause.*) What are you doing?

MONTEIRO (*pointing to José Luis and Ema*): Well, they're still at it. A little sour clarinet and then a little of the other. You know, talking. And *we're* talking about life, killing time. (*The Director starts to sit down on a pile of sand. Monteiro gets up and turns the mason's bucket upside down.*) Here, sit here, where your desk used to be, remember?

DIRECTOR (*sitting on the bucket*): I got a letter from my daughter. She's still in Brussels.

MONTEIRO: Some honeymoon, huh?

ESTELA: Oh, she was so lovely, even though she's just a little girl. At the church she looked as though she were taking first communion. Like a little Virgin Mary when she came in.

DIRECTOR: All my life I wanted to go to Europe. And now, well, yesterday I was saying to my wife, reading Ana María's letters, well, it's just as though I were making the trip I'd always dreamed of.

ESTELA: She's going to Venice, isn't she? They say it's so romantic.

DIRECTOR: They're going to take exactly the same trip that my wife and I planned. It's really a great joy. Every night I read all of the letters to Isabel, the whole collection. And when they're over I always say the same thing: "Well, woman, what do you think of our trip?" (*He laughs and sneezes, and José Luis tootles on his clarinet. Then he says to himself*) Lovely trip. (*He has gotten to his feet. The bucket has left a white circle on his rear.*)

ESTELA: What a dreary day. Is it much longer?

DIRECTOR: Just a few minutes. A little more than a quarter of an hour. We'll put in our hours until five thirty, and that'll be all.

JOSÉ LUIS: But I agreed with Esteban that he'd come for me at six.

DIRECTOR: It's too cold, and then there won't be any light in the evening. It gets dark so early nowadays.

JOSÉ LUIS (*to Ema*): I'll have to wait for him. It's on account of the registry. Imagine . . .

ESTELA: My feet are frozen.

MONTEIRO: For the life of me I don't know why it's so cold now. It wasn't that way in the old days. Excuse me . . . (*He swats the*

director on the rear to clean the white circle off his overcoat.)
You've got lime on your coat. (*Pause.*)

DIRECTOR: Monteiro, I'd like to talk to you . . . now or later . . .

MONTEIRO: Concerning the library?

DIRECTOR: No. What can you say about that! It's . . . ah . . . a personal matter.

CRITIC (*coming in*): They told me at the little shack up in front that you are the people from the library.

DIRECTOR: Yes.

CRITIC: Well, you could have said so! Who's in charge?

DIRECTOR: I'm the Director.

CRITIC: Manuel Jiménez, at your service.

DIRECTOR: Pleasure.

CRITIC: I must consult some manuscripts of Bartolomé Hidalgo. Do you have them here?

DIRECTOR: Here? Well, as you can see . . .

CRITIC: Oh, but they must be here . . . aren't they?

DIRECTOR: Well, whatever the case, Hidalgo is a published author and the manuscripts are somewhat difficult . . .

CRITIC: Oh, I'm looking for something much more important than you imagine! Now, do you have them?

DIRECTOR: Even though we did, at this time . . . well, put yourself in our place . . .

CRITIC: Am I to interpret your remarks to mean that these manuscripts have been destroyed . . . out of carelessness . . . or that they have been inadvertently sold in one of your lot sales?!

DIRECTOR: Now, now, now, sir, don't get that way. The books are gone, that is to say, they have been deposited or carried off to the official warehouse #1, down by the docks. Because, now . . .

CRITIC: To the point . . . please! Do you have the manuscripts I'm looking for or don't you? If you do, where do you have them?

DIRECTOR: If you'd let me explain, sir.

CRITIC: I . . . I don't need explanations. What I need are Hidalgo's original manuscripts. Consulting those manuscripts is a matter of vital importance to me.

MONTEIRO: Estela, what do you think of that? This is the first one to bother about the library in six years.

DIRECTOR: If you'll just try to follow my explanation. The warehouse hasn't been properly furnished yet. The salted hides, as I explained to all of you, didn't I, my friends . . . now, ah . . . as I explained, the salted hides have gone out. But we still have the wool to contend with! And as long as there's the wool there's no room for us. At the moment there is room for the boxes of books and the bales of wool and that's all! We won't be able to get in until the next shipment. It'll be a matter of days.

CRITIC: But I'm on the verge of a very important discovery. Do you realize that?

DIRECTOR: Of course! I understand perfectly.

MONTEIRO: You know, it's been years since we had a trouble-maker like this one.

CRITIC: But I'm after something really unbelievable! (*He continues, unaware of the interruptions.*) Do you remember that ballad which starts off, "The tarts that Vigodet keeps penned up in his sty"?

DIRECTOR: Yes, yes, yes. "Dance to the tune of his bagpipe."

CRITIC: Good, well, I am absolutely convinced that what Hidalgo wrote was not *tarts*, but *hearts*. "The *hearts* that Vigodet keeps penned up in his sty."

DIRECTOR: Oh, and that's why you want the manuscript.

CRITIC: You must realize that I've submitted my article to the ALPHA AND OMEGA REVIEW of Iowa University. And, as you well know, I'm the only scholar in this country with whom they maintain any correspondence whatsoever. For fourteen years now I have dedicated myself to the study of Hidalgo's poetry between 1808 and 1813.

DIRECTOR: Well, if you've been studying those five years for fourteen years, you can very well wait a few weeks longer. At this moment our reading room doesn't even exist! I beg you, please try to understand.

CRITIC: My dear sir, I don't understand anything about that or anything else. What I'm trying to tell you is that I'm going to change

forever the form of Hidalgo's poems. My discovery will fall upon
Iowa like a bomb. They think of our poetry as something coarse
and crude, but if we change the vulgar word *tarts* for the cultured
term *hearts,* and furthermore if we can prove that that is what he
meant . . . oooohh . . . one must then deduce *a fortiori* that Bartolomé Hidalgo was a learned and lucid poet and not just a happy-
go-lucky, whore-mongering guitar player. The change of *tarts* to
hearts can very well earn me the title of fellow at Iowa University!

DIRECTOR: Rest assured of the fact that I understand exactly what
you're trying to tell me. But it would give me great pleasure if you
too could understand what I am trying to tell you about our
situation.

CRITIC: Am I right in presuming that you do not wish . . .

DIRECTOR: For the love of heaven, sir, believe me! I beg you to
believe me! I . . .

CRITIC: With your permission. This library, is it public or not? (*And
he cuts the Director off as he starts to speak.*) It's public. Do I or
do I not have the right to consult that manuscript? Yes or no! Yes,
I do! You can't deny me that right! So please don't try. I want you
to understand that I am not asking, I am demanding my rights!

DIRECTOR: Please, put yourself in my place, sir. Try to understand
for one minute.

CRITIC: And let me warn you sir that I am a regular contributor to
the FREE TRIBUNE and that this denial of yours will be very thor-
oughly and negatively examined on our pages.

DIRECTOR: Could I please get a word in edgewise? It just can't be that
you don't understand me.

CRITIC: Ah? Are you insinuating that I don't . . . Oh! But this is . . .
this is unbelievable! It's an outrage! This is unbearable! It's unheard of!

ENGINEER (*coming on*): What you mean is insolent.

CRITIC: And who are you? The Subdirector?

ENGINEER: I'm someone who's going to kick you the hell out of here
on your ass if you don't leave immediately! Who do you think you
are?

CRITIC (*his temper dampening perceptively*): Now, there's no need to lose your temper, *s'il vous plait*. After all, this is the library, I presume.

ENGINEER: You presume wrong, this *was* the library! It is now the site for the Third International Committee for Refugees from the Near East in the Far East, the ICRNEFE, now under construction.

CRITIC: But I thought . . . um . . . well, the gentleman over there told me . . . really, I never dreamed that, uh . . .

ENGINEER (*grabbing the Critic by his coat and pushing him to the door*): I've got a lot to do and I have to finish demolition tonight. No time to lose. Get out! (*He pushes him out.*)

DIRECTOR: My dear Mr. Engineer, please accept my apologies. I tried to calm him down in every way I knew how, but . . .

ENGINEER: Forget it. I've been giving orders for so long! I'm used to dealing with personnel problems of this sort. It was nice swatting that mosquito.

DIRECTOR: I'm very grateful, Mr. Engineer, very grateful . . . and talking of mosquitos, I remember once in this very office, the Director's office, a Subdirector said to me, "Mr. Director, the council feels that your report on cleanliness and repairs . . ."

ENGINEER: Good, well, now, Mr. Director, the crux of the matter is, ah . . . well, I came up to tell you that you're going to have to get out.

DIRECTOR: But we can't.

ENGINEER: We're working three shifts! And to keep my men waiting around because of you . . .

DIRECTOR: But, Mr. Engineer, we have to put in our hours!

ENGINEER: Like I told you the other day, this is no longer the library. This is the site of the International Committee.

DIRECTOR: Excuse me. But we can't get into the warehouse down there by the pier because it's crammed with wool. Perhaps tomorrow, when they send out a shipment, but until then we can't get in.

ENGINEER: But we're involved in a demolition!

DIRECTOR: Until tomorrow, it is the library.

ENGINEER: By tomorrow, these walls will be knocked down.

DIRECTOR: Then we'll go down with the ship!

ENGINEER: No jokes, please. And don't hold up my work! How long do you intend to stay?

DIRECTOR: Five thirty.

ENGINEER: You've got five minutes. So . . .

DIRECTOR: Excu . . . you'll forgive me, but hours are hours! And work schedules are work schedules! And if they exist there must be some reason for them.

ENGINEER: All right. But will you give me permission in the meantime to send up a couple of men to clean things out here?

DIRECTOR: Of course! And believe me, Mr. Engineer, I'm most grateful. I mean, after all, what objection could I have? The problem's always to act! Act! (*Then almost to himself*) Things, fundamental things!

ENGINEER (*starting to leave*): You're going to freeze if you stay here. You're soaked.

DIRECTOR: Oh, don't worry about us. One gets used to the cold! (*The Engineer goes off.*) You know, I would have liked to have told him about my report on cleanliness and repairs. (*To Monteiro*) It was in 1929, remember? (*There is a squawk from the clarinet.*)

MONTEIRO (*impatiently*): How long are you going to keep making that noise? (*Pause. They do exercises to keep themselves warm. The clarinet again. Then Monteiro speaks to José Luis in a friendly tone.*) Hey, José Luis, do you want to rub shoulders?

JOSÉ LUIS (*angry*): What do you mean by that?!

MONTEIRO: Oh, now don't get angry! I'm serious. Oh, you meant . . . oh, you thought I meant . . .oh, no! (*He points to Ema.*) No, I'm talking about . . . ah, you know, rubbing shoulders. Coins. The game! Nickels. You know, bouncing them off the wall. We'll play forty throws.

JOSÉ LUIS: Oh, that. All right, wait a moment. Yeah, yes, I'll play, wait a minute.

DIRECTOR: Monteiro, I would like to talk to you.

MONTEIRO: Yes, sir. But let me warn you, I don't remember any of 1929. Along about that time, they were trying to push me out of the soccer team, and I don't remember anything. I was a nobody then.

DIRECTOR: Monteiro, I wanted to ask you a favor. Now, we've known each other for several years. Tomorrow's the twenty-fourth, the, ah . . .

MONTEIRO: Yes, Mr. Director.

DIRECTOR: The day my wife and I met . . .

(*Two Workmen come on. They are talking and laughing happily.*)

FIRST WORKMAN (*interrupting the Director*): Excuse me. (*He makes whoever is sitting on the bench for the moment stand up, and they begin to arrange the tools and various objects they are going to carry off with the plank and the sawhorses.*)

SECOND WORKMAN: Hey, the one for you is the old bag that runs the apartment house. She's got money to burn!

FIRST WORKMAN: Which old bag?

SECOND WORKMAN: The one that came over to complain. Didn't you see her? She's got one tooth and she's covered with warts, but, my God, what lungs! She complained for fifteen minutes straight without taking a breath.

FIRST WORKMAN: Well, what was she complaining about, huh?

SECOND WORKMAN: Bugs and things. Seems she went to get into the elevator and she found herself locked up with a huge rat! It just sat there staring at her!

FIRST WORKMAN: Yah, but what about *her*? What right's she got to stare at the rat?! (*They laugh. Estela, Monteiro, and the Director also laugh, somewhat feebly.*)

SECOND WORKMAN: It's this demolition. It's let loose an army of all kinds of rats and mice. Never seen anything like it! The whole neighborhood is infested.

FIRST WORKMAN: Ah, that's logical. You know, big cellar, lots of junk.

SECOND WORKMAN: Well, it doesn't matter. They're coming over today from public health to kill the rats. You know they use dogs to catch them?

FIRST WORKMAN: Yah, I've seen them. Little tiny ones, fox terriers, they're called. They train them.

DIRECTOR: Monteiro, did I tell you that tomorrow is the anniversary of the day when I met my wife?

MONTEIRO: Well, yes, yes, you told me.

DIRECTOR: Of course. Well, we've . . . we've been friends for a long time, you and I, haven't we?

ESTELA: Are you having a celebration?

DIRECTOR: No. No, no, it's not that. Monteiro, I need five pesos. Could you lend them to me? Since it's the twenty-fourth of the month, we're a little . . .

MONTEIRO: Well, old man . . . I mean, sir . . . it's the twenty-fourth of the month for me, too. Just now I tried to gamble my bus fare with José Luis to see if I could win enough for a cup of coffee. Where would I get five pesos?

DIRECTOR: Forgive me, I shouldn't have asked. It's not really important . . . honest. Forgive me . . . I . . . I really shouldn't.

ESTELA: Don't worry, Mr. Director, I can lend it to you.

DIRECTOR: Oh, no please, madam! Oh, that's not . . .

ESTELA: I really don't need it now. I mean it! I really don't need it! (*Waxing tearful again*) If you only knew how I *don't* need money . . . *now.*

DIRECTOR: Well, I really don't know if I should.

ESTELA: Just be grateful you've got someone to give something to. (*She hands him a bill and then blows her nose.*)

DIRECTOR: Thank you. It's . . . you know, because of the anniversary. I wanted to buy her some dates. We like dates, both of us. I'll have to write a poem to your . . . lovely spirit . . . so generous, Estela.

ESTELA: Please! Don't feel that . . .

DIRECTOR: Although I don't know. Nowadays people laugh at old fogies that write verses. It's all so materialistic!

MONTEIRO: In my day, you'd gamble everything down to your undershirt.

DIRECTOR: When I retire and have time, you'll see. I'll finish my book "The Low Blow of the Oboe." I wanted it to be a hymn in praise of the spirit and against materialism. If I hadn't given myself over to my work the way I did, well . . . I suppose it would have been finished by now. I've left my life within these walls. But now . . . now that I'm going to retire, it's going to be different. I'm sure. You'll see, I'll really *set to work!*

ESTELA: The very first day I came to the library, you recited some verses to me. This room was full of people. Your poems were so lovely!

MONTEIRO: Poor Martínez. He used to like them, too. He knew hundreds of songs, all kinds. He even made them up himself. Remember? (*He sings, rather listlessly, the song about the library in Act II.*)

> The library, the library
> The library, the library
> The library is going to move.

(*Pause.*)

FIRST WORKMAN: Would you mind moving, please. (*The librarians move disconsolately against the walls like prisoners about to be shot. We hear the barking of dogs offstage.*)

SECOND WORKMAN: Hear that? The dogs are here. When they start catching the rats, we've got to go look. Those fox terriers are really something! Two jumps and they corner them and then . . . crack! (*Then to the librarians*) Excuse me, would you mind moving, over that way. Move along, yes, that's right. Thank you. (*They have been cornered.*)

JOSÉ LUIS: You want to play?

MONTEIRO: Nickels only. (*They move to one side and get ready to pitch their nickels against the wall.*) Who got you started on the clarinet?

JOSÉ LUIS: It was my grandfather's. He blew it so well it paid for seven children and a whole house. What do you think of that?

MONTEIRO: And what are you going to blow? Bottles?

JOSÉ LUIS: I'm learning to play the clarinet because I'm ambitious. An uncle of mine knows the director of the municipal band. And then within a few years, with a little bit of luck . . .

MONTEIRO: You mean a lot of luck, don't you?

JOSÉ LUIS: Well, you've got to grab hold of something if you want to move ahead, if you're ambitious.

MONTEIRO: Sure. You grab hold of that, huh? Like a drowning man! . . . and you're right.

JOSÉ LUIS: Sure. Do you think I'm ready to stay here like you did? This is death!

MONTEIRO: And what do you think the municipal band is going to be? The same death with a lot more wind. (*He puts his hand to his mouth and trumpets comically.*)

JOSÉ LUIS: Oh, go on, throw, for God's sake!

EMA: We have to wait much longer?

DIRECTOR: Just a few minutes. A few minutes more and then we can all go home. (*Then talking to himself*) Isabel must have had her injection by now, although, well, the intern didn't come yesterday . . . I never thought I'd spend all the days of my life between these four walls until today. All the days of my life. Coming to the same place, seeing the same people. And what for? For nothing. Absolutely nothing. Or rather, *I* think it was all nothing. A game. A way of keeping busy, making time pass, until one is over and time goes on without one. We'll go home today and they'll knock down all these bricks. And there won't be any trace left of all those days! That's the way it is. Well, all those years of mine were all for nothing, not even rubbish. There won't be anything left in this place. Not one little scrap of me. The first breeze will carry away the air I breathed and there'll be nothing left. You know, I should write about that.

ESTELA: Poor Martínez! But he did have a nice wake. It was held in the garden because it was so hot, remember, Ema? I went with Claudio. Now there was a man who really knew how to be attentive. He didn't even know Martínez, but he spent the whole night there. He even managed to cry . . . to make me happy, I think. It was a lovely wake.

EMA: I should have worn woolen stockings. It's turning cold and it's started to drizzle again. Why don't we go home?

DIRECTOR: We still have a little longer to go. (*Estela opens her umbrella. The Director, Estela, and Ema all take refuge under it.*) We still have a little longer. It's nice to keep up the schedule. It used to be hard for me, but for some years now, it's been a great comfort. One knows that one leaves the office at a certain hour and until then there is nothing to worry about.

JOSÉ LUIS: You always win!

MONTEIRO: Because I always play to win and you . . . you're thinking of something else.

(*There is a sound of barking offstage. The workers leave.*)

SECOND WORKMAN (*as he goes*): They're starting now. Come on, you'll see, it's great!

EMA: José Luis, don't play if you lose.

JOSÉ LUIS: But Ema!

MONTEIRO: Come on, it's your throw.

JOSÉ LUIS (*to Ema*): One more throw, that's all, eh? One more.

EMA: Go ahead. Do what you want! You'll do it anyway.

JOSÉ LUIS: Just one more.

EMA: Whatever you want, you stubborn thing, you.

JOSÉ LUIS: But honey, he's already thrown.

MONTEIRO: Come on.

JOSÉ LUIS: Just this one, honey. Will you be angry at me if I throw it?

MONTEIRO: Come on! Don't be a piker.

EMA: You'll never change. And anyway, you're getting wet. Come here.

JOSÉ LUIS (*tossing the coin*): Well, you won that one, too. I won't play anymore.

MONTEIRO: You'll never play this or anything else, for that matter. At least not from now on.

EMA: That's right. Influence him, influence him! Go ahead!

JOSÉ LUIS: Mr. Director, do you know Sony Terra over at the registry?

DIRECTOR: Yes, I know him. He's the nephew of Izaguirre, the one who was Secretary General. He's the man who appointed me Director here. An extraordinary man! When he told me I had been appointed, I almost hugged him . . . happiest moment in my life!

EMA: If you could give José Luis a note of introduction to Sony Terra . . .

DIRECTOR: Oh, I will, of course. What for?

JOSÉ LUIS: There's a vacancy at the registry and I wondered if I could . . . ah . . .

DIRECTOR: You want to transfer?

EMA: It means twenty-five pesos more.

JOSÉ LUIS: It's just for the time being. You see, I'm . . . ah . . . a little ambitious. And I hope to become a musician and enter the municipal band.

DIRECTOR: And what about your seniority?

JOSÉ LUIS: It's just that twenty-five pesos more a month really speak. I need them to get married.

DIRECTOR: How long ago was it that you came to the library?

JOSÉ LUIS: Fourteen . . . fifteen years. But now I . . .

DIRECTOR: Do you mean to say that you have fifteen years seniority and you're going to exchange them for twenty-five pesos?

ESTELA: Is seniority that important?

DIRECTOR: Are you really talking about seniority? Oh, I see. No, no, please don't interpret it that way. I didn't mean to imply that you were old. To the contrary! But I'm surprised that you haven't realized that we government employees are very much like mummies. Each one of us is worth more the longer we've been in service.

EMA: But, Mr. Director. With twenty-five pesos more a month we could get married.

MONTEIRO: Can't you see, he's got the face of a ripe plum. What I mean is that he's a real ripe man ready for plucking.

DIRECTOR: Seniority is the most important thing there is! A fresh mummy isn't worth anything. On the other hand, if we allow ourselves to be wrapped in yards and yards of routine . . . if, over the years, one has cooked slowly on a low flame of procedures until we're well seasoned with boredom, exhaustion . . . then it's all different! Then one is ripe for promotion.

JOSÉ LUIS: But sir, it's just for the time being. That is to say, later, with my clarinet, if I'm lucky . . .

DIRECTOR: Seniority is a subtle liquor, it embalms us slowly. It takes more than a day to make the sleep of indifference flow through our veins. And it's an even longer journey to come to our total rest, to achieve what I call "the ecstasy of administration." It's true that there are some extraordinary persons who, within a few months of their appointment, have managed to mummify themselves completely! But it's not normal.

JOSÉ LUIS: But I . . . sir, I want to get married!

DIRECTOR: Take my word for it, boy. A man needs a certain seniority in order to retire without retiring. On the average it takes at least five years. And then what a lovely situation that is! It's wonderful to have seniority. Whether one be at home or in the office, nothing matters any more! One is protected from the world and its demands. One lives marvelously, sheltered by the eighth marvel of the universe: pyramids of paper. Under the custody of the impenetrable sphinx of regulation, one lives the life of a pharaoh in the sarcophagus of hierarchical presuppositions, resting forever in peace. Even when one is twenty years away from retirement.

FIRST WORKMAN (*entering with the Second Workman*): I told you those little dogs were great! They killed them all! Caught them and then . . . crack! (*Then turning to the librarians*) You'd better be going now. They really are going to knock the walls down.

DIRECTOR: It's time. Five twenty-eight. We can go now.

JOSÉ LUIS: I have to wait for Esteban because of the registry.

EMA: And me? I'm half frozen, José Luis.

JOSÉ LUIS: Wait for me at home. I'll be over as soon as I can, hon. But I told Esteban to come by at six. All right? (*He takes her hand and they stare into each other's eyes for a moment.*)

EMA: I'll be waiting for you, so don't be late.

(*We hear the dogs barking. They are closer now. During the following they bark two or three times.*)

ESTELA: Are we to report here tomorrow?

DIRECTOR: Well, if the warehouse has been cleared out, we'll put our time in there, but if not, we'll meet here as usual.

JOSÉ LUIS: Well, how will we know where to go?

DIRECTOR: We'll have to find out from the newspapers.

MONTEIRO: Do you think they'll bother with us?

EMA: What about calling you up on the telephone before we start out?

DIRECTOR: Well, how would I know? I suppose the best thing to do is to go down to the piers at one o'clock, and if they don't let us in, we'll come here.

ESTELA: I hope it doesn't rain tomorrow. What fun! Wandering about from one place to the other in weather like this!

(The Director, Estela, and Ema go off underneath the umbrella. Monteiro follows them a short distance behind. He puts up his collar.)

MONTEIRO: Aren't you coming?

JOSÉ LUIS: Didn't I tell you? I'm waiting for Esteban.

MONTEIRO *(ironically)*: My boy, you'll go far! I guarantee! *(He goes off. José Luis sits down on the plank and begins to practice his scales. One or two bricks fall on the piles of sand. The band breaks forth in a very short melody, at the end of which we hear the Voice of the Orator, offstage.)*

ORATOR: My dear Secretary Pro tem with the rank of Provisional Weekly Inspector, most excellent Mr. Ambassador from the Republic of Oslibrón, my dear Minister from Calachín of the Meridinal Bog, ladies and gentlemen. We are gathered today to lay the cornerstone for the new temporary site of the International Committee for Refugees from the Near East in the Far East, the ICRNEFE, initials that intertwine marvelously with the sinuousness of political vines in a tangle of indissoluble knots lowering in a perfect metropolitic without profaning or suprefying that ancient dream which billows florally into the sulphurous aspects of the future! Ladies and gentlemen, let us be armed and, in effect, in order that we may become camels of Ob Groves. It will be through this path alone, if we milify it, that the gross columnifications and camalitic evils will be overcome! On this point I am squarely solid! These are no poultry bags and baggage! In order that we may all be vaquitors . . . this is no time, no dry season wherein just anyone may emulate, according to my rights, the coloquious cabalistic of such strident inaction and intransigence. No, it is not nor will it ever be! For those have been the monicaterers and caterers of symprapatellic nonsense! And for this very reason, they must be indefatigably phosphorized! Therefore, let us admit frankly and unswervingly, let us speak with a pillarditic thright, voicing the world of the castellene in its immortal thrusala. Let us say, "Brothers, with ICRNEFE, a bordery! no munery! no tunery! no punery!" . . . I have spoken!

(The speech ends and is followed by a brief ovation that peters out. José Luis has continued his attempts to achieve the scale on the clarinet. The first shadows of night fall and it begins to rain.)

CURTAIN

In the Right Hand
of God the Father

A FOLK PLAY IN TWO ACTS

BY ENRIQUE BUENAVENTURA

Enrique Buenaventura is a director of the first rank. He has run a theater company in Cali, Colombia, for many years. Like Carballido in Mexico, Buenaventura has been influenced by presentational techniques of modern European drama as well as by Oriental techniques he managed to observe first hand on his visit to Japan during an international theater conference. One of Buenaventura's more recent plays, *Documents of Hell,* has been performed in Canada.

In the Right Hand of God the Father, first produced in 1960, may not be a wholly successful translation. The folk idiom of the original is so pithy that one may well wonder if it should be translated at all— it is precisely this sort of value that is lost in almost any translation. I confess that some of the flavor of the original has been altered in my translation. My efforts to compensate for this unavoidable loss have had to be cautious, for I wanted to translate the play rather than adapt it. Adaptation would have resulted in something foreign both to Buenaventura and the world in which his play has its roots. Regardless of my relative success or failure in translation, I was so impressed by Buenaventura's effort to take *costumbrista* material and Christian ideology as a means of developing a refreshingly irreverent statement of socialist implications that I had to proceed. It goes without saying that in this play Sr. Buenaventura has employed dramatic devices from the old Spanish moralities or *autos sacramentales.* The recommendation made by the play—to cheat—is the same as that made by the ending of *The Good Woman of Setzuan*. However, though the plays deal with similar myths and come to a similar conclusion, I see no point in comparing them further. They are both originals in the sense that the myths employed have been claimed by the authors and have been transmuted into utterly personal statements. The hero's final gesture—shrinking to the point of invisibility and leaping into the right hand of God the Father, which holds the orb of the earth, to cling to the Cross and plague God's own creativity is one of the most beautiful and ironic touches that I have read in Spanish American drama.

CHARACTERS:

The Ringmaster	*The Doctor's Wife*
Peralta	*The Gravedigger*
Jesus	*A Sanctimonious Biddy*
The Devil	*The Niece*
St. Peter	*Wife of the Rich Man*
Death	*Husband of the Old and Ugly*
Peraltona	*Woman*
The Leper	*Young Girl*
The Cripple	*First Beggar*
The Old Beggar	*Second Beggar*
The Blind Man	*Third Beggar*
Maruchenga	*Beggar Woman*

Setting: a peasants' hut. Above it, Heaven is represented by a large cloud with a door. Below, and to the side, is a Hell's Mouth.

PROLOGUE

(The Ringmaster—a clown of the sort one sees at folk fairs—enters carrying a flag. He is dancing to the tune of the folk music customarily employed in these popular entertainments. He places his flag at the proscenium.)

RINGMASTER: Ladies and gentlemen, here I am . . . !
to guide your gaze and claim your ears
for a wise old mojiganga
that's called in Colombia, where I'm from,
"In the Right Hand of God the Father."
It's a serious mojiganga—I assure you!
Now let the cast appear!

(The cast enters, dancing to music which they play themselves. They form a semicircle. Each one of the characters steps forward as he speaks. Those characters that wear masks remove them as they introduce themselves.)

PERALTA: Gentlemen, let me warn you,
and all the ladies, too,
there is no bull at all
attached to the end of my tale.
That's true ... no lie ... that's true!

I'm called (*the actor gives his real name*) and in this mojiganga I play the part of Peralta.

JESUS: It being the first time
I appear before this host,
let me sing now ...
glory to the Father, and to the Son,
and to the Holy Ghost.

I'm called (*the actor gives his name*) and in this mojiganga I play the role of Jesus the Nazarene.

DEVIL: If it's a lie
then let it lie.
If it's a truth
don't budge it.
Ears will hear and eyes will see
the things they'll tell
to you, of me!

I'm called (*the actor gives his name*) and in this mojiganga I play the part of the Devil.

ST. PETER: Knowledge is the root of knowing
and knowing is the root of knowledge.
Or so say the toothless ancients.
So listen well
so you may tell
your tale as I do mine—
exactly!

I'm called (*the actor gives his name*) and in this mojiganga I play the part of St. Peter.

DEATH: Everyone listens and is still
                     whenever I start to sing,
                     though few of you like
                     the sound of my voice.
                     Be quiet! You will!
                     You have no choice.

I'm called (*the actress gives her name*) and in this mojiganga I
play the part of Death.

RINGMASTER: Well, that's it. Now you've seen the leading figures of
our play. Come, little Jesus and St. Peter, climb up to your bird-
cage in the sky. And you, foul fiend, you get yourself below to the
caverns and the caves of your dominions! Aaall . . . get ready
to play your parts, for the show's about to begin!
(*The Ringmaster leaves and the mojiganga commences.*)

ACT ONE

PERALTONA: Why I bother to sweep up this shelter for stinking beggars is more than I know. How could it ever be clean? Who ever
heard of a man who didn't care one bit about himself . . . or his
house . . . or his clothing? Spends all his time washing wounds,
helping the sick, burying the dead. He takes the bread out of his
own mouth and the rags off his back and gives them to the poor.
But who worries about *him* . . . or about *me*? Here we are . . . poor
as church mice, and the whole house overrun with beggars!

LEPER: Water! A little gourd of water, please!

PERALTONA: Water? Ask the cripple over there to get it for you. And
stop bothering me! One of these days the Devil's going to take me
off for being so . . .

LEPER: Water.

PERALTONA: All right, all right, I'm coming! You'd think he was
crossing the desert. (*She goes out, but continues talking.*) Peralta,
what's the point of working like a mule, if you turn around and
throw away everything you've earned, feeding and clothing a whole
army of good-for-nothings?

PERALTA (*entering with a bag over his shoulder and a large spade*):
Stop your mouth, sister, and don't talk nonsense.

CRIPPLE: Oh, Peraltica, we've had no breakfast.

LEPER: We haven't had anything but the little sugar water you gave
us yesterday.

OLD BEGGAR: And all you'll find in my cupboard are the boards, the
bare boards!

PERALTA: These are the last ears of corn in the field. We'll cook up
something for you in a jiffy. The crops have been bad this year.
Bad luck.

OLD BEGGAR: Well, I had bad luck in town just now, no one gave me
anything! Charity's gone out of style! Tap a rich man on the elbow
and he'll give you a kick!

LEPER: Oh, what about Marialarga? Richest woman in town! They
tell me she wags her head from side to side just to save her fan!

PERALTA: I don't like gossip . . . you know that.

PERALTONA (*to the Leper*): Here's your water . . . poor thing. (*To
Peralta*) And you, you get married! Get married, man! Then at
least you'll have to take care of your own children instead of these
. . .

PERALTA: I don't need a woman . . . I don't need children . . . I don't
need anyone! I have my neighbors! They're my family. (*He goes
out with the corn.*)

PERALTONA: Your neighbors! Your family! Look at them, falling all
over themselves with gratitude, aren't they? Look at all they've
done to pay you back. There you are, ragged and more miserable
than any of the beggars you help. Why don't you buy yourself a
new suit? Or buy *me* one, for that matter? We both need new
clothes. Or if just once you'd bring enough food home so we could
fill our stomachs. But you never think of yourself. You've got the
blood of a worm.

OLD BEGGAR: Nasty old shrew!

LEPER: Skinflint!

CRIPPLE: Old snake!

PERALTONA: Grumbling again! Be quiet, all of you. There's nothing wrong with you. When it comes to wagging your tongues, you're not sick then!

PERALTA (*coming back*): You'll have to wait a bit. The water's coming to a boil. And you, Peraltona, stop your noise. I could hear you out in the yard.

JESUS (*emerging from the door in the cloud, with St. Peter*): Look, Peter. See that house down there? By the Camino Real? That's Peralta's house. We've talked long enough—now let's go down and do something. (*They descend.*)

(*Little by little, the lights are brought up around the whole house and music is heard, like a celestial bambuco.*)

PERALTONA: What's that?

CRIPPLE: I feel something too ... strange ... inside!

PERALTONA: And that smell, where's it coming from? It smells of orange blossoms, sweet basil . . . and rosemary, too. It seems like incense, or the odor of lavender on baby clothes.

BLIND MAN: Hail Mary, full of grace!

JESUS AND ST. PETER (*in unison*): Blessed art thou among women.

PERALTONA: Peralta! Peraltica! There are a couple of pilgrims at the door. (*She goes out.*) Peralta, come look at the pilgrims.

PERALTA (*entering*): What pilgrims?

PERALTONA: Didn't you feel something?

PERALTA: There is something. I haven't smelled an odor like that— ever—not in the jungle, or the gardens, or even the holy temple of God.

PERALTONA: Could it be? . . . Peraltica, do you suppose it's those pilgrims that just came up?

PERALTA: Oh, the pilgrims! Gentlemen, have you been waiting long?

ST. PETER: We're on a journey and we have no place to spend the night.

PERALTA: I'll take you in, with all my heart. But I warn you, it's not going to be very comfortable, because there isn't a speck of salt left in the house, not one lump of chocolate, not even the beginnings of a snack. But come in, come in. It's the good will that counts. Dear, go look in the cupboard . . . and snoop around the kitchen to see if there's a *little* something we can give these gentlemen.

PERALTONA: Oh, right away, right away! There's nothing to beat serving one's neighbor!

PERALTA: Forgive the inconvenience, gentlemen. Please forgive.

ST. PETER: The Master and I are used to it.

PERALTA: If it isn't rude to ask . . .

ST. PETER: But it is, Peralta.

PERALTA: How can you know? You didn't let me finish.

JESUS: You were about to ask who we were. Don't worry. You'll know soon enough.

PERALTA: Very well.

PERALTONA (*within*): Peralta! Oh my God, Peralta!

PERALTA: What's the matter woman? She's the noisiest woman! . . . What are you gentlemen laughing at?

ST. PETER: Never mind. It's a private joke.

PERALTONA (*entering*): Peralta, little brother, you'll never believe what I've seen!

PERALTA: Well . . . what have you seen? . . . A ghost? Or a jungle spook?

PERALTONA: What ghost or jungle spook! Nonsense. I saw . . . with these eyes that were almost struck blind by the sight . . . I saw a whole cupboard—full of food!

PERALTA: You're crazy.

PERALTONA: Crazy! I not only saw it, I touched it and ate it! The meat rack is groaning under the weight of jerked beef and bacon. (*The Old Beggar and the Blind Man come running on.*) The sausages and the salami hang down and curl up like snakes! The cupboard is crammed with dozens of cheeses and butter balls . . . You don't believe me? Look, I saw it, I touched it, I smelled it, I tasted it!

OLD BEGGAR: The gourds in there are full of ground chocolate and cinnamon. And the bread! The cakes! And the sacks are full of beans!

CRIPPLE: Help me! Take me! For God's sake let me see! Let me feast my eyes, and make my mouth water. (*The Old Beggar and the Leper help him.*)

LEPER: Hurry! Hurry! It's been ages since I've seen my shadow on a sausage.

BLIND MAN: I've touched it! My God, you'd never believe! The things I've touched! What have I touched? Whole piles of potatoes. Baskets full of juicy tomatoes. Nests of warm eggs. And whole trays full of rice fritters, so soft and crusty that they must have been cooked by magic! And my finger got stuck in the sweetest, sweetest preserves—mmmm—pure sugar!

PERALTA: God be praised! There's something to give my neighbors at last. Serve the gentlemen, and feed everyone! Everyone eat! I'll go fill some baskets to take over to the neighbors. (*He goes off.*)

PERALTONA: You gentlemen just be patient for a little while. I'll be back in a jiffy. (*She goes out.*)

JESUS: Put the gold over there, Peter, and let's get away. Eating would be like stealing food from the beggar's mouth.

ST. PETER: Well, I confess *my* mouth has turned to water with all this talk of food. What's the rush? Wait a little bit. It's been ages since I've had chocolate and cookies.

JESUS: Now, now, now, that's enough of that! Let's continue according to our plan. (*They start out.*)

ST. PETER: All our planning, and what does it come to? Oh, I can just taste that chocolate now! It must be wonderful . . . all foamy and hot!

JESUS: Stop grumbling, Peter, and follow me. There's a little clearing up ahead. From there we'll see everything. (*St. Peter follows him, grumbling.*)

OLD BEGGAR (*comes on carrying the Cripple, and assisted by the Leper*): I tell you, there's a snake in the woodpile somewhere!

LEPER: Why talk about snakes? The only snakes I saw are those strings of sausages, man!

OLD BEGGAR: Well, you tell me how a cupboard could fill up just like that, in less time than it takes to cross yourself.

CRIPPLE: Shut up and eat!

BLIND MAN (*coming on*): Son of a bitch, this cheese is as soft as a sponge! Melts in your mouth!

PERALTA (*coming on with a bag of groceries*): Mmm? Well, where are the pilgrims?

OLD BEGGAR: They've gone.

LEPER: When we came out, they'd gone.

CRIPPLE: Odd ones, they were.

PERALTA (*to Peraltona, who comes on with the food*): And the pilgrims?

PERALTONA: Aren't they there? I was just bringing them some things to munch on, before supper.

PERALTA: They've gone away. Be damned if it isn't true what they say ... a poor man stinks! But I wonder what their hurry was? Oh, look. They forgot this. (*He picks up a bag of coins.*)

PERALTONA: What is it? Look and see, it might be valuable.

PERALTA: My God! They're pieces of eight! Thousands of gold coins!

PERALTONA: And you're going to give them back, all of them. I bet they left them here deliberately!

LEPER: Pieces of eight?

OLD BEGGAR: Pieces of eight! Pieces of eight! That's what they are!

CRIPPLE: Pieces of eight! Pieces of eight! (*He gets up and moves, completely cured.*) Oh, let me see these pieces of eight! Pe ... Peralta ... what's this? Is this, is this me? Peralta, Peraltica, it's me ... I ... me ... myself! I'm walking! My legs! Look at them, the old stilts ... they're walking again!

BLIND MAN: Pieces of eight! Pure gold pieces of eight! Look at them shine!

LEPER: Can you *see* them shine?

BLIND MAN: Of course I see them! *I* see them? See them? Yes, yes, I *see* them, I *see* them!

CRIPPLE: But will you look at the leper! You're cured! You're all well! Here, give me your hand. See? Look! You see? You're cured! You're all well! (*He has made the Leper touch his own face.*) Feel how smooth? The rot's all gone. Your face is as clean as a whistle.

LEPER: You're right. I can't feel ... I can't feel the ... And my hands! My hands! ...

CRIPPLE: Look, they're absolutely clean!

BLIND MAN: So that's the way the world looks! Oh, Peralta, who'd ever believe it?

LEPER: A mirror! I need a mirror; I want to see myself in a mirror. (*He runs off screaming:*) I'm well! I'm healthy! I'm well! (*He comes back again.*) One, two . . . and I'm born anew! I'm born anew! I'm born again with a new face! My face, oh, my face! I'd forgotten about my face. I've got eyes, and I've even got a nose and a mouth, just like any old Christian! Oh, the whole world has to see this! (*He runs off.*)

BLIND MAN: And I want to see the whole world!

CRIPPLE: And they've got to see me run! They've got to see me jump!

OLD BEGGAR: And I, I'll have to go on begging, carrying my old age on my shoulders. These pieces of eight aren't for me.

PERALTA: The pieces of eight! I'd forgotten! Oh, I've got to catch up with them and return them!

PERALTONA: All of them? Won't you leave me one? Just one, to buy something?

OLD BEGGAR: Peralta be damned. (*He goes off.*)

PERALTA: Whoa, there, gentlemen! Come back. Come down! You've forgotten something important!

PERALTONA: You're a born loser, Peralta . . . but the worst is, he seems to enjoy it. If you ask me, that much honesty is a sin!

PERALTA (*to Jesus and St. Peter*): Well, gentlemen, here's your money. Count it. You'll see it's all there.

JESUS: Let's go back to your house. I want to talk to you. Come, let's get out of the sun.

PERALTA: It's not my fault if you went off and left . . .

JESUS: Sit down, Peralta, and listen.

PERALTA: After you, sir.

JESUS: Sit down! I must reveal some important things to you. And Peter, you sit over there and mind your own business. Now, Peralta, pay attention. We are not the pilgrims we appear to be. Don't you believe it. This gentleman over here is Peter, my disciple. And I am Jesus of Nazareth. We've come to earth with no other purpose than to put you to a test. And in all honesty, let me tell you, Peralta, you passed with flying colors. (*Peraltona sticks her head in and starts eavesdropping.*) Another man less Christian than yourself would have kept the gold. Well, the pieces of eight are yours, Peralta. Distribute them as you wish. And what's more, I'm going to grant you five wishes. Whatever you want, so long as it's *your* wish.

PERALTONA: Oh, gentlemen, I've done my little bit for charity too. I've sacrificed for charity. I've sacrificed my whole life, to accompany Peralta in his good works. Why don't the gentlemen give me a little something too?

JESUS: Take whatever you want, good woman.

PERALTONA: God will repay you, oh, God will repay you. God will repay you in heaven! (*She goes out.*) Oh, God will pay you kind, good gentlemen!

PERALTA: Holy Majesty, please forgive her.

JESUS: She deserves it, poor thing. She's put up with a lot. She's very different from you. But each one suffers life in his own way. Well, Peralta, make your wishes.

ST. PETER: Consider well what you are going to say so you don't end up in a stupid mess.

PERALTA: That's what I'm thinking, Your Grace.

ST. PETER: It's just that if you ask for something bad, and the Master grants it to you, once it's granted, you're done for, because the Master's word is good and it can't be recalled.

PERALTA: Let me get this clear, Your Grace, let me think it out. All right! Your Divine Majesty, the first thing I ask for is that I win at gambling whenever I want.

JESUS: Granted.

PERALTA: The second . . .

ST. PETER: I warn you, this is a very delicate matter and also a very weighty one.

PERALTA: Don' worry, Your Grace, I'm attacking it from all sides. The second is that when I am going to die I want you to send death to me face to face. Don't let her sneak up on me from behind.

ST. PETER: Now, what's the point of that? Where do you get ideas like that?

PERALTA: Now, Your Grace . . . let me . . . let me work this out! I know what I'm doing.

JESUS: Granted.

PERALTA: The third . . .

ST. PETER: Now, give this one some thought. It's the third one. You have three wishes left. Divine Grace is not to be frittered away.

PERALTA: Please don't interrupt me, because if you rattle me my skull turns to stone and I can't think at all. The third . . .

ST. PETER: Whoever heard of such a thing? Wasting wishes on games of chance and stupidities about death. I begin to sense a lack of respect in all of this!

JESUS: Peter, stop butting in . . . and be quiet. He's free to ask for whatever he wants.

ST. PETER: Well, that's true. I don't know why I bother. It's just that I can't stand to see . . .

PERALTA: My third wish is to be able to stop anyone wherever I want for as long as I want.

ST. PETER: What! What kind of addlepated wish is that?

JESUS: Be patient, man. Peralta, my friend, your wishes are rather unusual. But so be it.

ST. PETER: Holy Virgin of the Anchor! Ask for Heaven, man, don't be an idiot, ask for Heaven!

JESUS: Granted.

PERALTA: The fourth . . .

ST. PETER: If you'd only listen to me, just ask for Heaven and you're set for life!

PERALTA: The fourth . . .

ST. PETER: You've only got two left. Heaven for you . . . Heaven for your sister, and no more nonsense!

PERALTA: The fourth . . . but, Your Divine Majesty, before I make that wish, I want to ask you something. And you'll forgive me, Your Divine Majesty, if it's not well put. But just the same I want you to give me a straight answer. Clear and straight.

ST. PETER: No! He's fit to be tied! I can just hear it now. This one's going to be something. God-Almighty-on-His-throne have mercy!

PERALTA: Well, I want to know if it's Old Nick that rules the souls of the damned, or if it's You, or our Father in Heaven.

JESUS: My Father, I, and the Holy Ghost, together . . . and separately . . . rule everything. We kicked the Devil out and sent him down to Hell. He's master there and *he* rules the souls of the damned, just as you have power here where we've sent you . . .

PERALTA: All right, then, Your Divine Majesty, if that's the way it is, I'm going to make a fourth wish.

ST. PETER: I can't stand it! Divine Majesty, I can't stand another one of these foolish wishes. Give me permission to retire.

JESUS: Peter, sit down.

PERALTA: What I want, Your Divine Majesty, is for you to give me the power to keep the Devil from cheating on me in any kind of game.

JESUS: Granted.

PERALTA: And finally . . .

ST. PETER: Let him be damned. He can go to the Devil for all I care.

PERALTA: And finally . . .

ST. PETER: You'll be damned, that's what!

PERALTA: I ask Your Divine Majesty to give me the power to be able to shrink down to what ever size I want. Even if it be as small as an ant.

JESUS (*unable to restrain his laughter any longer*): Oh, Peralta, we broke the mold and threw it away after we made you! Everyone asks me for grandeur and you, a little crumb of a man, you ask me for insignificance. Very well.

ST. PETER: But can't you see? The man's crazy!

PERALTA: I'm not sorry I wished as I did. And what's done is done.

ST. PETER: Idiot. The last place I'll ever see *you* is in Heaven!

JESUS: I grant your last wish.

(*They start out.*)

ST. PETER: *And* . . . as far as I'm concerned, Your Divine Majesty, this is the last time you have to invite me on one of these peregrinations.

JESUS: He must have his reasons for wishing as he did. He doesn't sound like a fool.

ST. PETER: And he may be so clever all his wishes will backfire. (*He continues grumbling as they ascend to Heaven.*)

PERALTA: Just think of the greed that will start up in those money lenders and gamblers in the town when they see this pile of gold. All the thieves and crooks from miles around will come running. But they're not going to get a penny, 'cause then they'll see my wish carried out. I'll always win at cards whenever I want. They'll find out who they're dealing with. Just you see. (*He goes out.*)

PERALTONA (*coming on, dressed to the gills*): Maruchenga! Maruchenga!

MARUCHENGA (*loaded down with boxes and gewgaws*): I'm coming, Ma'am. It's just that I can't see where I'm going.

PERALTONA: Now you're going to tell me you're nearsighted! There are just no good servants to be had any more! Oh, the stink! Bring me that jar of perfume, so I can sprinkle a bit around here. It stinks to high heaven. (*Maruchenga puts the boxes on the ground.*) Oh, you cow! Look what you're doing! Putting the packages on the floor! And what a floor! Filthy and contaminated with the sores and wounds of the lepers, oh, dear me! Those rotten old beggars aren't coming back in here, I can tell you. Hand me that silk shawl, will you? What do you think of it? Perfect for visiting the queen. Now, let's see, oh, yes, arrange my bustle, will you? It's slipped to one side. Maruchenga!

MARUCHENGA: Ma'am?

PERALTONA: The bustle, you viper! Straighten my bustle! (*Looking in the mirror*) Don't you think I look younger, prettier somehow? I bet you I could even scare up a lover now. Now hand me the parasol. I've got to practice my new walk. And fetch me the curling iron. You know, one can't really dress up any more. By tomorrow all those good-for-nothing women that spend their lives hanging out the window will be imitating this outfit of mine.

CRIPPLE (*coming in*): Miss Peraltona! What's happened? . . . Ma'am?

PERALTONA: What do *you* want? But before you start, let me warn you that from now on I won't have anything to do with anything but ladies who wear silk stockings and shoes. And as far as you beggars are concerned, don't you even think of coming back here. Peralta can carry on his charity someplace else.

CRIPPLE: But do you know where he is?

PERALTONA: Who?

CRIPPLE: Don Peralta.

PERALTONA: How could anybody tell where that idiot would be?

CRIPPLE: Well, he's in town. He started a card game in the casino.

PERALTONA: So now he's gambling away his gold. Well, they'll skin him alive.

CRIPPLE: Skin him? He's the one who's cleaning them out. When he's through with them they'll have to put nails in their pockets to make them jingle. And I'm talking about the best gamblers in the country. They've come from all over. The best. Real sharks. They cheat him! They palm cards! They mark the deck with their nails! They even change games on him! They roll dice. Then they play monte, bis bis, cachimona, roulette, just to see if they can beat him by changing the game. But it doesn't work! He collapses every once in a while from pure exhaustion, only to come back and win some more.

PERALTONA: And I bet you he hasn't bought himself a new suit of clothes. Not even that.

CRIPPLE: Not a thing. He's still wearing his old poncho. And you can still see his ass peeking out of the hole in his trousers. Just the same.

BLIND MAN (*coming in*): What I've seen! Oh, what I've seen! You'd never believe!

PERALTONA: All you seem to do lately is to go around seeing. Well, what *did* you see?

BLIND MAN: Peralta! And he was skinning all the gamblers and card sharks alive! And they all grumbling and cursing. But every hand they play is a hand they lose.

PERALTONA: We've heard. Nothing he does surprises me.

BLIND MAN: Well, that's nothing! There he was, throwing out aces, when the messenger from the king comes up. The king has sent for him!

PERALTONA: There you have it. That's what he gets for being so greedy.

BLIND MAN: Wait, Ma'am. You'll see. You'll see. "Let's go see the king," said Peralta, as though it didn't frighten him a bit. So off he went just as calm as could be. He's got the blood of a worm, that's what.

PERALTONA: Silly fool.

BLIND MAN: Well, then I made out like I was a blind man and I followed them. And you should have seen the commotion in the palace.

PERALTONA: And you mean to say he went to the palace in his old poncho and his . . . oh, there's no cure for that man!

BLIND MAN: And he walked in just like it was nothing. I climbed up and peeked through a window, and guess what I saw! You'd never believe!

PERALTONA: Oh, stop teasing and tell your story.

BLIND MAN: Well, then, I saw . . . I saw them invite him to sit down at the table with the king!

PERALTONA: The king's table?

BLIND MAN: And they sat him between the king and the queen!

PERALTONA: Between the king and the queen?

BLIND MAN: The king and queen were having chocolate and cookies . . . and a little bit of cheese. And you know what? His highness gave him some to drink out of his own golden cup.

PERALTONA: You're lying!

BLIND MAN: And then they toasted him with some of the prettiest little words you ever heard. You'd think that he was the bishop himself. Nothing less than the Bishop Gómez Plata!

PERALTONA: Maruchenga!

MARUCHENGA: Ma'am?

PERALTONA: Get a move on, we're going to the palace! If that barefoot noodle of a brother of mine, in his old poncho, drank from the king's cup . . . well, just think what I'll drink from! The king himself will turn to wine and I'll swallow him in a gulp! (*She goes out and screams from outside*) Maruchenga!

MARUCHENGA: Coming, Ma'am. (*She follows her.*)

CRIPPLE: The pieces of eight have gone to her head.

BLIND MAN: I never thought I'd open my eyes to see all this. You know what they're saying in town? They say that Peralta is in cahoots with the Devil.

CRIPPLE: You suppose our cures are the Devil's work too?

BLIND MAN: Well, we're cured, and that's what matters. But as for the pieces of eight, well, in my opinion, I think . . .

CRIPPLE: They're the Devil's work too?

BLIND MAN: Well, so what? They're pieces of eight no matter where they came from. I'm saving the ones he's given me. And if I save enough of them, maybe I'll be able to pull myself out of this poverty. But if you ask me, all this charity . . .

CRIPPLE: Yes . . . but just think of it, to clean out all those gamblers, those crooks. They didn't stand a chance.

BLIND MAN: Well, if you ask me, he had a little help.

CRIPPLE: I'm told he commits all kinds of horrible things in secret, sins against God. Blasphemous. There's an old woman I know . . . you know, sort of a half witch? And you know what she told me? That she's flown over the roof tops with that man.

BLIND MAN: Do you mean Camila?

CRIPPLE: That's the one.

BLIND MAN: Ooo, friend! She's flown around with a lot of men. But lately her flying's wearing down the broomstick, I can tell you.

PERALTA (*coming in*): Well, my friends, how are you? How do you feel?

CRIPPLE: Don Peralta, what are you doing here?

BLIND MAN: We were just talking about you.

PERALTA (*handing them some gold coins*): Here, go buy some new clothes. And give some to charity . . . your neighbors.

CRIPPLE: Bless you, Don Peralta, bless you.

BLIND MAN: You're a saint, Don Peralta, a real saint!

CRIPPLE: God will repay you in Heaven.

PERALTA: Oh, don't be foolish. Go distribute your alms.

BLIND MAN: Yes, yes, of course. Charity for all, Don Peralta.

CRIPPLE: God repay you. God grant you Heaven. (*They go.*)

PERALTA (*arranging the coins into large piles*): There, now, this will
  pay for a big house, large enough to take care of all those people
  who have come here looking for help. Damn it, there are lots of
  poor people in this world. They've even come from as far as
  Jamaica . . . and Jerusalem, too. And this, this is for the injured
  who cry out and the misfits and the strange ones. They should en-
  joy the gold of the Lord too . . . as well as the gambler's money.
  (*The wind begins to whistle and we hear a strange, unpleasant
  music.*) Oooo, it's cold.
  (*Death appears*).
DEATH: I've come for you.
PERALTA: For me? And isn't there someone else around that . . .
DEATH: It's your turn, because you're a good man, and a kind man,
  I'm giving you warning. You should be grateful.
PERALTA: Well, friend, I . . . I am grateful. But do me a *whole* favor,
  and give me time to confess myself and to make my will, won't you?
  Look at all my money. I've got to see that it's well distributed.
DEATH: Well . . . don't take too long, I've got lots to do today.
PERALTA: Why don't you take a little walk around while I get ready?
  I bet you'd enjoy looking at our town. It's a lovely view. Look, you
  see that avocado tree out there? It's nice and high. You climb that
  tree and you'll see a lovely sight. That's the way, that's the way.
  Now, be careful. Be careful. And sit in the fork of the tree. I won't
  be a minute. There, that's right. That's where I want you. Now,
  old woman, you rest up there. Make yourself comfortable up there
  because there you'll stay till I decide to let you down. Not even
  Christ Almighty and his heavenly host could get you down off the
  fork of that tree. I must say he's kept his word. Death came to meet
  me head on and I can make anyone stay wherever I want them to
  stay whenever I want them to stay . . . Well, now, on with my
  charities! (*He goes off.*)
  (*Fiesta of Death: Men covered with sores, paralytics, sick people
  enter, along with an enormous figure of Death. They are beating on
  old jars and assorted junk. The Old Beggar enters with a woman
  disguised as Death. The Leper is dressed as a medicine man. There
  are several doctors in the group as well.*)

FIRST DOCTOR: We've banished death with potions and laxatives and enemas.

SECOND DOCTOR: Of course, there's still sickness, but we'll scare it away little by little by little.

LEPER: You see this face? Clean as a newborn babe's. And who cleaned it for me? Who cured it for me? My own secret formula! Here you have it, ladies and gentlemen, my own special ointment. Leaves of crocus and a hornet's nest, and then some borrachero roots, all of them simmered in boiling lard!

OLD BEGGAR: Alms for the love of God.

WOMAN: Just you wait, I'm going to give you more than you ever asked for.

OLD BEGGAR: I'll take whatever you can give me.

WOMAN: Well, here it goes!

(*The Old Beggar and the Woman do a Dance of Death.*)

LEPER: Then add scorpion claws, small lizards, and the marrow of a pig. And a leaf or two of sorrel to keep it nice and pink.

(*The Doctors and Patients pantomine a ridicule of Death.*)

PERALTONA: Maruchenga! Maruchenga!

MARUCHENGA (*offstage*): Coming, Ma'am.

PERALTONA: Bring me another fan, this one is beginning to shred. And fetch me my other shoes, my feet are killing me.

MARUCHENGA: You never stay at home any more, Ma'am, that's the trouble.

PERALTONA: Oh, but I have so many obligations. If it isn't the bishop's palace, it's the king's . . . or to the flower club, or a wedding. Oh, I'm breathless! And then you have to walk around stiff as a board inside these stays and crinolines. Just like a saint in an Easter procession. Here a bow, there a bow, with a little buzzy-buzzy-buzz to a lady from the club. And then another little buzzy-buzz to the great gentleman over there, because it's all buzzy-buzz and fancy words like "madame" and "monsieur" and rosewater and patchouli and fancy meringues. Today I'm invited to a ball given by the Mogollones. And let me tell you, that's one ball I don't intend to miss, because they really know how to put on airs. Oh, for

God's sake, hurry and bring me my fan and my shoes. (*Maruchenga goes off.*)

OLD BEGGAR (*coming in*): Hail Mary.

PERALTONA: Full of grace.

OLD BEGGAR: You're so dressed up and beautiful, you get younger and younger and younger every day. You're going to end up fifteen years old.

PERALTONA: Oh, what a flatterer you are. What's the gossip?

OLD BEGGAR: Some things against your brother.

PERALTONA: Wouldn't you know it? That's the way they repay his charity. Well . . . if you shelter crows, they'll pluck your eyes out.

OLD BEGGAR: At first, you know, everyone was happy and celebrating because there was no more death. The doctors couldn't *give* their medicine away. But now everybody goes around pining for just a little bit of death.

PERALTONA: There you have it! That's why I don't want any truck with humanity. I take my strolls, enjoy the air, and have a good time. And the rest of the world can sink or swim for all I care. The most dangerous thing in this awful world we live in is to be good. Take poor old Peralta there. They won't be happy until they rip his heart out and smash it on the stones.

(*Maruchenga enters, with fan and shoes.*)

MARUCHENGA: Almost all the shoes have broken heels.

PERALTONA: Well, what do you expect? I've never put my feet into such torture in all my life. The things people invent!

OLD BEGGAR: And if that crowd comes over here clamoring for Death, will you give her over? Will you let her go?

PERALTONA: Don't mention it! What on earth would I have to do with that old bag of bones? Good heavens!

MARUCHENGA: Have you seen her lately? Poor old thing! She looks so miserable up there in that tree.

PERALTONA: Whenever I go by there, I keep my eyes down and I cover myself with blessings. Good gracious saints preserve me!

MARUCHENGA: Her bones are getting all moldy and green, from sitting all these days up there in the tree.

PERALTONA: Christ in Heaven preserve me!

MARUCHENGA: She's all covered over with spider webs, and dead leaves, and birdshit, and the wasps made a nest, right by her left eye. So the poor old thing can only see out of one eye now. Everyone's saying that Don Peralta has to be the damnedest witch that ever was to keep her up there in the tree that way.

PERALTONA: Holy Mary, Mother of God, Maruchenga, you keep your mouth shut!

DOCTOR'S WIFE (*entering*): Peralta. Peralta ... God grant you a very good day, Miss Peraltona. You couldn't by any chance tell me where the devil your brother is hiding, could you?

PERALTONA: Now is that a way to ask a question? You just pull yourself together and then tell us what's the matter.

DOCTOR'S WIFE: Well, what do you think's the matter? I'm the wife of Dr. Pantaleón, the legitimate one, the *legal* one. The others are tied to him only by the bedsheets. To use the vulgar expression ... mere concubines! Now, for a long time there's been all kinds of sickness, disease after disease, and not a single Christian soul has kicked the bucket. At first my husband gave enemas all over the place, but then little by little I began to suspect that all this didn't have anything to do with doctors and their enemas. You can't fool me, I know them. I've *seen* the people they cure to death. Now, Madam, you listen to me ... the whole world says that your brother has hidden death away somewhere. Don't misunderstand me, I don't want him to get rid of her altogether ... oh, no, but if he would just let her out once in a while, let her stroll around, you know ... here and there ... because as far as my husband is concerned, no one calls on him anymore. And his horse died. And the knives and pliers he uses for operating are getting all rusty!

(*The Biddy and the Gravedigger enter.*)

PERALTONA: Well, I'm very sorry Ma'am, but I'm not lighting any candles at this funeral.

GRAVE DIGGER: What funeral?

PERALTONA: What I mean is, that's none of my business.

GRAVE DIGGER: Oh, Ma'am, you gave me such a start, I was so happy,

I thought that Peraltica had remembered me, that he'd taken pity on me, and given Death permission to make a few friends again. You remember me, Ma'am? You may have seen me sometimes at the graveyard? Why, I was the man, no one else, who buried your sainted mother, God rest her soul. And as for Peralta, I buried his father, and your whole kin. May God keep them in their glory.

BIDDY: Holy Mary, Mother of God.

PERALTONA: Free of sin conceived. Well, Miss Eduviges.

BIDDY: Ooof! I'm all out of breath climbing that hill. My heart's in my mouth.

PERALTONA: Maruchenga!

MARUCHENGA (*offstage*): Ma'am?

PERALTONA: Fix a little orange-leaf tea for the gathering, won't you, dear?

MARUCHENGA: Yes, Ma'am.

BIDDY: Well, you see, the priest sent me because his reverence and the sacristan are really miserable. They're as hungry as a pair of mangy dogs.

PERALTONA: The priest? Hungry? Oh, now don't give me that, Miss Eduviges.

BIDDY: It's the truth, as sure as I'm standing here, Ma'am. Not one burial, not one responsory, not even a little bitty requiem in all this time. Saints preserve us! They think it's the doings of the Devil.

GRAVEDIGGER: And what about me? I haven't put a shovel in the dirt in ages. I don't have the strength to clean out the graveyard. Why, it's all overgrown, with lizards everywhere, sunning themselves on the tombstones.

NIECE (*entering, followed by the Wife of the Rich Man*): What's this, Miss Peraltona? All dressed up? With high heels and walking roughshod over the hearts and hopes of the poor people?

PERALTONA: Why, you snooty thing! What's gotten into you? How dare you talk to me like that?

NIECE: It's four years since my uncle Román fell very ill with an attack of rheumatism. And we pray away and pray away for him to die, but here he lies, stinking, with his insides rotting away. And since he's a loan shark, he's been getting richer and richer on Peralta's gold.

PERALTONA: That's no affair of mine.

NIECE: Well, my mother sends you a message. She wants you to lend her Death for a little . . . just a little hop or two.

WIFE OF THE RICH MAN: The very thing I came for myself. My husband's had trouble with his water, you know . . . kidneys. And every night, why, it's . . . irrigation! Our money, as you know . . . we made that together. But now he's giving it all away to the husband of that lady here. And all he does is to poke some little straws into him so that he can take care of the overflow.

DOCTOR'S WIFE: You shut your mouth, Ma'am. Besides, he's the only client we've got left. And that's only because his disease is a damp one.

WIFE OF THE RICH MAN: Well, as far as I'm concerned, I'd give anything to lay my hands on Death and drag her down from wherever she's hiding, because there's no point at all in being a widow if there isn't a penny left in the purse.

HUSBAND OF THE OLD AND UGLY WOMAN (*coming in with the Young Girl*): Death, I need that Death right now, because my wife, who was as old as the hills when we got married . . . well, you should see her now! She's crazy as a bedbug and as wrinkled as a piece of parchment. All I'm asking for is to let her rest so that I have some rest myself.

YOUNG GIRL (*who has come with him*): You see, we want to get married like God says. I mean, we're tired of sneaking around without the sacraments, always exposed to the knives of evil tongues.

PERALTONA: Yes, but your wife, old and ugly as she was, had a nice little pile of money when you married her.

HUSBAND OF THE OLD AND UGLY WOMAN: True enough, but I paid my debt. Thirty years of taking her scolding and her whining. And rubbing her joints with cocoa butter!

PERALTONA: Well, I'm very sorry but I can't help any of you. All these affairs are for my stupid brother to settle. I'm going over to the Mogollones now. And as for you, well, settle it whatever way you can. (*She starts out.*)

MARUCHENGA: I'm coming too. I just can't stand this gaggle any longer. (*She leaves.*)

DOCTOR'S WIFE: Look at her! Ribbons and bows, and insults to boot. And all of that money taken from the poor. (*She leaves.*)

HUSBAND OF THE OLD AND UGLY WOMAN: What's the good of all that money? Right into the pocket of the loan sharks, and the cash boxes of the gamblers.

GRAVEDIGGER: And now there are more rich people than ever before ... but more poor people too. It's just the same as always ... except that no one dies and that's the real calamity. (*He leaves.*)

NIECE: We can't stand this state of affairs much longer. (*She goes.*)

BIDDY: It's against my better nature to say so, but as far as I'm concerned, that Peralta is leaning toward a Mason and has all the signs of excommunication on his head. (*She leaves.*)

OLD BEGGAR (*makes little piles of coins*): One little pile, for loans at twenty percent. Another for gambling at the cantina. Now let's see, I loaned eighty to the fellow with the broken nose. And a hundred and fifty to the gimp. And as for you, you old hag, I pray God nobody ever helps you out of that tree. I'm going to collect my coins for a hundred years.

CURTAIN

ACT TWO

DEVIL (*stumbling out of Hell*): What accounts are you keeping, you damned sinner!

OLD BEGGAR: God in Heaven! It's the Devil himself! (*He runs out, leaving his coins behind.*)

DEVIL: Ah! What have we here, the famous pieces of eight! What a hell of a mess this milk-sop ass has let loose!

PERALTA (*coming in*): Good day, Your Highness, what are you doing around here?

DEVIL: Don't make out as though you didn't know.

PERALTA: And this gold?

DEVIL: What should it be but the gold you've been throwing around just to make trouble!

PERALTA: Not trouble, Your Grace . . . charity. But what brings you to these parts?

DEVIL: You know very well.

PERALTA: I do?

DEVIL: Tell me, where's Death? Where have you hidden her?

PERALTA: She's in the avocado tree. Does Your Grace need her for something?

DEVIL: Can't you tell? You've put me, my lieutenants, and the whole crew of Hell out of work! There we sit with our arms crossed and nothing to do. The other day I sent a spy on the road to Heaven, to find out if all souls are being saved nowadays! "What salvation and what damnation!" St. Peter told him! "The whole thing has gone to wrack and ruin!" So I snooped around a bit more and I found out that you were the cause of it all.

PERALTA: Look, Your Highness, I can't let Death go, because the first one she'll take will be me. But . . . I tell you what I'll do. I'll bet her against any of the souls that you want to put up from your place . . .

DEVIL: You want to gamble with me? You really think you're good, don't you?

PERALTA: I wouldn't say that, Your Highness.

DEVIL: You know that ever since I became the Devil, *no one* has won a game against me?

PERALTA: That may be. But you see, gambling's my special sin. I can't stop gambling even when I know I'm going to lose.

DEVIL: Very well, you've got yourself a game. But on one condition: that along with Death you gamble your own wretched soul too.

PERALTA: Done! (*They gamble.*) Forty! Ace and three. You can't beat that no matter how hard you play.

DEVIL: What? Well, don't get your hopes up. I'm just giving you a little lead, that's all. (*They play again.*) Hum . . . Now, this is a different matter altogether!

PERALTA: All right, here goes! Seven of trumps. Draw one, and I get the ace!

DEVIL: What the devil! You're a treacherous snake, aren't you?

PERALTA: No more a snake than you, Your Highness. Now, let's play it out.

DEVIL: Very well. Show your hand.

PERALTA: One moment.

DEVIL: Listen, you scum, you show your hand.

PERALTA: Patience, Your Grace.

DEVIL: The hell with patience! Now show me your hand, I can't stand it any longer!

PERALTA: Four kings!

DEVIL: Damn it! Why the hell can't I cheat you! Why? Don't you laugh at me, or I'll break your ass!

PERALTA: I'm not laughing at Your Grace.

DEVIL: You're not going to get the better of me! Double or nothing!

PERALTA: All right. Double. But this time you'd better bet something good.

DEVIL: All right. All right! I'll go the whole way. I'll bet one whole cauldron of souls against your death . . . and Death herself, of course.

PERALTA: What's a cauldron?

DEVIL: A cauldron . . . well, it's a . . . cauldron. More or less thirty-three thousand million souls . . .

PERALTA: Fair enough. (*They play.*)

DEVIL: Take that.

PERALTA: Trumps. Change.

DEVIL (*growls*): I can't do it! It can't be! Not one little cheat! I can't do it! Not one!

PERALTA: Your Highness is going to have to play an honest game for once.

DEVIL: You've got some evil power.

PERALTA: Forty, ace and three, one again; no matter how poor my score, I'll always win.

DEVIL: You won!

PERALTA: So it seems.

DEVIL: And now you've got Death and my cauldron of souls as well.

PERALTA: Fair and square.

DEVIL: And you beat *me*, the best card player in the world? You've got some secret power, you con man, you!

PERALTA: No, Your Highness, I've got nothing.

DEVIL: You've ruined Hell. It's bankrupt!

PERALTA: Not I, Your Grace. You're the one who likes to gamble. If you want, I'll give you a chance to make it back.

DEVIL: No. No, I won't play you any more. I'm not going to let you catch me again. (*As he starts to leave*) I'll get even with you. You've got some sort of power, I know! But you'll lose your witch-craft, and when you've lost it, we'll see! You flyspeck! (*He departs into Hell.*)

PERALTA: Well, that wish was granted, too. The Devil can't cheat me, at cards. Now I've got Death, and thirty-three thousand million souls. Whooee! There's going to be hell to pay in Hell tonight! With the Devil crying like a snot-nose! And the lieutenants and the whole crew of Hell releasing souls by the million!

(*Jesus and St. Peter enter through the door in the cloud.*)

JESUS: He's got to be the one who's got her. It couldn't be anyone else. Go down to him then, and treat him with a great deal of care and respect. See if he'll lend us Death for a while, because if he doesn't, we've really done ourselves in!

ST. PETER: All right . . . but I told you that man was crazy.

JESUS: Do as I say, Peter, and go down. Take care how you treat him.

ST. PETER: All right! I'm going. But if it were up to me . . .

PERALTA (*with his coins*): I don't have to gamble any longer. The problem is to get rid of it all. Well, back to charity . . . with my eyes closed!

ST. PETER: Peralta!

PERALTA: Oh, what a miracle to see you again, Your Grace!

ST. PETER: Miracles, shmiracles! Tell me something, Peralta. Why are you like this?

PERALTA: What's the matter?

ST. PETER: What's the matter? Do you think you're fooling us?

PERALTA: I haven't thought about it.

ST. PETER: What have you done with Death?

PERALTA: The good Lord gave me permission to fix something any-where I want for as long as I want.

ST. PETER: So that's why you made those cock and bull petitions! You set out from the very beginning to make a mess of everything!

PERALTA: A mess, Your Grace?

ST. PETER: Don't you realize that we haven't had a single blessed soul come up there? That Heaven is at a standstill? I went to the Master and I told him, "Master, you can take this job of porter, and give it to someone else, because I'm not the kind of man to spend eterni-ty sitting around doing nothing." Then the Master sent me down to you, in order to get you to let Death loose. I got my orders and you can't say they're not important.

PERALTONA (*entering*): Maruchenga!

MARUCHENGA (*behind her, loaded down as always*): Coming, Ma'am.

PERALTONA: Mercy be! Here's the pilgrim with all the gold. Maru-chenga!

MARUCHENGA: Ma'am?

PERALTONA: Take all that stuff inside there, and make some hot chocolate for the pilgrim, but hurry, hurry!

MARUCHENGA: I am! I am!

PERALTONA: Oh! The help one gets nowadays! Well. Now you can see how much good your gold has done.

ST. PETER: Yes, I can see.

PERALTONA: Charity everywhere. We don't know what to do with so much charity. It's coming out our ears. If Your Grace will excuse me, I've just got to take off this girdle. And this crinoline. Ah! I'm exhausted. I can hardly breathe. (*Then, with great airs*) Begging Your Grace's pardon. (*She leaves.*)

ST. PETER: All right, now what were we saying?

PERALTA: That the Master had sent you down ...

ST. PETER: Oh, yes. Well ... now ... I want you to take into recog-nition that this is an order from our Lord.

PERALTA: Very well. I'll let her go . . . with pleasure. On condition that she doesn't do anything to me.

ST. PETER: As the Master says, granted.

PERALTA: Wait for me here and I'll bring her to you.

ST. PETER: That Peraltica's a slippery one. If I didn't have a better grip on my temper I would have bashed him one in the face.

MARUCHENGA: Here you are, mister pilgrim. And please excuse the service. Here, sit down and eat. Madam will be with you at any minute.

PERALTONA (*from within*): Maruchenga!

MARUCHENGA: Coming, Ma'am! (*To St. Peter*) She's all in a dither.

PERALTONA: Maruchenga!

MARUCHENGA (*leaving*): Coming, Ma'am!

ST. PETER: Mmmm. Now this is what I call food! A steady diet of glory is more than a man can bear.

PERALTA (*with Death*): Here she is, Your Grace. Look at her, all crippled up. Covered with birdshit. Fainting from hunger. She can barely walk.

ST. PETER: Oh, for goodness sake, get her out of my sight. Don't you see I'm eating?

PERALTA: Oh, Your Grace, I'll have her cleaned up in the time it takes to say "thanks and amen." Forgive me. (*He goes out.*)

ST. PETER: Well, now he's turned my stomach and spoiled my chocolate. Whoever heard of a thing like that? Bring in a bag of bones like that when a man is eating. (*We hear the music of Death.*) Ooooee! It's cold.

DEATH: Wheee! Wheee! (*She screams with brutal joy, jumps about, runs around, and then runs off like a shot.*)

PERALTA: The bitch was hungry from all that fasting. The minute I cleaned her up she got her strength back, snatched up the butcher knife, and ground it sharp on the stone in the patio.

ST. PETER: Don't you see? Now I've got to climb all the way back, because she's going to start sending up all kinds of people. And I've got to be on duty at the door. You're too much, too much!

PERALTA: That's as may be . . . but there's more, Your Grace.

ST. PETER: More? What?

PERALTA: Well, just a little while ago I beat the Devil at a game of cards, and won a whole parcel of souls.

ST. PETER: A whole parcel . . . of what?

PERALTA: Well, Your Grace, it was actually a cauldron. Some thirty-three thousand million, um, uh . . .

ST. PETER: What's that you said? . . . Where are they?

PERALTA: How should I know?

ST. PETER: God Almighty, grant me patience! How many did you say?

PERALTA: Thirty-three thousand million.

ST. PETER: Thirty-three . . . oh, God in Heaven!

PERALTA: You should really go see if you've got room for all those little people.

ST. PETER: Little people? Dear Master of mine, this man belongs in a loony-bin!

PERALTA: I won them all from the Devil, fair and square. And let me warn you, no old fossil is going to boss me around, even if he comes from Heaven.

ST. PETER: Old fossil! You, you pig! I told the Master. I told him! God Almighty! God the Father! God Immortal in all His Heavens! (*He climbs up to his cloud.*)

MARUCHENGA (*within*): Oh, Madam, oh, Ma'am, oh, my poor mistress! (*Enters.*) Don Peraltica! My mistress, Peraltona, she's dead! There she lies, stiff and cold, like a dead bird. Oh, what a tragedy!

PERALTA: The old bitch took revenge. Oh, well, requiescat in pace.

MARUCHENGA: Amen.

(*They leave. Enter a funeral procession.*)

BIDDY: Requiescat in pace.

THE OTHERS: Amen.

BIDDY: God have mercy on faithful souls
    on their way to Purgatory,
    oh, God take pity upon their pains.
    They were what I am today,

and I am soon to be as they.
Pray God for me,
as I will pray for thee.

ALL: Amen.

MARUCHENGA: Oh, please, why don't you stay a little? Come in here
and pray for my mistress, Peraltona.

DOCTOR'S WIFE: This whole thing has been Peralta's doing.

MARUCHENGA: That may very well be. Much difference it makes to
her.

BIDDY (*entering the house with the cortege*): Requiescat in pace.

ALL: Amen.

BIDDY: Souls in Purgatory
who are suffering now,
intercede, we pray, for us,
as we will pray for you.

DOCTOR'S WIFE: The poor man never had a moment's rest. On his
feet, running about till the very end, fighting diseases.

NIECE: But the diseases caught up with *him* in the end.

DOCTOR'S WIFE: The smallpox in one place, measles in another,
whooping cough and ringworm someplace else. And over there a
fever and here a pain in the side . . . Blessed souls in Purgatory!

BIDDY: Blessed souls in Purgatory, pray for us!

ALL: Amen.

DOCTOR'S WIFE: And all this time he was as healthy as an ox! And
now there you have him, fallen among his patients. He was always
such a kind man. Souls in Purgatory!

BIDDY: Souls in Purgatory, pray for us.

ALL: Amen.

DOCTOR'S WIFE: It's God's vengeance.

YOUNG WOMAN: Vengeance of the Devil. That's the way my old man
died. Death hooked into him and dragged him into the grave. It's
all witchcraft. It's all Peralta's doing. *He's* the doctor . . . doctor
of witchcraft!

BIDDY: Holy Mary, Mother of God! Souls in Purgatory! Child, don't
say such things . . .

> In the name of the Father,
> in the name of the Son,
> in the name of St. Marcial,
> keep me free from harm
> and protect me. Amen.

ALL: Amen.

NIECE: For my uncle Román to die, that was all right. His time was come, and it was our time to inherit his money. But for my mother and my uncles and all my family to go with him? Well, now, that's what I call a downright injustice.

YOUNG GIRL: Peralta's taken our whole world and mixed it up. He ruined life with his gold, and death with his witchcraft.

BIDDY: Let's be on our way, for the road to death has no end. There isn't time enough to bury them all. There they lie, half covered with earth.

DOCTOR'S WIFE: As for you, my friend Eduviges, give us your prayers —here a prayer, there a paternoster, here another prayer.

BIDDY (*without paying attention begins the exit*):

> Souls in Purgatory
> flying o'er our heads,
> remember us below
> and plead for those
> you have left behind.

ALL: Amen. (*They leave.*)

JESUS (*standing in the door of the cloud*): Damn it to Hell, Peter, you're stubborn. Now get down there and talk to him.

ST. PETER: I told you, Master, I told you he was crazy.

JESUS: Stop babbling and go down and talk to him.

ST. PETER: I don't want to have any more to do with that devil of a man. I'll be doorkeeper for you, Master, as long as you wish. And you know how much I've put up with at that doorway recently.

JESUS: I've never had to complain against you, Peter! Now you go down and talk to him, as I told you to.

ST. PETER: All right. I'll do as you say. And no back talk. All I say is this, if I break one of my keys on his head, I'm not to blame.

JESUS: Oh, stop grumbling and stirring things up. He's not to blame. The long and the short of it is, he's been nothing more than an instrument.

ST. PETER: Well, that's a fine instrument Your Divine Majesty has managed to dig up. And didn't you give him all these opportunities yourself?

JESUS: We give them to all men.

ST. PETER: Yes, but you gave him some that were better than most. And look what he did with them.

JESUS: Get a move on, Peter. And try to wear your holy patience, with patience.

ST. PETER: Holy patience! Who ever heard . . . that bag of rags . . . to look at him, so meek and quiet. He seems all right if you don't know who you're dealing with. Peralta, that son of a . . .

MARUCHENGA: Jesus, Mary, and Joseph, what's coming now!

ST. PETER: Good-for-nothing! Damn nuisance! Where's that Peralta?

MARUCHENGA: I'll go fetch him right away, mister pilgrim, then I'll bring you a drink of chocolate. (*She leaves.*)

ST. PETER: Who ever heard of such a thing! Make a treaty with that bag of nothing. What are we coming to!

PERALTA: At your service, sir. Here I am.

ST. PETER: Well, the Master sent me. But between you and me, if it was up to me I'd . . .

PERALTA: Now, now. Don't get upset. You're much too old for that kind of thing.

ST. PETER: The very idea of having to explain anything to you . . .! But the Master has ordered me to make everything clear to you.

PERALTA: And what's not clear, Your Grace?

ST. PETER: You know very well.

PERALTA: I'm sorry; I don't.

ST. PETER: Now, look, you, don't make me lose the last bit of patience I've got left. You know very well that you won those thirty-three thousand million souls from the enemy.

PERALTA: It was a fair game.

ST. PETER: Shut up.

PERALTA: Very well.

ST. PETER: You haven't got the least notion of the tangle of higher theology you got us into.

MARUCHENGA: Here's some cheese and a cup of chocolate. Just like the mistress used to fix you, bless her soul. Oh, she was so good, even though she did have a bad temper.

PERALTA: All right, now, you go in there. We're talking.

MARUCHENGA: Oh, you don't know how much I miss her, with all of her airs and all of her pickiness. (*She goes out.*)

ST. PETER: Well, she's paid for her airs . . . all of them . . . She came up to heaven, you know, and I had to let her in. You know what a gossip she is. If I hadn't . . . (*He changes the subject.*) My God, this is good! If it weren't for this chocolate . . . it's the only thing that makes my job worthwhile. But now, *you* tell me, haven't you any idea what it is you've done?

PERALTA: I distributed the gold the Master gave to me.

ST. PETER: And what good did it do? Hmm? Just look at the brouhaha you've started.

PERALTA: Don't let your right hand know what your left hand is doing. That's what it says in the Bible.

ST. PETER: Ha! So now you're quoting scripture, huh? (*He takes a piece of bread and wipes out the inside of his chocolate cup.*) Excuse me, but this is so damn good, and I'm nothing if not thorough.

PERALTA: What was all that about thology?

ST. PETER: *The*-ology. If you're going to say something, say it right. It's one of the greatest mix-ups we've ever had up there. But to tell you the truth, as far as that's concerned, I don't understand beans. Theology, well, that's just heavenly music to me. But to give you an idea, they had to call St. Thomas Aquinas to solve the problem, because the Master said that the damned were damned and damned they'd stay for all eternity.

PERALTA: Well, how did they solve it?

ST. PETER: You've got a sense of humor, too, huh? Questions! Questions!

PERALTA: I'm not trying to be funny.

ST. PETER: Now don't you get insolent with me! Don't you get wise with me, because if you do, I'll pin your ears back!

PERALTA: Now, now, Your Grace. Don't get upset. Don't get upset! Next thing you know, you'll get indigestion and spoil your chocolate. But please, tell me what happened.

ST. PETER: Well, those souls, the ones you got out of Hell, where were they going to go?

PERALTA: To Heaven.

ST. PETER: But can't you get it through your thick skull, they are damned! So St. Thomas began a discourse, up one side and down the other, for ten celestial minutes. That's more like one year in your time. And then he said he wanted to get together with the Master and St. Teresa. And that really did it! He got all the lady saints in Heaven stirred up, because even if it is Heaven, women will be women. You could hear them grumbling and gossiping all over! The noise got louder and finally they all gathered in the square.

PERALTA: What happened next?

ST. PETER: Now don't push me. Don't push me. St. Teresa, she sat down at a desk and started to scratch away with her pen. St. Thomas read on and on and she pushed and pulled at the pen. Now there's a scribe for you if ever there was one. If anybody ever needed proof that she can really write, well, there it was.

PERALTA: But what did she write?

ST. PETER: Stop interrupting! There she sat on her stool, writing away, writing away on the lectern. And as she wrote, this long piece of paper came crawling up over the top of the lectern and hung down and then it began to curl up, and curl up.

PERALTA: I'm waiting, I'm waiting.

ST. PETER: Well, let's hope you're not going to have to wait through eternity in the place where I'm pretty sure you're going to have to wait, you knucklehead.

PERALTA: All right. Go on with your story.

ST. PETER: Pretty soon, about five celestial minutes later, she scratched a big flourish with her pen, and made a sign to the Master that she was finished.

PERALTA: And then?

ST. PETER: Can't you be patient? We've certainly been patient with you. Well, then, the Master called for a general assembly and they began to beat on all the drums in Heaven, and to pull everyone off his cloud, because we were going to hear something unheard of. To give you some idea of how unusual this all was, not even St. Joachim, the Master's grandfather, had ever heard of anybody reading a proclamation in the plaza of the celestial court.

PERALTA: But what finally happened? For the love of God! How did it all end, Your Grace?

ST. PETER: Well, how should it end? In the long and short of it, the document said that you had won all those souls from the Devil fair and square, in a very straight and honest game.

PERALTA: I'm glad they recognized that.

ST. PETER: Ah, but you should have heard the little old saint read it! "We, Thomas Aquinas and Teresa of Jesus, being of age, and residing in Heaven, by mandate of our Lord, have gathered to resolve the very difficult problem . . ."

PERALTA: Um, uh . . . we were at the point where they said I had won the souls from the Devil . . .

ST. PETER: Ah, but you should have heard the pretty little voice with which she read it! It was just like when . . . um, young mountain shepherds get together to play the gelder's whistle.

PERALTA: Very well, if you don't want to get on with the story it's all right with me.

ST. PETER: Now don't you be insolent. Even though you won those souls legally, it'll be a cold day in Hell when they get into Heaven.

PERALTA: Why is that?

ST. PETER: Because it doesn't matter how sharp you are, you're not going to make the good Lord go back on his word.

PERALTA: Well, that isn't it. I mean . . .

ST. PETER: Those damned souls are condemned to stay wandering around in circles . . .

PERALTA: Circles? Where?

ST. PETER: Don't shout.

PERALTA: I'm simply demanding to know . . .

ST. PETER: What? What? I'm going to break your head in two! Oh! Oh, dear me! Oh! (*He falls back.*) Now look what you've done! Look what you've done! Don't you know I suffer from heart trouble! It's all this climbing up and down!

PERALTA: It's your own fault you got angry. Who asked you to do that?

ST. PETER: God grant me patience! Bring me a drink of water!

PERALTA: Here it is.

ST. PETER: Well, to make a long story short, those damned souls are not going to return to the flames and the sufferings. Instead they are condemned to a newfangled Hell. And if you ask me it's just as good a Hell as the one they left behind.

PERALTA: Oh, that's another matter. And what's that Hell like, Your Grace?

ST. PETER: Well, it's a very particular kind of penance, I can tell you. Give me a little more water, will you? Well, this is what they did. God all of a sudden flung into the world thirty-three thousand million bodies, and into those bodies they popped the souls that you won out of Hell. And those souls, even when their mothers and fathers think their bodies are going to go to Heaven . . . well, they're already damned in life. And that's why even holy baptism won't do them any good, because when their bodies die, their souls will go into other bodies. Over and over again until Judgment Day. And when it's all over they'll be damned to fly around and around Hell, per secula seculorum, amen! How about a little more water? I'm almost dead.

PERALTA: In other words, you're telling me that even in life those souls are going to be in the service of the Devil?

ST. PETER: Yup. And the Hell in which they burn is jealousy. Envy.

PERALTA: That sounds like a good idea. And it's a very good punishment, too, the one they invented.

ST. PETER: Oh, get me some more water. You've left me as dry as a bone.

PERALTA: If you want a little more chocolate, I'll have it fixed for you.

ST. PETER: No, thanks. Look . . . I'll tell you a secret. Your sister? Well, I had to *smuggle* her into Heaven. 'Cause I've just got to have more of her chocolate. Let me tell you, eating glory all the time is much too rich a diet for an old man like me . . . Maruchenga!

MARUCHENGA: Sir.

ST. PETER: Bring me a little corn meal, will you? Peraltona says she needs it for the griddle cakes.

MARUCHENGA: Right away, sir.

ST. PETER: And as for you, Peralta, well, you didn't pay attention to me. Now your wishes have gone up in smoke. They've evaporated. How many have you got left after all this hurly-burly?

PERALTA: One, Your Grace.

ST. PETER: Oh, yes, the one where you turn yourself into a speck.

PERALTA: That's the one, Your Grace.

ST. PETER: There's no making you out, Peralta.

PERALTA: Sometimes I can't make myself out, Your Grace.

MARUCHENGA: Here's the corn, sir. But what was all that about Miss Peraltona?

ST. PETER: Peralta will explain it to you. Well, I better be climbing back. It's about time for tea.

MARUCHENGA: Don Peraltica, this is all so mysterious. Where's it going to end, I wonder?

PERALTA: How should I know, Maruchenga? (*He goes out.*)

FIRST BEGGAR (*entering with the Second Beggar*): Do you happen to know what time Don Peraltica will be back?

MARUCHENGA: He should be back any minute now. It's just that he keeps running around like a little elf. Here to there and back and forth, from one house to the other, laying out the dead, consoling and succoring the live ones.

SECOND BEGGAR: He smashed the beehives and now he's trying to catch the bees.

MARUCHENGA: You ungrateful thing, shut your mouth!

FIRST BEGGAR: Well, he could have given away the gold without making such a mess of it.

MARUCHENGA: And what do you know about anything? These affairs are God's business.

SECOND BEGGAR: I suppose it's God's business to hang Death in an avocado tree . . . and then to let her down!

FIRST BEGGAR: And just like that to have put an end to all Christians!

SECOND BEGGAR: And then to leave such a crop of corpses. Why, they were like worms at harvest time. Not all the chickens in the world could eat 'em up.

MARUCHENGA: The ones he helped most are the ones who grumble loudest.

FIRST BEGGAR: He hasn't helped me that much.

SECOND BEGGAR: Nor me.

MARUCHENGA: You're a pair of leeches, that's what you are. And if it were up to me, I'd take a broom to the both of you.

FIRST BEGGAR: You know the ones who really made a profit? . . . with all this dying around here, it's the ones who inherited the money. They've got so much they don't know where to put it.

SECOND BEGGAR: And now they spend all their time having parties and orgies. Do you think the world can be made better with a little gold?

FIRST BEGGAR: And with miracles and with witchcraft? And tricks?

MARUCHENGA: I don't know anything! Let God's will be done.

THIRD BEGGAR (*entering*): Hail Mary, full of grace.

MARUCHENGA: Blessed art thou among women.

THIRD BEGGAR: See? Look! *Look*! See? Look at me! That's the way they left me. That's the way they left me! Right in the middle of the Camino Real . . . almost naked! Took everything I had. Everything! Everything Peraltica had given me.

FIRST BEGGAR: Well, that's not surprising, with all the robbing that's going on.

SECOND BEGGAR: Everything's gone rotten! The whole world's bad.

THIRD BEGGAR: And here come more! There are clouds of them, whole clouds of bad beggars as greedy as lobsters.

BEGGAR WOMAN (*entering*): Praise be to God.

MARUCHENGA: Praised and blessed on high.

BEGGAR WOMAN: Isn't Peraltica around somewhere?

MARUCHENGA: He's out doing good deeds.

BEGGAR WOMAN: Well, let's hope he has some left over for me. The money he gave me boiled away like magic. I met this gentleman along the way, he had a very honest face . . . and I gave him all the gold Peralta had given me. The fellow promised he would double it for me in a month. A month passed and I never saw him. Another month went by and I had to go back to begging.

OLD BEGGAR (*entering*): God Almighty, what a terrible, terrible mess!

MARUCHENGA: What now?

OLD BEGGAR: It's a disgrace, that's what it is! A calamity!

MARUCHENGA: Well, what is?

FIRST BEGGAR: Now, there's one that made a profit. The gold was really meant for him all along!

SECOND BEGGAR: What with his money-lending and his good long nails, there's one man who knows how to scratch himself rich.

FIRST BEGGAR: Hoarding and hiding his money under his rags. Look at him, all covered with rags.

OLD BEGGAR: I suppose you haven't made any profit. I know the little games you've been playing, so let's not talk about profit, because it would be like giving a rope to a man who's going to hang.

MARUCHENGA: Oh, don't pay any attention to them. Tell us what's happened.

OLD BEGGAR: Well, after he'd buried all the dead, Peralta went into town, and what does he find? A great big orgy of all those who got rich on their inheritance. The ones who got fat on death. So he went to the cantina where they were gambling and it was just running over with people. Running over!

SECOND BEGGAR: And you know how he hates gambling.

FIRST BEGGAR: Yes, with all the tricks he knows.

THIRD BEGGAR: They found his weak spot like a pit in a mango.

BEGGAR WOMAN: Let the man tell his story, you . . .

OLD BEGGAR: Well, he started playing cards and he began to take those sharks one by one. And he started piling up the gold . . .

BEGGAR WOMAN: Oh, God bless him! He's such a kind man.

FIRST BEGGAR: He doesn't know where to put it, he's won so much.

SECOND BEGGAR: Here it goes, all over again!

OLD BEGGAR: And then the hornet's nest broke. There they were, knives and razors, and he as calm as could be: "Trumps! Forty, ace and three!"

MARUCHENGA: And? What happened?

OLD BEGGAR: Then in comes the king's messenger. He's supposed to go to the king's palace. His most royal majesty is waiting for him. Out he goes, followed by that crowd of people, screaming and squealing like souls in Hell . . . that Peralta had powers! That they should drown him for a heretic! That he used loaded dice!

MARUCHENGA: And then what happened?

OLD BEGGAR: Why, he gets to the palace, and there sits the king, high up on a platform, with the queen by his side. And behind them there were a bunch of people, oh, you know, very well dressed and very white. They looked like bigshots or bosses. And off to one side there were some women . . . very pretty, very rich . . . like princesses! And then a man in black stands up. He was wearing a funny kind of hat and he says: "Peralta, the king's going to pass sentence." And the king fixed the crown on his head, and then in a great big voice he shouts out, "Peralta, you gave us all a big scare. You had us all believing that the kingdom was going to come to wrack and ruin. And you are the cause for all this hurly-burly." And then somebody handed him a rolled-up piece of paper for him to read. "We all know that the world can't be changed, and the best thing to do is to leave it the way it is, because that's the only way the rest of us, you know, the kings, can govern it." Son of a bitch, you should have heard what happened then! *Everybody* began to accuse poor old Peralta! They all had their crack at him. And the king told Peralta to gather up his things and sentenced him into exile.

MARUCHENGA: Ungrateful dogs that they are. Just think of the good Peralta's done them.

FIRST BEGGAR: Wherever they exile him, that's where the money goes.

SECOND BEGGAR: Why didn't they lock him up around here so he could keep on making money?

THIRD BEGGAR: Well, I'm getting to him before they throw him out of the kingdom, that's for sure.

BEGGAR WOMAN: Christ Almighty, what a stupid government we have! His royal majesty doesn't know which side of the bread his butter's on.

OLD BEGGAR: Here he comes! (*Peralta enters.*) He looks worried. He looks sad. Oh, Don Peraltica, have mercy! A little something, please!

FIRST BEGGAR: Don't forget your poor folk, Don Peralta.

SECOND BEGGAR: God'll repay you in Heaven.

THIRD BEGGAR: Look how the thieves left me! Naked as a jaybird, Don Peralta . . . God will repay you.

BEGGAR WOMAN: Here I am again, in utter misery, Don Peralta. Help me, in the name of God. God will repay you . . .

MARUCHENGA: I bet you haven't eaten a thing. Wait a bit. I'll bring you a little corn stew. (*We hear the music of Death. She enters jumping.*)

DEATH: Hmm . . . You look frightened out of your wits . . . if not to death. You're a bunch of chickens! Haven't you gotten used to me yet? Which ones are going to come with me this time? I don't like them sad and dreary. I like them happy and gay. See? I've even brought the ghosts of some old musicians to play a serenade for my old friend Peralta. All right, strike up! They're the best I could find but they died of hunger and they haven't the strength to play. I said play! Play, you good-for-nothings! Ah, but you're all so droopy and downcast! Well, here goes a little tune for you . . .

> Vengeance tastes best
> when it's cold
> and I love vengeance
> more than gold.

And now, Señor Peralta, will you deign to go with me?

PERALTA: With pleasure. I've lived a lot and I've enjoyed it.

DEATH: You certainly managed to stir things up, damn you.

PERALTA: They can judge me any way they want. I tried to do what was right. Am I to blame if it didn't turn out? But now let me make one last request. Pay for my shroud for me, and then, make a little bag for me, and put it in my shroud. And in that bag I want you to put my cards and my dice. I want to be buried without a coffin at the gate of the cemetery, so that everybody'll step on me. You're my witnesses, and I hold you responsible for carrying out my last will and testament. And now, Ma'am, let's go.

MARUCHENGA: Oh, dear me, Death is taking him away!

BEGGAR WOMAN: Peraltica is leaving! Who'll take care of us now?

OLD BEGGAR: Requiescat in pace.

ALL: Amen.

BEGGAR WOMAN: Rest in peace with the holy company at your head.

ALL: Rest in peace.

BEGGAR WOMAN: With St. Michael and his sword of justice . . .

ALL: Rest in peace.

BEGGAR WOMAN: With the key that opens everything and the hand that closes all . . .

ALL: Rest in peace. (*Exit all.*)

EPILOGUE

RINGMASTER (*entering*): And so it was that Peralta snuck into Heaven, but God the Father called him up to His cloud and spoke to him: "Peralta, choose whatever place you want. No one has won such honor as you, for you are humility itself . . . you are charity itself. You needn't be humble any more, for now you're saved." However, since Peralta hadn't used the last wish the Master had given him, of turning himself into a little speck, he chose to use it then. And he got smaller and smaller until he became a tiny little Peralta no more than three inches tall. And who'd believe it, with all the strength of a lucky man, he jumped a mighty jump right onto the globe of the world that God the Father holds in His right hand. Then he made himself comfortable against the Cross and hugged it. And there he stays to this day, right there in the right hand of God the Father. And there he'll stay for all eternity.

(*All the characters enter as they did in the beginning.*)

JESUS: And that's the end
                  of our story,
                  with Peralta in glory.

ST. PETER: A good lesson
                  for those who listen.

DEVIL: False or true,
                true or false;
                please forgive us
                all our faults.
DEATH: Bless us all;
                our play is done.
                We pray to God
                you found it fun.
RINGMASTER: We beg your leave now
                to retire,
                we players must be off
                in search of hire.
                For your applause
                we humbly thank you,
                so go with God
                my lovely ladies,
                and gentlemen go with Him too.
                And we will promise
                to remember you,
                forever, and ever, amen.

                                                            CURTAIN

The Mulatto's Orgy

BY LUISA JOSEFINA HERNÁNDEZ

Luisa Josefina Hernández of Mexico has acted in and directed plays, and has written many novels and dramas as well. Hers is a practical and broad knowledge of the theater. She studied for some time at Columbia University, served as chairman of the theater seminar at Havana in 1963, and has taught drama in various theater centers and universities. *The Mulatto's Orgy*, written in 1966, is more theater than literature. What I mean is that the play will not render itself effectively to literary criticism. This play is a significant spectacle or ritual; it comes to life upon the stage. It demands music, startling changes of scene, impressive lighting effects, expert dancing, and all the devices of drama that inflate our gestures to the dimensions of a compelling ritual. Any effort to interpret this play on a purely realistic level is sure to invite failure. It is a vision of protest and a plea for liberty on its most significant and instinctual level. The subject matter of this play in the hands of a Germanic author of "epic" inclinations might prove more dense on a politcal and philosophical level; in the hands of an American author caught up in the civil rights protest, the treatment of the subject would almost certainly prove shrill and strident. It is very Latin American that Miss Hernández' play should address us with ironic optimism and a lyrical grace somewhat foreign to our nordic drama.

CHARACTERS:

The Indian	*The Mulatto*
The Friar	*The Mulatto's Wife*
First Miner	*First Woman*
Second Miner	*Second Woman*
Third Miner	*Third Woman*
The Mayor	*First Musician*
First Priest	*Second Musician*
Second Priest	*Third Musician*

A night sky, huge and full of stars, like a composition of electric lights. Presently the stage lights come up. Dawn. We find ourselves in the city of Guanajuato, 1799. The city can be indicated by a map of the period and, if worst comes to worst, by a placard indicating the place and time. As soon as this has been established, we hear a cacophony of voices, street calls, coaches, and the clangor of sounds that issue from the mines. The Friar enters. His costume must not represent a specific order. He wears sandals and has a beard. It is hard to tell whether he is young or old. There is something luminous about him. He seems capable of understanding everything but is nevertheless able to defend his principles. He walks with the slow gait of an exhausted man and is about to sit on the ground when the Indian enters. He too seems of an indeterminable age. The Indian is a very practical man but he too has a certain spiritual quality.

INDIAN: Good morning, Father.

FRIAR: God be with you. How far is it to Guanajuato?

INDIAN: You can see the first houses from here. And over there, beyond the wood, you can see the whole city. Where is your coach?

FRIAR: The men of my order travel on foot. We have no coaches.

INDIAN: Who's carrying your baggage?

FRIAR: I travel with what I wear on my back. What's so funny?

INDIAN: Father, what's the good of being a Spaniard?!

FRIAR (*touched to the quick*): There should be no advantage in being a Spaniard. All people in this world are free to choose the path that leads to God.

INDIAN: Some paths are harder than others.

FRIAR: What do you mean? Have you been baptised?

INDIAN: That's the first thing they do! I've been baptised since I was a kid.

(*The Friar stares at the Indian and says nothing. He is not sure if the Indian is being ironic. He is about to ask him, but then changes his mind.*)

FRIAR: Guanajuato is a big city ... or so I'm told.

INDIAN: It's glorious, Father. Back in Spain your countrymen dream of nothing else ... or so I'm told. People make money and they spend it. It's a pity it's not Saturday, because if it were, you'd go from one fiesta to another. You should see how the money flows! ... like water!

FRIAR (*not offended, but thinking of something else*): I'm sorry I missed it. I could have gathered lots of alms for my order ... but I came to see the trial of the mulatto. You know anything about it?

INDIAN (*evasively*): They talk of nothing else, Father.

FRIAR: Am I late?

INDIAN: Did you come to confess him?

FRIAR: I bring an order from the Viceroy ... who is a great friend of mine. He takes an interest in everything that happens in New Spain.

INDIAN (*smiling*): Father, if *you* tell me what the Viceroy says, *I'll* tell you all about the mulatto and what he did.

FRIAR: Did you actually know him? If you didn't, I'd better wait and find out about him at the trial.

INDIAN: I am the mulatto's servant.

FRIAR: Good God! Do you mean to say that you were with him through all of it?

INDIAN: I stuck to him every second of the day and night. And that's why, now that you're coming, I am going! The trial is tomorrow.

FRIAR: Don't you want to testify?

INDIAN: No one will ask me anything. When someone calls an Indian to testify, it means that the judges have already made up their minds and the case is settled. That's the way things are.

FRIAR: Where are you going now?

INDIAN: To a cave I know about. I'll hide there for fifteen, maybe twenty days, till they have forgotten about the trial. People forget things in a hurry around here. (*The Friar gives him a despairing look and searches for a place to sit down.*) You've walked a long way today, haven't you, Father?

FRIAR: Eight leagues.

INDIAN: What's the good of being a . . . How long has it been since you've eaten?

FRIAR: Someone gave me some fruit last night.

INDIAN (*serious at last*): I'll tell you about the mulatto and you tell me about the Viceroy. (*He smiles.*) Charity is for the Indians and the friars. Let's give each other alms for a change.

FRIAR: Is your cave far off?

INDIAN: Father, you're standing in front of it. I've got some food, wine, and fresh water. Been saving it ever since it happened. Here, sit over here on this log. What do you want? You Spaniards eat ham and jerked beef. But since you're so different . . .

FRIAR (*sitting down exhaustedly*): Give me what you will and let's talk. God is with me, you see. I was about to faint . . . and I owe my finding you to His wonderful kindness. May He bless us in all we say and do here, that it may be for your good and mine.

INDIAN: And my master's too, the mulatto.

FRIAR: So be it.

(*The lights dim and the starry sky shines brightly once again. The Indian and the Friar are seated upstage and to the side, so that it is easy for the Indian to step from his role as narrator into the action whenever it is necessary.*)

INDIAN: It happened in the middle of spring before the rains and the wind come. The weather is so nice then, you sleep out of doors in the open. Lots of the miners do it. It happened right here, Father, right here on this hill where we are sitting. So you'll get the names straight, it's called Mari Sánchez. Father, this hill is made of pure gold. When you walk on it, you're stepping on the richest veins of gold anywhere in the sierras. But you know what a miner's life is like.

(*Three men with soot-blackened faces come on. They carry picks and shovels and are dressed in a strange assortment of rags: fine shirts in tatters, satin trousers stained and dirty, silk stockings drooping and torn. While the Indian is talking, the men move with their heads down like sleepwalkers, but the minute he utters the last word they turn to the audience and speak with vitality in a rhetorical tone, as though they were performing some kind of operetta.*)

INDIAN: They can spend weeks digging with their picks and shovels without finding anything. Then again, I've seen it with my own eyes, sometimes they'll dig out two whole pounds of pure gold. That's what happened with Mari Sánchez.

FIRST MINER: That's the way it was until one day . . .

SECOND MINER: We found the great vein.

THIRD MINER: Gold. Not silver, but gold!

FIRST MINER: We felt we'd discovered America!

SECOND MINER: We felt like Cortés when he was appointed Captain General.

THIRD MINER: The vein was endless. There was enough for three months. Three months' worth of gold!

FIRST MINER: We went crazy. We ran screaming out of the mine.

SECOND MINER: But we stole some first.

THIRD MINER: We hid the gold and two hours later we came back, dug it up, and sold it.

SECOND MINER: Then we ran off to buy clothes!

(*We hear delicate music played on the clavichord. The miners go off with mincing steps and the mannered movements and gestures of the minuet, as though they were courtiers. The lights come up on the Indian and the Friar.*)

INDIAN: That's how they are. When they find gold they go out and buy everything they dream of. Buy on Saturday, sell on Monday.

They'll take their shirts of fine Dutch linen and wrap them around their pick handles to keep their blistered hands from bleeding. You see, Father, it's because they're mestizos. You understand?

FRIAR: All men are alike in the eyes of God.

INDIAN: But not in the eyes of man . . . and nothing could be farther from a mestizo than a mulatto. When the word got out they'd found the vein of gold, I ran for my master but he wasn't at home. His wife was, though.

(*The lights come up on a beautiful mestiza dressed in Spanish costume. She looks like a painting and it should be surprising that she moves and talks. The Indian crosses to her.*)

INDIAN: I came to talk with my master, the mulatto.

MULATTO'S WIFE: I haven't seen your master for two days. And where have you been all of this time?

INDIAN (*evasively*): Me? Oh, at the mines . . . out in the fields . . . looking after my master's interests.

MULATTO'S WIFE (*ironically*): Oh, yes, of course, your master's interests! One exhausted mine under a mountain of mud . . . and it isn't all his anyway! You were out guarding one third of a mud mine! What's happened?

INDIAN (*evasively*): I wonder where my master could be now?

MULATTO'S WIFE (*becoming annoyed*): He went off to the woods. But before he left he said, "Woman, I want to sleep out in the open and talk to the gods in the center of the earth. I've got to ask them to save my life from becoming something dreary, dark, and empty. I want them to shine it up for me with joy." (*As the woman speaks she loses her resentment and her eyes begin to shine. She shares her husband's dream.*)

(*The lights come up once more on the Indian and the Friar.*)

FRIAR: That's an invocation! They can accuse the mulatto of making a pact with the devil. Does the Holy Office know this?

INDIAN: It knows, and their priests have argued the matter one way and the other.

(*The lights come up on the priests. Each one carries the hood of an inquisitor in his hand.*)

FIRST PRIEST: Oh, come now. Are you really going to wear this . . . this costume?

SECOND PRIEST: It depends.

FIRST PRIEST: On what?

SECOND PRIEST: It's not just any old masquerade, you know. But I'll seek the Mayor's opinion first, just to make sure. You must keep in mind that we have sentenced two blacks, six mulattoes, and ten Indians for crimes of heresy, witchcraft, and general paganism. And so, actually, in order to continue setting a good example, what we need is a mestizo and not a mulatto.

FIRST PRIEST: You're right. This mulatto, like all mulattoes, is a damned nuisance.

SECOND PRIEST: But tell me, what do you think? Do you really believe that he summoned up the spirits of the mine? Do you think he's guilty of witchcraft?

FIRST PRIEST: Unquestionably.

SECOND PRIEST: My dear sir, your imagination seems alarmingly paganized of late!

(*The lights come up on the Indian and the Friar.*)

INDIAN: Well, what do you think of that, Father?

FRIAR: Nothing. What can I say? I believe in good and not in evil.

INDIAN: A new religion! There's no end to them! But let me get on with it. I *found* my master . . . in the woods, sleeping on the wet ground. His chest was naked. He wore a white blanket wrapped around his waist and he had his machete at his side.

(*The lights come up on the Mulatto. Almost more than a person, he is an "entity": dark-skinned, beautiful body, passionate, and given to excess. He sleeps like some god of the forest. The Indian looks at him for a moment before waking him.*)

INDIAN: Master, wake up. It's me. (*The Mulatto moves.*) Wake up.

MULATTO (*without opening his eyes*): If you only knew what I was dreaming. O gods, I thank you for the color! I was dreaming red but before that I went wild with green and yellow and blue. Oh, my gods, what color!

INDIAN: When black and white mix in the blood, the results are always wild.

MULATTO (*jumps to his feet laughing and puts his arm around the Indian*): What do you want? Money? I haven't got any. Not one coin.

INDIAN: At this very moment you are richer than any of the six Spanish families that live in the city.

MULATTO: Play jokes on me and I'll break your head!

INDIAN (*quickly*): They've found a huge vein of gold at the Marí Sánchez.

MULATTO: What did you say?

INDIAN: That you're the richest man in the city.

(*We hear a Spanish dance played by a full orchestra. The Mulatto begins to dance, jumping about wildly in every direction.*)

MULATTO: And here I was, begging for life, dreaming of colors! Screaming in the night to be saved from the habit of being a mulatto in a colony of slaves. There I was, screaming that I'd rather be dead!

(*The lights come up on the Friar and the Indian.*)

FRIAR: Blasphemy! And a direct attack on the government of His Excellency, the Viceroy! Is this known?

INDIAN: The Mayor knows it.

(*The lights come up on the Mayor, who also looks like a painting of the period. Perhaps it would be best to dress him a little more luxuriously than normal, for he is the chief authority of Guanajuato.*)

MAYOR: As far as I'm concerned, *anything* out of the ordinary is an attack upon the government of the Viceroy! At the bottom of every crime is dissatisfaction, and the dissatisfaction of those who are not Spaniards is, in this country at any rate, directed at those of us who are Spaniards. Strange! (*He assumes a solemn demeanor.*) For this reason one can say that the distance between a judge and the accused narrows down to an abstract thought. Repression ferments the very situation of the colonies or, to put it another way, provokes expressions of rebellion everywhere. There is no solution. (*He returns to his pose. The lights come up on the Friar and the Indian.*)

FRIAR (*very upset*): But that's the dilemma of all government! The Mayor's right. Nevertheless, it's very difficult to assume responsibility when a man's life is at stake.

INDIAN: Father, doubts will always be doubts . . . even when they're honest, like yours. The best thing is not to have them. For example, my master never had any doubts, ever!

(*The lights come up on the semi-nude Mulatto. He holds his machete in his hand now. He is beautiful and frightening. He stands, poised, in an attitude of command, and it is difficult to tell exactly how seriously he takes himself. The Indian comes over and stands by his side.*)

MULATTO: I order you to bring me musicians, servants, food, and drink. I want you to invite all the workmen in the mine.

INDIAN: Very well. Where will I tell them to go?

MULATTO: Tell them to come here. The fiesta will be here . . . near the mine! My fiesta's going to be too big for a house or a walled city. It's a fiesta for everyone! I'm inviting the winds, and the salamanders will come too. And . . .

INDIAN: What else?

MULATTO (*almost childlike*): Know what I want?

INDIAN: Tell me, sir.

MULATTO: Have you seen that painting of the Marquesa de Cruilles? The one that hangs in the waiting room of the Mayor's palace? The one you can see from the street?

INDIAN: I've seen it.

MULATTO (*hesitating, then making a nervous gesture with the machete*): Well, I want the Marquesa de Cruilles.

INDIAN (*joking but not pushing the joke*): Live or dead?

MULATTO: Live! White! Trembling in my arms! With her black hair and that smile! That smile! Yes, yes, I must have the Marquesa de Cruilles! (*He raises the machete.*)

INDIAN: You'll have her.

MULATTO: And music, wine, lamb, beef, songs, servants, porcelain plates, silk, satin, perfume, and the Marquesa de Cruilles.

(*The lights come up on the Indian and the Friar.*)

FRIAR: How could you promise him that? The Marquesa was the wife of the old Viceroy! She's a respectable old dowager by now.

INDIAN: If a man asks for an illusion, then it's an illusion he wants, don't you think?

FRIAR: Perhaps. What did you do?

INDIAN: I went to my mistress and told her to dress herself like the Marquesa. Oh, it was easy enough. My mistress is very beautiful. She even looks like the Marquesa in a remarkable way.

(*The lights come up on the Mulatto's Wife. She is now the very image of the Viceroy's wife in a white wig and all of the finery of the period. The Indian comes to her side.*)

MULATTO'S WIFE: The dress is identical but the wig is hot and the powder makes me sneeze. And these shoes are not made to go wandering in the woods! My skirts are going to be covered with mud!

INDIAN: Well, then, take your shoes off and pull up your skirt.

(*The Mulatto's Wife hesitates for a moment, then kicks off her shoes and hikes up her skirts, revealing the lace-trimmed under-garments. She runs off with great agility. The Indian steps down and very carefully picks up the little silver shoes with the tips of his fingers. The lights come up on the Indian and the Friar.*)

I arranged that fiesta all by myself. I bought the meat, the wine, the pulque, and I rounded up the women to cook the food and serve it. I delivered the invitations and I hired the musicians.

FRIAR: They're going to accuse you of being an accomplice.

INDIAN: Father, I'm here now, in this cave . . . I'm not standing in front of the Mayor.

(*The lights come up on the stage, which has been surprisingly set. The musicians stand at one side. There is a violin, a guitar, and some wind instrument. On the other side are the three miners we have already seen, but they are now wearing clean clothes. Off to one side there are three Indian women grinding corn, each at her metate. The Mulatto, who now wears a red sarong, is seated down center on the ground and he looks depressed. There is no joy even though the musicians have been playing dance music constantly and the cooks have been making tortillas incessantly. And the miners have been strutting about giving themselves airs. Above them we make out the starry sky and the light that comes from the furnace.*)

MULATTO: Let wealth spread out through the world like rain, as though it were destruction, death. Let the gold from the mines pour down on us, and clean us and leave us shining and new! Newborn!

FIRST MINER: Today's Saturday.

SECOND MINER: Just Saturday?

THIRD MINER: We need tomorrow. Sunday's everything rolled up in one.

MULATTO: Let the gold rain down on our heads and let's have ourselves a baptism at last, a baptism of metal, not blood, not fire! We've got to become the stone, the earth, the seeds, the air of the muddy night!

FIRST WOMAN: I'm going to take home a whole bag of gold!

SECOND WOMAN: My children will have gold to buy bread.

THIRD WOMAN: We'll eat and we'll eat until . . . the vein runs out!

SECOND WOMAN: Bread comes up from the center of the earth. Blessed be the bread of gold and silver.

MULATTO: I never wanted to be unique. I never wanted to be something special in this world. Never. All I ever wanted was to belong to a place where the colors of my body could dissolve and mix, even the red or blue. If we were all just blood-colored or the color of our teeth or the hue of our bones . . . I want a world like that. Between white and black there's nothing! Nothing! (*Suddenly desperate*) Oh, Marquesa . . . Marquesa de Cruilles! (*The Mulatto falls to the ground as though he meant to cry long hours for the absent Marquesa.*)

MUSICIANS ONE AND TWO (*singing*):

> Marquesa, most beautiful Marquesa,
> With the rose of spring on her mouth,
> And a laugh of mystery and delight.
> Hair darker than the forest,
> Teeth brighter than snow,
> A spark of sunlight shot in the night.

(*The Mulatto stands up. We can see that he has actually been crying.*)

MULATTO: Enough. I want a fiesta now, a great fiesta! Happy fiesta! No more songs to a Marquesa we never knew. No more tears for an old woman who may be dead for all I know. No more, no more, no more!

(As if in reply to the screams of the Mulatto, the musicians pick up the tempo. The miners begin to dance and the women work furiously. The Mulatto stands with his machete in his hand like a statue and looks at them with a trace of irony in his face. The lights come up on the Indian and the Friar.)

FRIAR: But do you mean to say that no one had ever told the mulatto that he did not own all of the mines' output?

INDIAN: Believe it or not, Father, no. No one even knew who the other owners were . . . off in Mexico City. His woman knew . . . but she had other things to worry about.

FRIAR: The sentence will be severe. I don't think your master has a prayer of a chance, or a shred of defence.

(The lights come up on another part of the stage. An imaginary trial is taking place. The action of the trial is conducted in the light of the Friar's remarks. We see the Mayor flanked by two priests. The priests always hold in their hands the hoods of the Inquisition. The Mulatto kneels before them. He no longer wears his red sarong.)

MAYOR: The political authorities of New Spain accuse you of a breach of trust, of corruption of customs, and, finally, of having incited the workers at the mines as well as other persons to indulge in and carry out pagan rituals in the middle of the night and in the solitude of the jungle. Answer me, are you guilty?

MULATTO: I admit to an unbridled imagination and to having forgotten that the mine had two other owners and, finally, of having not wanted my fiesta under a roof.

FIRST PRIEST: Your statement is a dangerous one! You realize that?

SECOND PRIEST: Everything that's confused, everything that's not obvious, clear, and normal lends itself to the very worst interpretations!

(The three men turn their backs on the Mulatto and talk in private.)

FIRST PRIEST: Does the Mayor feel that it's worth the effort to take the worst interpretations?

SECOND PRIEST: Doesn't the Mayor feel that what seems called for most urgently are the best interpretations?

MAYOR: My opinion is that, for the moment, it seems precisely the better part of valor not to make my opinions known!
(The three face the Mulatto once more.)
More questions will be put to you as we study the case in depth. To the dungeon!
(The lights come up on the Indian and the Friar.)

INDIAN: My master was sad, you see, because he didn't know how to enjoy his fiesta. The miners danced and ate and drank, but my master seemed turned into a statue as he watched them . . . watched everything.
(The lights come up on the Mulatto and his machete. He is dressed once more in his red sarong and stands as described, like a statue. The other nine persons who are on the stage are divided into small choruses and they sing according to their accompaniment in three different rhythms.)

WOMEN: Golden bread, silver bread,
             Rice of stone and of mud.

MINERS: Hidden city
             Below the ground!
             My city
             And my town . . .
             City where I live,
             Long and dark and winding streets
             With corners full of blackness
             Where I burn my life
             Hidden from the sun.
             No riches for me,
             No happiness at all.
             All my dreams are of silver
             And silver lights up my dreams.

MUSICIANS: Money, silver and more money,
             You've got to make money, money, more money!
             You've got to make money, you've got to save money,
             You've got to keep playing the game of silver!

MINERS: Beneath the cathedral
             Under the courthouse

And the monuments in the park
Under the palace
And the avenues
Hidden away from the sun.

WOMEN: Golden bread, silver bread,
Rice of stone and of mud!

(*Presently they seem to forget their lyrics. They speak, they sing, all at the same time, creating very quickly the sense of chaos, which is supported by the dimming of the light. The voices die out, and in silence the lights come up on the Mulatto. He has not moved and stands alone. Very softly at first, we begin to hear the music of the song of the Marquesa de Cruilles. She comes on stage dressed as we have seen her. When the Mulatto sees her his expression is more of triumph than of amazement. He has prayed for this gift with fervor and it has been granted him.*)

MULATTO: Marquesa de Cruilles. (*His statuesque demeanor seems to disappear. He is about to kneel before her but instead he kisses her hand. She smiles as the painting must have smiled.*)

MULATTO'S WIFE: What a pleasure to see you again.

MULATTO: Your Excellency remembers me.

WIFE: How could I forget?

MULATTO: And just what was it brought me to mind?

MULATTO'S WIFE: A summer afternoon. We were in a boat, sir, you and I. But, sir . . . how strange . . . it wasn't in Spain, nor was it here, but rather in Italy. You and I have spent an afternoon together . . . in Venice.

MULATTO (*not daring to believe it*): And then, remember? . . . tell me, what does the color blue mean to you?

MULATTO'S WIFE (*without hesitating*): My dress that afternoon was blue and you praised the faintly olive tint of my skin. You said to me, "Blue is a magnificent color on women with olive skin." And then . . .

MULATTO: What happened then, most excellent lady?

MULATTO'S WIFE: You kissed me, a long kiss.

(*The Mulatto stares at her in the full hunger of sex. She returns his gaze.*)

MULATTO: María Antonia, do you know where we are now?

MULATTO'S WIFE: On top of a muddy hill, covered with jungle and stuffed with gold. It's a kingdom.

MULATTO: It's our kingdom. Will you accept it?

MULATTO'S WIFE: Haven't I, for centuries, accepted everything you have given me?

MULATTO: That's true. María Antonia, let me kiss you.

(*They kiss for a long time. The lights come up on the Indian and the Friar.*)

FRIAR: What a strange woman. And how could she have brought herself to imitate the Marquesa de Cruilles?

INDIAN: She *was* the Marquesa . . . for several days.

FRIAR: Oh, surely that's going to complicate the trial! Has his wife testified?

(*The lights come up on the Mayor and the two priests. Standing before them in her dress of the Marquesa is the Mulatto's Wife.*)

MAYOR: You confess yourself guilty of having imitated the dress of the Marquesa? Having used her name? And of having taken her place?

MULATTO'S WIFE: Yes. No! No, it wasn't that way at all. I am the mulatto's woman. We made love then . . . in the jungle. What sin is that? We were *married* in the cathedral! It was on Sunday, eleven o'clock, and the sun was out. I was the most beautiful bride and he . . . what can one say about him?

FIRST PRIEST (*coughing*): Yes, that's true, my dear, that's true. But we're not questioning the fact that you were married. His excellency the Mayor only wishes to find out why it is you put on that dress, and adopted a personality so different from your own.

MULATTO'S WIFE: Don't you understand? He was waiting for the Marquesa. I dressed myself like her so that he'd want me.

SECOND PRIEST: Are you mad, woman! What earthly connection could your husband have with the poor old wife of the Viceroy? You are defaming a person of the highest rank and you made yourself accomplice to a very extravagant act. The most trivial explanation would be that you were bewitched into acting like the Marquesa.

MULATTO' WIFE (*vehemently*): Don't say that, please! I have always known who I am! I'm the mulatto's woman, married to him in a white mantilla at Sunday mass. I've always known who I am!

MAYOR: Would you swear that on the Bible?

MULATTO'S WIFE: Yes! I'll swear that I always knew I was I and no one else!

MAYOR: Very well, bring in the mulatto.

(*The Mulatto's Wife does not expect this. She covers her mouth with her hand. The Mulatto appears without his sarong or machete. He goes to her and kisses her hand.*)

MULATTO: María Antonia. (*She allows him to kiss her hand immediately. Almost without thinking of it she begins to play the part of the Marquesa.*)

MAYOR: Mulatto, this woman you see here dressed up like the Marquesa de Cruilles, wife of the old Viceroy of New Spain . . . this woman is willing to swear by God that she is your legitimate wife and that her impersonation of the Marquesa is a masquerade and nothing more.

(*The Mulatto and his Wife look at each other for a long time.*) Woman, are you ready to make your sworn statement?

MULATTO'S WIFE (*speaking in a more refined manner*): No, Your Excellency. You must forgive me. Instead, I swear before God that I am the Marquesa de Cruilles and that I belong body and soul to this man.

FIRST PRIEST (*screaming*): Perjury! She knows very well who she is!

SECOND PRIEST: She's been invaded by an evil spirit! By evil itself! How could she possibly swear that she belongs body and soul to a *man*?

MULATTO (*speaking firmly*): Thank you, María Antonia.

(*Her smile is almost imperceptible but it is a passionate one.*)

MAYOR: Take that man away. (*The Mulatto leaves the stage and the Mayor returns his attention to the Wife. Speaking angrily*) Do you know what you've done?

(*The Mulatto's Wife breaks into sobs. The lights come up on the Indian and the Friar.*)

FRIAR: There's a fantastical vein runs through these people of New Spain! Absolutely fantastical!

INDIAN: Oh, come, now, Father, you don't mean that! Are you telling me that you and I can't plant a tree?

FRIAR: Of course we can. But *that* kind of tree won't grow in the ground of reason, it's a proven fact.

INDIAN: I wish you could have seen that fiesta. There was music and food and wine day and night for three whole weeks. The miners themselves would show up on Saturday, spend whatever they had in their hands by the fistful! But on Monday they'd return to their work with nothing but the clothes on their back . . . and sometimes without their clothes.

(*The miners enter. They are now dressed in rags and they walk across the stage slowly.*)

THE MINERS (*singing*): Hidden city
　　　　　　　　　Below the ground!
　　　　　　　　　My city
　　　　　　　　　And my town . . .
　　　　　　　　　City where I live,
　　　　　　　　　Long and dark and winding streets
　　　　　　　　　With corners full of blackness
　　　　　　　　　Where I burn my life
　　　　　　　　　Hidden from the sun.

(*The miners go off and the lights come up over the kneeling women. They talk softly and upstage one can hear a faint music.*)

FIRST WOMAN: Quickly!

SECOND WOMAN: We mustn't get tired. There's no such thing as exhaustion!

THIRD WOMAN: Part of that gold is ours. I'm going to take lots of it home!

FIRST WOMAN: I just don't get tired! I don't get sore and my arms don't hurt.

SECOND WOMAN: I don't care how long I kneel!

THIRD WOMAN: I don't care if I sleep or if I eat. It doesn't matter!

FIRST WOMAN: No one talks anymore. Nothing matters except our hurry.

SECOND WOMAN: If I faint, they'll call another. They'll pay her and the money will be for *her* house and *her* children. And then other people will buy food and clothes.

THIRD WOMAN: No animal works harder than us because only we know the agony of being poor.

SECOND WOMAN: Get on with it, quick! Quickly! We mustn't lose a second!

(*The lights come up on the opposite side of the stage. This time we see the musicians. They enter playing a lively tune. But presently, as though their exhaustion would not permit them to continue, their eyes close and they prop each other up and play slowly. Then they rouse themselves, shake their heads, and recover their lively tempo. This happens at least twice. The lights come up on the Indian and the Friar.*)

INDIAN: My master slept by day, out in the jungle. So did my mistress . . . but at home. Every night I followed her to this place.

(*The lights come up on the Mulatto's Wife, her skirts hiked up, barefoot, running through the jungle. She is followed by the Indian, who carries her shoes.*)

INDIAN: Now just why are you running? There's no hurry!

MULATTO'S WIFE: Oh, there is! There's a great hurry! (*She stops.*) I don't know who I am any more. I've got a joy inside me that's so huge, all I can think about is dancing. All I want is to laugh. And I don't know why. It's as if my *body* had turned happy all of its own! . . . And I used to be sad all the time! But then there's something even more strange! I don't know if I should tell you about it.

INDIAN: There is nothing strange to an Indian.

MULATTO'S WIFE: That's true. You know, I'm convinced that I am the Marquesa. (*The Indian is surprised, and smiles.*) Don't look at me that way. It's as if my face, my body, were really those of the Marquesa. I know what she was like! I know how she talks, the things she says. When I am not the Marquesa, all I do is think about her. And that's why . . . oh, I don't know if I should tell you.

INDIAN: If you've done something bad, I'm going to find out about it sooner or later anyway.

MULATTO'S WIFE: Two days ago, on the way home, I passed the Mayor's palace to look at the painting of the Marquesa once more.

The doors were open wide. The servants hadn't come yet and the men at the door were talking to a street vendor.

INDIAN: What did you do?

MULATTO'S WIFE: I took the painting off the wall and carried it home. No one saw me.

(*The lights go out on the Indian and the Mulatto's Wife, who look at each other, he surprised, she almost afraid of herself. The lights come up on the Friar.*)

FRIAR: Madness! Now the trial is hopelessly complicated. How can they ever pass judgment?

(*The lights come up on the Mayor and the priests. The Mulatto's Wife stands before them accused.*)

MAYOR: You are accused of having stolen a very valuable painting ... property of the governor of New Spain.

MULATTO'S WIFE: I had to have that painting.

FIRST PRIEST: Paganism! Haven't you heard, sir, that these people make images of their neighbors in order to perform witchcraft?

SECOND PRIEST: Of course! What did you do with the painting?

MULATTO'S WIFE: I hung it in my room ... at the head of my bed.

FIRST PRIEST: In place of the Virgin Mary?

MULATTO'S WIFE: I worship that painting.

SECOND PRIEST: Do you mean to say that that painting was for you actually an object of worship?

MULATTO'S WIFE: When I look at it, I forget everything.

FIRST PRIEST: Your Excellency, in my opinion both the mulatto and his wife should be judged by the Holy Inquisition! For her behaviour is in every way singular and in no way natural!

SECOND PRIEST: And I confess that I am scandalized!

MAYOR: For the time being, because of the absence of precise conclusions, I declare you formally under arrest, let us say, for theft. To the dungeons with her. (*The Mulatto's Wife goes off and the Mayor turns on the priests with a look of disapproval.*) What was needed for an example was a mestizo, not a mestiza! Whenever the Holy Inquisition has taken action against women who are not of black blood, the results have always been disastrous! Let's say that we accuse this woman of witchcraft. Will she make a good example or will we simply aggravate the situation?

FIRST PRIEST: That's a very delicate question, Your Excellency.

SECOND PRIEST: There are those who would say it was one and there are those who would say it was the other.

MAYOR: You're not helping me! Something happens that clearly demonstrates corruption and rebellion . . . and here we stand bedeviled and in the middle, frightened into petrifaction. Yes, frightened! Not the faintest notion what to do. The mulatto keeps the earnings of his partners because they're Spaniards. And then he spends them on an orgy that lasts weeks . . . out of pure contempt for the Spaniards. He throws the money away on the people because the people are not Spanish. Then he disguises his wife as a Marquesa in order to offend the Spanish lady. And finally, they steal a painting . . . a deliberate provocation . . . an insult to the government of Spain. Now if this isn't hatred, what is it?

FIRST PRIEST (*frightened*): Do you think they're planning an uprising against the government of New Spain?

MAYOR: I believe that this scandal is proof of a general and far flung attitude, of which all those who participated in this fiesta are definitely guilty!

SECOND PRIEST (*alarmed*): I hope you are not thinking of putting them all in jail.

MAYOR: What? The entire town? Do you want them to cut us to ribbons? Remember, there are six thousand Spanish families in this colony, and the number of Indians, mestizos and mulattoes is far greater than that!

FIRST PRIEST: Quite right.

SECOND PRIEST: No doubt about it.

(*The priests make a motion of agreement and fold their arms in front of them. Their hoods are still in their hands. The Mayor looks at them indignantly.*)

MAYOR: Oh, the devil!

(*He goes off in a fury while the two priests look at each other in amazement. The lights come up on the Indian and the Friar.*)

FRIAR (*as though he were reading*): From a Spaniard and an Indian is born a mestiza; from a Spaniard and a mestiza a castiza; from the Spaniard and the castiza is reborn the Spaniard. From the Spaniard and the Negress is born a mulatto, from a Spaniard and a mulatta is born a morisco, from the Spaniard and the morisca is born an alvino, from a Spaniard and an alvina we go back once more to where we started. From an Indian and a Negress is born a cambujo, from a cambujo and an Indian is born a lobo, from a lobo and an Indian we get an alvarasado . . . (*Suddenly impatient*) Oh, all these denominations and their refinements prove too subtle for me! The distinctions are so thin that soon we will not be able to make them!

INDIAN: Some day they just may call us Mexicans. (*Speaking nostalgically after a pause*) You couldn't even talk to my master. If I looked for him by day, I'd find him sleeping like a baby, a smile on his mouth. If I went to him at night, I found him living such a strange life. Even his words no longer seemed in step with the life we live. One night he and the Marquesa danced until dawn . . . like demons.

(*The lights come up on the Mulatto and his Wife. She is now dressed as the Viceroy's wife; he is naked from the waist up, barefoot, without his machete or sarong. The musicians stand at one side and play. The cooks nod and doze without stopping their work. The miners, exhausted, try but cannot keep up the dance. Their movements are disjointed and grotesque. They are dressed in all their finery. The Marquesa and the Mulatto dance a French quadrille in a solemn way. They are both very much aware they are beautiful. They cut a lovely shape as they dance. They love each other intensely. The dance should be long enough to indicate the passage of time. At the end of it, still under the starry sky, we begin to see the coming dawn. The Indian enters.*)

INDIAN (*speaking in the manner of a courtier, which is not natural to him*): M'lady. Sire. The night is wearing thin, the sun will soon be out.

(*The Mulatto makes a sign and the music stops. The musicians, the miners, and the cooks fall exhaustedly as if they were puppets. The Mulatto is surrounded by his Wife, the Indian, and three mounds of human beings, breathing heavily.*)

MULATTO'S WIFE (*to the Mulatto*): Good morning. (*The Mulatto looks at her, his eyes full of tears.*) Why do you cry? . . . Because I'm leaving?

MULATTO: We've lost another night, María Antonia. Another night that we've lived . . . together.

(*The Marquesa puts her hand over his mouth to make him be still.*)

MULATTO'S WIFE: We have no past. We can't. The night is not lost, we belong to each a little more, that's all.

INDIAN: M'lady, may I lead the way?

MULATTO'S WIFE: The sun is up. We'll call attention to ourselves if we go together. (*To the Mulatto*) You and I never say "until tomorrow." We say, "till today."

(*The Mulatto is very moved. He kisses her hand. The Indian holds out a black mantilla and she puts it over her head.*)

INDIAN: You look as though you were going to mass.

(*The Mulatto's Wife runs back once more to embrace him and kiss him on the mouth, and then leaves. The Mulatto wraps himself in the red blanket and takes his machete in hand.*)

Are you tired?

MULATTO: I don't know what that means. (*He points to the mounds of exhausted people.*) Do you think that's exhaustion? You think exhaustion is something that happens to your body, don't you? Well, it's not true. Exhaustion is what I feel after I've danced all night without being tired. Exhaustion is what I felt when I turned off the sun and lit up the night. It's what happened when the poor and desperate mulatto became the lover of the Marquesa de Cruilles.

INDIAN (*speaking softly*): And what were you tired of?

MULATTO: Of New Spain. (*Pointing again at the sleeping people*) Exhausted Indians . . . cheating, fawning, lying mestizos, in love with the gold that trickles through their fingers . . . stupid people with no sense.

INDIAN: But sir, you have no common sense either.

MULATTO: Who would expect it of me? Mestizos, Indians, mulattoes, we have no right to intelligence and good sense. That's the privilege of the conquistador. When one people rules another, it becomes their duty to become intelligent, farseeing, and wise. But when that rule begins to decay, then we begin to show the color of reason.

INDIAN: You seem to know a lot of things today.

MULATTO: Today and every day.

INDIAN (*familiarly*): Don't you ever think about what you are doing?

MULATTO: I live a different way, surrounded by my imagination . . . figures that have become things, persons. I am alive like no one else! Desires, thoughts, and feelings of other men are scattered about in all directions. But in me they all gather together. I think and feel at the same time! The world is full of people who would give everything to live one of my nights.

INDIAN: You're very lucky, then.

MULATTO: Just the opposite. I pay for them and I suffer. I'm a man taken to his limits. No man has ever been more man than I. It's all one: to cry, to eat, to dance, to make love . . . thinking at the same time—always!—how terrible it is to be born in a Spanish colony!

(*The lights come up on the Friar, who speaks while the Indian returns.*)

FRIAR: His words frighten me. How can one live after having known how it feels to live entirely? Your master's fiesta was his death.

INDIAN: That's wrong, Father. The trouble with your religion is that it doesn't recognize the many shapes of the soul. It recognizes only one or two.

FRIAR (*surprised*): You think so?

INDIAN: A week ago I got them to let me visit my master in the dungeon.

(*The lights come up on the Mulatto stretched out on his red blanket without his machete. His arms are folded under his head. The Indian is by his side.*)

INDIAN: Sir, I brought you food.

MULATTO: My thanks, but to tell the truth I haven't thought of food since I've been here.

INDIAN: What do you plan to do, sir?

MULATTO: I don't know. I think I understand everything. All those things that were said to me and were never meant to be clear. Things that have yet to be made. Ways of explaining the movement of stars . . . and the foul temper of women . . . the stuff of which wood is made, and stone . . . and bodies.

INDIAN: Can I do something?

MULATTO (*smiling*): No. Thank you. By some miracle . . . I have been granted everything.

INDIAN: So you have.

(*The lights come up on the Friar, and the Indian returns to his place.*)

FRIAR: A miracle.

INDIAN: Perhaps not your kind.

FRIAR (*quite proud of it*): But that is exactly my kind of miracle! Oh, let me pray a moment. (*The Friar kneels, the Indian remains standing by his side.*) Dear God, if it's true that Your shadow falls upon the owner of this jungle-covered hill, if Your presence is revealed in these parts, I, Your humble servant, beg You that the miracle which now lives in the mind of a mulatto be allowed to run its course until it flows into each and every one of us. Amen.

INDIAN (*before the Friar can get up, touching his shoulder*): Couldn't you ask for the miracle to spread over all of New Spain?

FRIAR (*moved*): Yes. Of course. (*And he returns to his position of prayer.*) Heavenly Father, if it is possible, spread Your grace over all of New Spain . . . and dignify her sons.

(*The lights come up on the Mayor and the two priests.*)

MAYOR: The devil take all the sons of New Spain! Our beloved Charles V should have prohibited intermarriage!

FIRST PRIEST: Oh, now how could anyone watch over the human frailty of every soldier?

MAYOR: They never should have imported Negroes! They were an absolutely unnecessary ingredient. A double pollution of the blood!

SECOND PRIEST: But Negroes were an economic necessity. The Indian didn't work well.

MAYOR: And these races, if they had any pride at all, if they had the least speck of shame, would never have mixed their passions, and their foolishness, and their ugliness, and their ignorance, and their confounded imagination! They would have kept the Goddamn things to themselves!

FIRST PRIEST (*shocked*): Your Excellency seems to do nothing but fume and curse!

MAYOR: Why didn't Spain maintain itself aloof in these colonies the way the French do, and the Dutch? No doubt of it, one of our worst defects is a certain excessive gregariousness . . . familiarity!

SECOND PRIEST: Or some relatively strong animal instincts.

FIRST PRIEST: A certain lack of scruples with regard to Negresses and Indian women.

MAYOR: What do you mean? Are you with me or against me? It's your job to point out to me the spirit of New Spain. Why don't you just come out with it and defend the mulatto!

FIRST PRIEST: Your Excellency, in my humble opinion the mulatto is absolutely indefensible. He is a worthless wreck, absolutely abandoned to the worst vices. Correction seems out of the question. My colleague and I have gone to visit him together *and* separately and have heard nothing from him but blasphemy and raving.

SECOND PRIEST: If the colony weren't in such a bad way, they would be burnt alive . . . the mulatto and his woman. On far lesser charges, the Holy Inquisition has been known to . . .

MAYOR: What are you saying? Are you telling me that the colony is powerless, that the colony is decadent?

SECOND PRIEST (*covering up*): Not exactly, Your Excellency.

MAYOR: We all know it's true, but no one dares say it! So don't you start saying it! But, well, just the same, here between ourselves, tell me, what sort of sentence should one pass in a colony that is on its last legs? Should I use a strong hand or a gentle one?

FIRST PRIEST: I'm sorry, but I can't advise you on that point, Your Excellency.

SECOND PRIEST: It's really a metaphysical question.

MAYOR (*angrily*): Hypocrites!

(*He goes off and the priests look at each other in amazement, as they did before. The lights come up on the Indian and the Friar.*)

FRIAR: You haven't told me whether or not they summoned the others who participated in the fiesta.

INDIAN: It was impossible to tell how many people came to the fiesta. It always looked like the same people but the truth of the matter is that there were very few people that did not attend . . . let's say, women in childbirth and people on their deathbed. That's why they didn't arrest any more than they did. They had to settle for taking testimony and they weren't very happy with that.

(*The Mayor and the priests, and, standing before them, the musicians.*)

MAYOR: Now . . . you were with the mulatto all the time . . . certainly you should know what went on at that fiesta.

FIRST MUSICIAN: The mulatto didn't pay well but he made us play without a break.

MAYOR: I can believe that. What other reason would he have to call upon your services and look upon your wretched . . .

SECOND MUSICIAN: It was just enough to live on, we haven't managed to save a thing.

MAYOR: What I am trying to find out from you is what it was the mulatto was doing while you were playing.

THIRD MUSICIAN: Now, now, for example, Your Excellency, how much would you pay to hear us play twelve hours in a row?

FIRST MUSICIAN: We played all kinds of dances and songs without a pause, without a break.

SECOND MUSICIAN: How would Your Excellency like us to serenade the mulatto girl . . . the one you've been visiting after dark?

MAYOR: What's that! Enough, enough! Out, out! Good for nothings! . . . Bring in the cooks.

(*The priests smile and the Mayor grumbles. Three Indian women come on. They are very frightened.*)

Come in, come in. Sit down.

(*The Indian women are overcome with a fit of the giggles. This upsets the Mayor but he does not lose his composure.*)

I hope to use you as witnesses against the mulatto and his wife. Consequently I want you to tell everything you may know about them.

(*The Indian women suffer another fit of giggles. The Mayor stomps the floor.*)

Silence! What are you laughing at? What's so funny?

(*They have another fit of giggles, which they manage to control. Then one by one they step forward.*)

FIRST WOMAN (*speaking with some difficulty*): If you come to *our* house you are going to have to pay.

MAYOR: I don't understand.

SECOND WOMAN: And in gold!

MAYOR: I don't need cooks, I have eight of them already.

THIRD WOMAN: Well, we can cook whenever you want, and we can feed you, but you're going to have to pay.

FIRST WOMAN: And our children get all the leftovers.

MAYOR: Children? What children?

FIRST WOMAN: She has three, I have two, and that one has six . . . all of them fatherless. But you have enough gold to pay. I can tell by your clothes.

MAYOR (*perplexed, but without daring to speak his thoughts*): Gentlemen, do you by any chance understand these women better than I?

FIRST PRIEST: Your Excellency, these women do not understand our language. The only words they know are the ones they need in order to . . . well, to live . . .

SECOND WOMAN: One gold coin and we'll cook for you too.

(*The Mayor approaches the second priest and speaks into his ear.*)

SECOND PRIEST: Ooof! No doubt about it, Your Excellency. How could you even think they were otherwise?

MAYOR (*now very sure of himself*): Well, my dears, that'll do. Go with God. But tell the guard at the door where you live. When next we meet I promise to give you far less trouble! (*then in a sudden burst of Iberic gallantry*) . . . or perhaps I'll give you a little more trouble, hmm? Hard to tell.

(*The women giggle as before. The Mayor is very pleased with himself, and stares out of the corners of his eyes at the priests, who in*

turn look scandalized. No sooner do the women leave than the
miners enter. They are now dressed in rags.)

MAYOR (*somewhat alarmed*): Well, who are these people, now? (*He
goes to the priests.*) They must be highwaymen. Look at their
clothes.

FIRST PRIEST: Your Excellency, they are the workmen of New Spain.
Every month of the year a galleon sails out of Veracruz and under
your very orders, loaded to the gunnels with gold. You mean to
tell me you don't recognize the men that take that gold out of the
mines?

MAYOR (*threateningly*): Be careful. During the six months I have
held office I have not really left my house. I was warned in Spain
to keep off the streets. I know how dangerous they are. Now . . .
how *does* one deal with these tatterdemalions?

SECOND PRIEST: Ask them what you wish to know.

(*The miners, overcome with drowsiness, lean on each other in
ungainly and disrespectful attitudes. After a moment or two they
decide to speak.*)

FIRST MINER: Hey, tell me something. Is it true that when you're in
jail they feed you and that you sleep all day and you never have
to work?

SECOND MINER: Is it true that there are only three or four men to a
cell and that you smoke marihuana and talk and tell stories?

THIRD MINER: And is it true that the government gives each prisoner
two suits of clothes and a pair of shoes?

MAYOR (*really frightened*): What's the matter with you? Are you . . .
are you crazy?

FIRST PRIEST: They're out of their minds. Now they're pretending to
know the advantages of our jails!

SECOND PRIEST: They're trying to make us believe that there's a certain disadvantage to living *out* of jail.

MAYOR: That's what I was afraid of. Insolence! Rebellion! In short,
a revolution!

FIRST MINER: We have no houses. We live in the jungle or in the
mine . . .

SECOND MINER: On Saturdays we leave the mine with gold in our pockets and by Monday we've spent it all.

THIRD MINER: Oh, we've had everything! Owned it all . . . but very quickly. Food, fancy clothes, women, dances! But you know . . . in a hurry.

MAYOR: It's as though they were talking another language altogether. But one thing I'm certain of . . . when people start talking about these things they give them flesh and blood. A reality!

FIRST PRIEST: Of course. Poverty, hunger, and exploitation, why, it's nothing more than word-mongering! An invention!

SECOND PRIEST: If men would only keep silent, these things would never exist.

MAYOR: The problem is to keep them silent!

(*As the Mayor says this, the musicians enter, as well as the cooks, and they are followed by the Mulatto and his Wife. There is great disorder and confusion.*)

FIRST MUSICIAN: My mouth is swollen and my fingers are blistered.

FIRST WOMAN: My children have nothing to eat.

FIRST MINER: I've lived my whole life in a weekend.

SECOND WOMAN: I sell everything—the work of my hands, my skin, my eyes, even the creaking of my joints.

SECOND MUSICIAN: I don't wear out. I amaze myself!

THIRD WOMAN: What's all that about resting your head on a pillow and closing your eyes?

THIRD MUSICIAN: Death must be pretty.

THIRD MINER: *I* dream of going to jail! I bet your jails aren't as dark as the mines.

FIRST WOMAN: When I dream, I dream of throwing myself on the ground and crying on the mountain.

FIRST MINER: We have no hope. We've got to invent a future every weekend of our lives.

SECOND MINER: You breathe better in jail than at the bottom of a mine. The air could never be as stale and the roof of the jail doesn't cave in!

THIRD WOMAN: I'm in pain, I can't breathe, my fingers hurt. My fingers are worn down to the bone.

SECOND MUSICIAN: I play music with my teeth! with my bones!

SECOND WOMAN: I don't suffer. What hurts is the future, my sons' future. All I want is my daily bread.

(*The Mulatto and his Wife come over and stand among them.*)

MULATTO: I love music and I organized the fiesta because that fiesta was an imitation of the infinite order I have never lived. I planned the fiesta in order to live the things that should be and not the ones that are. I gave it so that the world, for once, could be measured and keep time exactly evenly. We create only when we manage to force our *own order* on the world of chaos and warring things. I am an artist!

MULATTO'S WIFE: And I am half of him, his soul, his thought, I have done nothing but follow him. And how could I break that order, his order . . . when it was newly born? Without him, when we were separate . . . we were no more than an angry mulatto and a grumbling mestiza. Within that order, I am the Marquesa de Cruilles and he is a great gentleman who carries me about in Venetian gondolas.

(*Throughout all of this the Mayor and the priests have tried to control their fear and not lose their composure.*)

MAYOR (*making a great effort*): Forgive the interruption, but the problem is something else altogether! It's good you've shown your true colors. You've unmasked yourself. As we suspected, you seek to topple the crown of Spain. But the real problem, as I have said, is not that . . . but one altogether different. What is the best way to deal with an outbreak of independence? An open repression or a tolerance that is designed to lose it all? Hum?

(*All those on stage except for the priests turn their backs on him.*)

I take it then that the best course would be a feigned tolerance?

(*The lights go out and come up again on the Indian and the Friar.*)

FRIAR (*rubbing his eyes*): It seems like a nightmare.

INDIAN: It's a nightmare that's gone on for three centuries, Father.

FRIAR: And it will take at least three more before these men learn to live in order naturally . . . and not in the way of the mulatto. (*Pause.*) How did they arrest your master?

INDIAN: They didn't arrest him. It happened another way. It was around midnight.

(*The lights come up on the Mulatto and his Wife. She is seated on a throne and he is at her feet leaning on her knees. As before, she looks like a painting of the period. We hear the Marquesa's music.*)

MULATTO'S WIFE: You're quiet tonight.

MULATTO: I breathe, I feel, I suspect. Some nights fall so heavily they seem like the last night of the world.

MULATTO'S WIFE: The last what?

MULATTO: The last night of harmony, feeling, and beauty, caught in the moment of being alive.

MULATTO'S WIFE: There are nights like that, yes. But there's also the blessing of not knowing when we have done something for the last time. Lovers never know their last kiss.

MULATTO: But then there's the misfortune of knowing. María Antonia, what would you do without me?

MULATTO'S WIFE: I'd climb back into the painting and wait for you.

MULATTO: How long would you wait?

MULATTO'S WIFE: Many years . . . all of them . . . centuries, perhaps. Don't you believe me?

MULATTO: Yes, I do.

(*The Indian comes on and calls to the Mulatto, who goes to him.*)

INDIAN: They are coming to arrest you. (*Pause.*) Why don't you say something?

MULATTO: Because I've had too many thoughts . . . all at once.

INDIAN: Some men have come from Mexico City, with papers that prove you're not the only owner of the Marí Sánchez mine. They say you shouldn't have taken all the gold but only a third of it.

MULATTO: I never touched that gold, any of it, not even what belongs to me. It was enough to watch it run about and divide. Instead of going to Spain it stays here with us.

INDIAN: Keep that opinion to yourself. Where are you going to hide? There's a cave . . .

MULATTO: Hide?

INDIAN: You want to go to jail?

MULATTO: Why not? The fiesta is over. (*He smiles sadly.*) She was right, you know. There's no telling when one kisses for the last time . . . Take care of her.

INDIAN: Aren't you going to say farewell?

(*The Mulatto's face registers pain. He shudders and then shakes his head.*)

MULATTO: I can't. Look after her.

(*The Mulatto starts off. The Indian tries to stop him but cannot.*)

INDIAN: Sir.

(*Since the Mulatto does not come back, the Indian turns to the Wife seated on her throne. She appears more a painting than before. The Indian leans against the throne and we hear soft music, gentle, a waltz. The miners, dressed in all their finery, appear, and the cooks and the musicians. They dance each by themselves, as though in ecstasy. The Marquesa and the Indian remain absolutely immobile. Blackout.*)

VOICE OF THE INDIAN: That was the last moment of order and herein ends the story of what the mulatto did. The charges against him can be of all kinds.

(*The lights come up on the Mayor and the priests.*)

MAYOR: I accuse him formally of . . . breach of contract . . . and his wife stands accused of the theft of the painting of the Marquesa de Cruilles, a painting which is, admittedly, not of great worth because it was done by an artist of no consequence who wished to curry favor with the Viceroy.

VOICE OF THE FRIAR (*out of the scene from the place where he had been sitting*): That's not bad. That's not bad at all.

PRIESTS: They stand accused of witchcraft, of conjuring spirits in the middle of the night, of employing the Marquesa de Cruilles' name in order to perform black magic on the top of the mountain. We must recommend the intervention of the Holy Inquisition.

VOICE OF THE FRIAR (*still out of the scene*): Now that's not wise at all! It's been years since the Inquisition has held a grand trial. It's going out of style!

MAYOR: They stand accused of propagating subversive ideas among the poor and also of fomenting disorder and rebelliousness. They are accused of ridiculing the royal power of Spain . . . witness the strange uses to which they put the name of a Marquesa. And above all they stand accused of sowing a terrible nostalgia for liberty by means of extreme abuses of liberty itself!

VOICE OF THE FRIAR: Now it's getting complicated. Infractions that are unclear provoke accusations that are equally confused. The results are always hideous. And when people start talking of such things they can destroy cities or whole countries . . . or at least half of the country.

(*The lights come up on the Indian and the Friar.*)

INDIAN: I told you the story of my master. Now you tell me the opinion of the Viceroy.

FRIAR: Grand principles of justice that correspond to grand ideas shrink when they are applied to concrete events. The problem of applying justice is to preserve the grandeur it had in the abstract.

INDIAN: Is that what the Viceroy said?

FRIAR: No. But is it just for Spain to rule New Spain from afar, to live off the work of its people, to feed upon its poverty? Wherein is it just to accuse the mulatto of setting a worse example with his liberty?

INDIAN: Father, is that what the Viceroy thinks?

FRIAR: No. But since the first idea is the more just, it follows that it is just for the mulatto to go free.

INDIAN: Did the Viceroy say that?

FRIAR (*looking at him with raised eyebrows*): No.

(*The lights come up on the Mayor and the priests. The Friar stands before them.*)

FRIAR: Therefore I take the liberty of recommending to you the most sensible course of action. Free the mulatto and his wife. Make the other owners of the mines recover their loses from the profits that have been made during the months of the mulatto's imprisonment. (*The Mayor and the priests look at each other.*) Money which undoubtedly is now in your hands.

MAYOR (*nervous*): Provisionally, of course . . . temporarily, that is . . . while we, uh . . . uh . . .

FRIAR: Punish the mulatto by means of a fine, which should be charged to the remainder of his profits, in order to pay for the costs of the trial—which, by the way, will not be pursued to its conclusion, by the express order of the Viceroy.

(*At the mention of the Viceroy, the Mayor and the two priests rise to attention and arrange themselves in a row.*)

Oh, yes, and have the mestiza return the portrait of the Marquesa.

MAYOR: But that's not necessary. Ah . . . we'll give it to her. The painting isn't worth anything, it has always been a great bother.

FRIAR: That's all.

(*The three men nod and the Friar retires.*)

MAYOR (*ironically*): Well, heaven heard my prayers. No one was helping, not you, nor the witnesses, nor the accused. But now the Viceroy has rescued me by means of his trusted servant. (*He looks at them aggressively.*) Of course, I admit that the state and the church lost a little money. (*The priests try to look indifferent.*) And . . . (*He starts to laugh.*) Where did those cooks say they lived?

(*The priests are scandalized, and cover their faces with their hoods for the first time. The lights come up on the Indian and the Friar.*)

INDIAN: Father, what *did* the Viceroy say?

FRIAR: The Viceroy knew that it didn't matter which way the judgement went. One way or the other, it was all the same because this colony's dying. But I don't agree with him.

(*The Mulatto and his Wife enter. They are carrying the portrait of the Marquesa. The Mulatto speaks to the Friar.*)

MULATTO: Father, why did you set us free?

FRIAR: Repression has always nourished independence, and I don't feel that New Spain is ready for it.

MULATTO: How long must she wait?

FRIAR: Ten years or so.

MULATTO: Even though you've set me free, there's still a possibility that I might live to be part of that movement.

FRIAR (*smiling*): That can't be helped. (*Pointing to the portrait*) Where are you taking it?

MULATTO'S WIFE: It's my . . . it's just a painting. A reminder, one of those things we use when we want to step off into . . .

(*The Mulatto picks up her sentence, and while he is speaking the cooks, the miners, the musicians, the Mayor, the priests come on-stage. Along with the Indian, the Friar, and the Mulatto's Wife they form a tight and strange and promiscuous group, a unit. From afar we hear soft music. It is no longer Spanish. It is a tropical melody reminiscent of Lecuona's music.*)

MULATTO (*speaking slowly*): . . . into the future, into something great, lovely, new, and ours . . . and free!

(*Once more we are looking at a period painting, one of those quaint pictures that illustrate the various forms of costume in New Spain.*)

Viña: Three Beach Plays

BY SERGIO VODÁNOVIC

Sergio Vodánovic, born in Yugoslavia, has become one of Chile's leading playwrights and critics. He studied at Yale and Columbia on a Rockefeller grant in 1957 and 1958. The timeliness of his writing is indicated by the title of his latest work, *Nos tomamos la Universidad* (We've Taken Over the University). Vodanovic's *Viña,* first produced in 1964, aroused my interest because of the strong sense of anxiety that its three one-act plays convey over the dissolution of the old class system. I was also interested in the relationship they bore to the early work of Tennessee Williams. *Viña* has been performed in English at the University of California at Berkeley and also at the Sausalito Little Theater. On both occasions I found it interesting to note how difficult it was for the American actresses who played the role of the Lady in "The White Uniform" to give orders to the servant in anything like a "normal" way, a phenomenon that brought home to me the distance that separates our two cultures. This distance, however, does not weaken the effect of the play—to the contrary, when the part is well acted, the brutalizing superiority of the Lady is quite believable and dramatic. These plays speak about the decay of an old system, but in "People like Us" and "The Exiles" one can detect a genuine and valid concern over the ruthlessness and materialism of the "new way" that is replacing the old system. It is to Vodánovic's credit that he does not take sides.

The White Uniform

Setting: the beach. Upstage, a canvas tent. Seated on the sand before the tent are the Lady and the Maid. The Lady is wearing a terry cloth robe over her swimming suit. She sports the tan of a long summer. The Maid wears a white uniform.

THE LADY (*calling out to her little boy, who is supposedly playing by the seashore*): Alfie! Alfie! Don't throw sand at the little girl! Why don't you go swimming! The water's wonderful! No, Alfie, no! Don't kick the little girl's sand castle! Play with her . . . that's right, Alfie, play with her . . .

THE MAID: He's such a little . . . fighter.

THE LADY: He's his father's boy . . . there's just no holding him. He has such a strong personality, comes to him through his father, his grandfather, his grandmother, too . . . especially his grandmother!

THE MAID: Do you expect the master to come tomorrow?

THE LADY (*shrugging her shoulders*): I don't know. Here it is March already, all my friends have gone back, but Alfred keeps me couped up here at the beach. Tells me he wants the kid to get everything he can out of the vacation. If you ask me, he's the one who's getting everything out of it. (*She takes off her robe and stretches out to sunbathe.*) Sunshine! Sunshine! Three months of sunbathing. I'm drunk with sunshine. (*She looks intently at the Maid.*) How do you keep from burning?

THE MAID: I stay indoors . . .

THE LADY: Oh, well, what did you expect? You came for work and not a vacation. You're paid well enough, aren't you?

THE MAID: Yes, Ma'am. I was just answering your question.

(*The Lady stretches out once more and resumes her sunbathing.*

The Maid picks up a bag and takes out an illustrated true romance magazine and begins to read.)

THE LADY: What are you up to?

THE MAID: I'm reading.

THE LADY: Did you buy it?

THE MAID: Yes, Ma'am.

THE LADY: Well, you're not so bad off then if you can afford magazines, eh? (*The Maid makes no answer and resumes reading.*)
Go on! Go right ahead! Go right on reading! Let Alfie blow up! Let him drown!

THE MAID: But he's playing with the little girl . . .

THE LADY: I didn't bring you to the beach to read. I brought you to watch Alfie. (*The Maid gets up and starts to go toward Alfie.*) Wait! You can see him well enough from here. I want you to stay with me, but keep an eye on him just the same. You know, I like coming to the beach with you.

THE MAID: Why?

THE LADY: Oh, I don't know. I suppose for the same reason that I like coming in the car even though the house is only a couple of blocks away. (*She chuckles.*) I like them to see the car. It never fails. Every day someone stops to look at it and admire it. Of course you wouldn't notice a thing like that. I suppose you're used to it . . . in a way. Tell me, what is your home like?

THE MAID: I have none.

THE LADY: Well, you weren't born a maid, were you? You must have been brought up somewhere. You must have had parents. Are you from the country?

THE MAID: Yes.

THE LADY: And you wanted to come to the city, eh?

THE MAID: No. I liked it in the country.

THE LADY: Then why did you come to the city?

THE MAID: My father couldn't make enough . . .

THE LADY: Oh, don't give me that. I know all about tenant farmers. They've got it easy. They're given their own little lots to farm, there's free food, they even have some left over to sell. Some of them even have their own little cows. Did your father have cows?

THE MAID: Yes, Ma'am. One.

THE LADY: You see? What more could you want? Alfie! Don't go so far out. Be careful of the waves. How old are you?

THE MAID: I?

THE LADY: I am talking to you, aren't I? You'd think I was crazy, talking to myself.

THE MAID: I'm almost twenty-one . . .

THE LADY: Twenty-one! I was married when I was twenty-one. Have you ever thought of marriage? (*The Maid looks down but makes no answer.*) Oh, that was stupid of me. Why should you want to get married? You've got everything you want with us. Plenty of food, a good room, clean uniforms. Get married and then see what you've got. A raft of kids, that's what.

THE MAID (*almost to herself*): I would like to get married . . .

THE LADY: Oh, don't be silly! That's the kind of idea you get from those cheap true romance magazines. Just remember, there are no more true blue knights in shining armor. What matters is not the shine of the armor but the shine of their money. I used to be furious when my parents would turn down my boyfriends because they didn't have any money. But then along came Alfred with his industries and factories and estates, and my folks didn't rest until they married me to him. I didn't like him. He was fat and he had a disgusting habit of clearing his nose and then swallowing. But then, later, in marriage you get used to everything. And I suppose you have to come to the conclusion that it all adds up to the same thing, except for money. I have money, and you don't. That's the real difference between us. Don't you think?

THE MAID: Yes, but . . .

THE LADY: Oh! So you do agree? Well, it's a lie! There's something even more important than money: one's class. You can't buy that! Either one has it or one doesn't. Alfred has no class. I do. I could live in a pigsty, but people would still know that I was someone. Not just anyone, but someone! You see that, don't you?

THE MAID: Yes, Ma'am.

THE LADY: Here . . . let me look at your magazine. (*The Maid hands it to her and the Lady thumbs through it. She spies something and laughs out loud.*) So this is what you read?

THE MAID: I like it, Ma'am.

THE LADY: Ridiculous! Utterly ridiculous! Look at that clod dressed up in a dinner jacket. He looks as comfortable as a hippopotamus in a girdle. (*She returns to the magazine.*) And he's supposed to be . . . the Count of Lamarquina! The Count of Lamarquina! Well, let's see what the Count has to say for himself. (*She reads aloud.*) "My child, I will never permit you to marry Robert. He is a commoner. Remember that the blood that flows in our veins is blue." And this must be the Count's daughter?

THE MAID: Yes. She's called Mary. She's a simple girl, good and sweet. And she's in love with Robert, the gardener at the castle. The Count won't hear of it. But you know, I have a hunch it's going to come out all right in the end. Because in last month's issue, Robert told Mary that he had never known his parents, and when the parents aren't known you can just bet that they are rich and aristocratic, and that they lost their son when he was little or that the little boy was kidnapped . . .

THE LADY: And you believe all this?

THE MAID: It's nice, Ma'am.

THE LADY: What is?

THE MAID: That things like that should happen. That suddenly one day you discover you're someone else, that instead of being poor, you're rich, that instead of being no one, you're someone.

THE LADY: That just can't be, don't you understand? Look at the daughter. Did you ever see me wearing hoops like that? Have you ever seen one of my friends wearing something as ghastly as that? And her hair, it's hideous. Don't you realize that a woman like that can't be an aristocrat? Let's see . . . is there a picture of the gardener?

THE MAID: Yes. Near the end. (*She takes the magazine, finds the place, and shows it to the Lady, who laughs.*)

THE LADY: And so this is the man you think may be the son of an aristocrat? With a nose like that? And hair like that? Look . . .

just suppose that tomorrow someone should kidnap little Alfie. Do you think that for one minute he will lose his air of distinction?

THE MAID: Oh look, Ma'am! Alfie just kicked over the little girl's sand castle.

THE LADY: You see? He's only four years old, and already he knows how to give orders, how not to care about other people. You can't learn that. It's in the blood.

THE MAID (*getting up*): I'll fetch him.

THE LADY: Let him be. He's having fun.

(*The Maid unbuttons the top button of her uniform and fans herself.*)

Are you hot?

THE MAID: The sun has a sting to it.

THE LADY: Don't you have a swimming suit?

THE MAID: No.

THE LADY: Haven't you ever worn one?

THE MAID: Oh, yes.

THE LADY: When?

THE MAID: Before hiring out. Sometimes, on Sundays, we'd take a trip to the beach in a truck that belonged to the uncle of one of my friends.

THE LADY: You'd go swimming.

THE MAID: On the big beach at Cartagena. We'd rent swimming suits and spend the whole day at the beach. We'd take our lunch and . . .

THE LADY (*amused*): Rent swimming suits?

THE MAID: Yes. There's a woman who rents them right there at the beach.

THE LADY: We had to stop once at Cartagena for gas, so we got out to look at the beach. It was really funny! And those rented swimming suits, some of them were so big they hung like bags all over! Others were so tight, the women's breasts were nearly popping out! What kind did you rent? A loose one or a tight one? (*The Maid looks down, embarrassed.*) It must be strange seeing the world from a rented swimming suit or a cheap dress or a maid's uniform the way you do. Something like that must happen to those people who pose for the photographs in your magazine. When they put on a dinner jacket or an evening gown, I'm sure they must change inside. They must see people differently. When I put on my first pair of stockings the whole world changed. Everyone seemed different. I was different. And the only real change was that I had put on a pair of nylons. Tell me, what does the world look like from behind that white uniform?

THE MAID (*timidly*): The same . . . the sand has the same color . . . the clouds are the same . . . I guess . . .

THE LADY: But it isn't . . . it's different. Look. Wearing this swimming suit and this robe, stretched out here on the sand, I know that I am in "my place," all this belongs to me. On the other hand, you, dressed as a maid, you know the beach is not your place, and that alone must make you see things differently.

THE MAID: Maybe.

THE LADY: Listen. I've got an idea. Give me your uniform.

THE MAID: What?

THE LADY: Give me your uniform.

TIIE MAID: But . . . why?

THE LADY: Because I want to see what the world looks like. I want to see the beach from behind a white uniform.

THE MAID: Now?

THE LADY: Yes. Now.

THE MAID: But it's just that . . . I . . . I don't have anything on underneath.

THE LADY (*tossing her the terry cloth robe*): Here. Put this on.

THE MAID: But I'm only wearing panties . . .

THE LADY: The robe is long enough to cover you. At any rate, you'll be showing off less than you did in those suits you rented at the beach at Cartagena. (*She gets up and pulls the Maid to her feet.*) Come on, into the tent and change. (*She forces the Maid into the tent and later throws the robe into the tent. She walks downstage and calls to her son.*) Alfie, why don't you go into the water? Wade a little . . . get your feet wet. Don't be such a stick-in-the-mud! That's right! Isn't the water nice? (*She returns to the tent and calls inside.*) Are you ready? (*She goes inside the tent.*)

(*After a moment, the Maid emerges, dressed in the terry cloth robe. She has put her hair up, and her whole manner has shifted from that of the timid girl we have seen. Delicately, she stretches out on the sand. The Lady comes out buttoning the top buttons of the uniform. She moves to sit down in front of the maid, stops, turns back, and takes a place behind her.)*

THE LADY: No. Not in front. At the beach a maid always sits behind her mistress.

(She sits down and looks about in all directions, highly amused. Delicately, the Maid changes her position. The Lady picks up the Maid's magazine and begins to read it. She smiles ironically, but the smile disappears as she becomes interested in the story. Quite naturally, the Maid reaches for the beach bag that belongs to the Lady. She takes out a bottle of suntan lotion and begins to apply it to her legs. The Lady sees her, starts to scold her, but cannot manage to say more than)

What are you doing?

(The Maid does not answer. The Lady decides to continue reading, but from time to time she spies upon the Maid to see what she is doing. The Maid is now sitting up examining her fingernails.)

Why are you looking at your nails?

THE MAID: I need a manicure.

THE LADY: I never saw you look at your nails before.

THE MAID: It hadn't occurred to me.

THE LADY: The uniform is hot.

THE MAID: They're of the best. They never wear out.

THE LADY: I know. I bought them.

THE MAID: It fits you.

THE LADY *(amused)*: You look pretty good yourself. *(She laughs).* It would be quite easy to mistake you. You'd catch the eye of any young boy. Oh, now wouldn't that be a wonderful story!

THE MAID: Alfie's going out a little far. Go look after him.

THE LADY *(jumping up and moving downstage rapidly)*: Alfie! Alfie! Don't go in so far. Be careful of a wave. *(She catches herself suddenly and turns back to the maid.)* Why didn't you go?

THE MAID: Where?

THE LADY: Why did you tell me to look after Alfie?

THE MAID (*quite naturally*): You're wearing the uniform.

THE LADY: So you like the game, eh?

(*The little boy playing nearby throws a rubber ball that rolls to the feet of the Maid. She looks at it but makes no movement to pick it up. The Maid looks at the Lady. Instinctively the Lady moves to the ball, picks it up, and throws it back in the direction from which it came. The Maid looks in the Lady's beach bag and finds a pair of sun glasses, which she then puts on.*)

(*Annoyed*) Who gave you permission to put on my glasses?

THE MAID: How does the beach look from behind a white uniform?

THE LADY: Oh, it's cute. And you? How do you see the beach now?

THE MAID: Oh, it's cute.

THE LADY: How so?

THE MAID: Because there's no difference.

THE LADY: What do you mean?

THE MAID: You with your white uniform are the maid; and I with this robe and these glasses am the lady.

THE LADY: How dare you? What do you mean?

THE MAID: Would you have bothered to pick up that ball if you hadn't been in a uniform?

THE LADY: We're playing a game.

THE MAID: When?

THE LADY: Now.

THE MAID: And before?

THE LADY: Before?

THE MAID: Yes. When I was dressed in the uniform . . .

THE LADY: That's no game. That's reality.

THE MAID: Why?

THE LADY: Because it is.

THE MAID: It's just a game . . . a longer game . . . like cops and robbers. Some have to be cops, and some have to be robbers.

THE LADY (*angry*): You're becoming insulting!

THE MAID: You're the the one who's insulting. Don't scream at me.

THE LADY: What do you mean? How dare you talk to me like that?

THE MAID: And you don't talk to me that way, do you?

THE LADY: I?

THE MAID: Yes.

THE LADY: That's it! The game is over!

THE MAID: I like it!

THE LADY: It's finished! (*She advances threatingly on the Maid.*)

THE MAID (*quite definitely*): You get back!

THE LADY (*stopping short*): Are you going crazy?

THE MAID: I'm going to be a lady.

THE LADY: I can fire you whenever I want.

(*The Maid bursts into laughter as though she had just heard the funniest joke in the world.*)

What are you laughing at?

THE MAID (*still laughing*): It's so ridiculous!

THE LADY: What? What's so ridiculous?

THE MAID: That you should fire me . . . dressed like that! Who ever heard of a maid firing her mistress?

THE LADY: Take off those glasses! Take off that robe! They're mine!

THE MAID: Go look after the baby!

THE LADY: The game is over. Give me back my things or I'll take them away from you.

THE MAID: Be careful! We're not alone on this beach.

THE LADY: And what of it? You think because I've got this white uniform on, they're not going to know the lady from the maid?

THE MAID (*calmly*): Don't raise your voice to me.

(*The Lady lunges at the Maid and tries to tear the robe off of her.*)

THE LADY (*while struggling*): You slut! I'll show you who I am! I'll show you! I'll have you thrown in jail!

(*The fight draws a group of bathers. The group is composed of two young men, one young girl, and an older gentleman of distinguished appearance. Before they can interfere, the Maid gets the better of things, pinning the Lady on the sand. The Lady continues screaming such things as: "You tramp," "Wait till my husband gets hold of you," "I'm going to put you in jail," "This is what happens when one tries to be . . ." et cetera.*)

FIRST YOUNG MAN: What's the matter?

SECOND YOUNG MAN: Is she having a fit?

YOUNG GIRL: She's gone crazy.

FIRST YOUNG MAN: They do sometimes. They're so lonely.

SECOND YOUNG MAN: May we help you?

THE MAID: Yes. Please. There's a comfort station nearby . . .

SECOND YOUNG MAN: I'm a medical student. I'll give her an injection so that she'll sleep for awhile.

THE LADY: Idiots! I am the mistress! My name is Patricia Hurtado. My husband is Alfred Jiménez, the politician . . .

YOUNG LADY (*laughing*): She thinks she's a lady.

FIRST YOUNG MAN: She's crazy.

SECOND YOUNG MAN: It's just an attack of hysterics.

FIRST YOUNG MAN: Let's take her away.

THE MAID: If you don't mind, I'll stay here . . . I have to look after my little boy. He's over there, wading.

THE LADY: That's a lie! We exchanged costumes just as a game! She isn't even wearing a swimming suit. All she's got on under that robe are panties! Look at her!

SECOND YOUNG MAN (*with a gesture to the first young man*): Come on! You take her feet and I'll take her arms.

YOUNG GIRL: Oh, how funny! She says the lady's naked . . .

(*The young men take the Lady and carry her off in spite of her kicking and screaming.*)

THE LADY: Let go of me! I'm not crazy! She's the one! Call Alfie! He'll recognize me!

(*The two men carry the Lady off. The Maid stretches out on the sand as though nothing had happened, making herself ready for a long sunbath.*)

THE GENTLEMAN: I suppose it's a sign of our times. No one seems to notice it, but every time you turn around something like this happens.

THE MAID: Like this?

THE GENTLEMAN: They're destroying the established order of things. Old people want to be young; young people want to be old; poor people want to be rich; and the rich people want to be poor. My daughter-in-law goes every week to weave with some women of the working classes. And she likes it! (*Slight pause.*) Has she been with you for a long time?

THE MAID: Who?

THE GENTLEMAN: Your maid.

THE MAID (*trying to remember*): A little over a year.

THE GENTLEMAN: And this is the way she pays you back! Pretending to pass for a lady! As though one couldn't tell a lady at a glance! (*Pause.*) Do you know why these things happen?

THE MAID (*very interested*): Why?

THE GENTLEMAN (*with a mysterious air*): Communism . . .

THE MAID: Ah!

THE GENTLEMAN (*reassuringly*): But we don't need to worry. Everything is back to normal again. Order is always re-established in the end. That's a fact. There's no doubt about it. And now if you'll excuse me, I must take my constitutional. I've got to, at my age. The circulation, you know. And don't you worry, the sun is the best sedative. At your service, ma'am. (*He starts out but then turns back.*) And don't be too hard on your maid. After all, maybe we're to blame for some of it . . . you can't tell.

(*The Distinguished Gentleman leaves. The Maid stretches out on her back to sunbathe. Suddenly she remembers Alfie, and sits up. She looks at Alfie tenderly and calls to him.*)

THE MAID: Alfie . . . if you're going to sit on that rock, be careful, you might get a scratch. Yes, that's better, run on the sand. That's right, Alfie, that's right, my son . . .

(*The Maid stares tenderly and maternally at Alfie as he plays on the seashore. The lights dim and the curtain closes.*)

People Like Us

A clearing at the edge of the highway from Viña del Mar to Limache. A few tree trunks and some bushes are the only necessary scenic elements. It is night. The stage is empty.

After a moment the Lady and the Gentleman enter. She is about fifty years old. She wears a summer coat and carries her bag on her arm. She has an air of cold indifference. The Gentleman is dressed in dark colors and seems somewhat irritable.

Freddy enters a moment later. He is twenty-three years old and walks in angrily, his hands in his pockets. He is dressed with a somewhat studied elegance, though his manner and gestures reveal him to be somewhat common.

Caroline enters next. She is eighteen years old, and she seems to be wrapped in thought.

FREDDY: Well! I suppose we'll have to wait here until the driver finishes repairing the cab. There's a moon out, at least. These taxis that take groups are nothing short of a calamity. I knew there was something wrong from the time we left Viña. (*He looks at his watch long enough to discover that it has stopped.*) What time is it? (*No one answers. He speaks directly to the Gentleman.*) Can you tell me what time it is?

GENTLEMAN (*who has, along with the Lady, moved some distance from the other two*): It is two fifteen.

FREDDY (*sets his watch*): Not exactly the time for a picnic. Would you believe it, this all happened out of sheer stupidity on my part? I could have gone back to Limache in the Impala of a friend of mine, but I said no. He got angry, but I'm stubborn. When you've got a friend, you've got to show him who's boss, otherwise it's no good. Right? (*No one answers. Freddy is irritated and begins to whistle a dance tune as he looks the place over. From time to time he looks at Caroline as though trying to recognize her.*)

LADY: I don't like that fellow.

GENTLEMAN: Well, I couldn't very well select the rest of the passengers.

LADY: What if they try to hold us up?

GENTLEMAN: Bah!

LADY: You're the one who had to go to Viña in spite of the fact that the car was acting up.

GENTLEMAN: It's been acting up for months.

LADY: And of course it had to stop on us tonight! Just precisely as we were coming out of the Casino! I didn't want to come.

GENTLEMAN: Don't start that again.

LADY: I start anything? I'm a mute. I haven't spoken in ages. I've lost the habit.

FREDDY (*to Caroline*): I've got it! Now I know. (*He goes to Caroline and points at her teasingly.*) It was at the Night Owl, right? (*Caroline pretends not to have heard and looks away.*) You don't have to be ashamed!

CAROLINE: I'm not ashamed!

FREDDY: Then why didn't you speak to me?

CAROLINE: Because I don't want to.

FREDDY (*aping her*): "I don't want to!" The airs you give yourself! Honey, I've seen you in the buff.

(*The Lady and the Gentleman look at Caroline in surprise.*)

CAROLINE: Very funny!

FREDDY: You don't talk to strangers, eh? In that case, allow me to introduce myself. (*He holds out his hand.*) Freddy Salamanca, at your service. (*Caroline shakes hands and then looks away.*) And you . . . what's your name? They didn't even announce you.

CAROLINE: Caroline.

FREDDY (*laughing suddenly*): Hey, tell me . . . did it hurt?

CAROLINE: Did what hurt?

FREDDY: When I pulled the chair out from under you.

CAROLINE (*turning angrily on him*): Were you the one?

FREDDY: That was a good one! (*He speaks to the Lady and the Gentle man.*) Listen, listen, that was really good. I was with Tito at the Night Owl. Tito is my friend, the one with the Impala, ugly as sin, but rotten with money. And anyway, after a while, who should come walking down the ramp right in the middle of the show but our friend here. (*He points at Caroline.*) She's going to do a striptease. We were sitting in the front row right behind her, and when Caroline went to sit down to take off her panties, I nudged the chair away with my foot, and then "splat," down she went on the floor . . . You should have seen it! It was wild! Ab-so-lutely wild! (*To Caroline*) I bet you blew up!

CAROLINE (*annoyed*): No.

FREDDY: Are you mad at me?

CAROLINE: No.

FREDDY: Performers have to put up with everything, don't they? They owe themselves to their public, so to speak. And anyway, they've got it pretty easy.

CAROLINE: But *you boys* have it made!

FREDDY: We? What do you mean by "you boys"?

CAROLINE: You know what I mean.

FREDDY: No. What do you mean?

CAROLINE: The announcer, Tony, he told me what kind of men you were.

FREDDY: Tony? With a history like his, he's a fine one to talk.

CAROLINE: Why guys like you go see a striptease is beyond me. If men did the striptease, I could understand.

FREDDY (*stung*): You think I'm not a man?

CAROLINE: Of course not!

FREDDY: I could take you to a hundred ladies who'd gladly tell you how good I am!

CAROLINE (*sardonic*): Ladies!

FREDDY: Yes, ladies! Respectable, too! Don't think I'm going to waste myself on little virgins!

CAROLINE: Why not?

FREDDY: They fall in love and they want to get married! Knock one of them up, and that's the end of Freddy! Furthermore . . . young girls, they just don't have it . . . they just don't have it . . .

CAROLINE: Have what?

FREDDY (*rubbing his fingers together*): Money, Honey, money! Or are you one of those who believes that the best things in life are free? No, sir, one has to pay for things, and they pay me. So you see, I'm not so useless after all.

CAROLINE (*snide*): What about the men? Do they pay?

FREDDY (*undisturbed*): What do you think?

CAROLINE: The least you could do is to be ashamed.

(*Freddy looks at her and smiles ironically. He lights a cigarette and moves off, trying not to appear upset. During the previous dialogue, the Lady and the Gentleman have remained more or less still without looking at Freddy and Caroline but obviously listening to the conversation.*)

LADY: Go see if the driver has fixed the car.

GENTLEMAN: Can't you see for yourself? Look, there he is. His head is still stuck inside the motor.

LADY: I've never heard so many filthy things in my life.

GENTLEMAN: Nor I.

LADY: People like us . . .

GENTLEMAN: Yes.

LADY: Yes, what?

GENTLEMAN: What you said. "People like us . . ."

LADY: I didn't finish.

GENTLEMAN: Well, anyway, you were right.

LADY: One has to be stranded on a highway in the middle of the night in order to discover the obscenity that surrounds us everywhere.

GENTLEMAN: It's one thing to see it in the movies or in the theater or in the newspapers.

LADY: What newspapers?

GENTLEMAN: The ones with the big red letters that you see at the news stand. I don't read them.

LADY: You're wise.

GENTLEMAN: People like us . . .

LADY: Yes. You're right.

FREDDY (*going over to Caroline in a friendly way*): Why are you so
angry? You had a rough time?

CAROLINE (*after a pause*): Yes.

FREDDY: Maybe I can help you. The Night Owl isn't the only cabaret
in Viña. I have a friend who owns two of them in the port. If you
want, I'll recommend you.

CAROLINE: I'm just no good.

FREDDY: No good? You're young, you've got a good figure . . . what
do you mean, you're no good?

CAROLINE: I don't know. I just don't go over. They make fun of me.

FREDDY: You live in Limache?

CAROLINE: No. Just outside.

FREDDY: What did you do before?

CAROLINE: Nothing. My father's a widower. He goes off for months
at a time. I used to sew, but I don't like sewing. I . . . I want to
travel, to have my pictures in magazines, to be someone . . . and
what chance did I have? One day I went to Viña to see a friend,
and I told him all about it. He took me to see Tony and I got a contract for the summer . . . It seemed easy . . .

FREDDY: Tell me . . . the first time . . . weren't you ashamed?

CAROLINE: I used to be more ashamed in Limache when they'd see
me with a torn dress. (*She shows him her dress.*) I bought this with
my first pay. Pretty, isn't it?

FREDDY (*winking at her*): Feel this. It's Palm Beach, English. Ten
dollars a yard! I know what it feels like to go around with patches
on my pants.

CAROLINE: But you've got it made. They pay you.

FREDDY: And I suppose they don't pay you? You strip down to the
boobies just for the fun of it, huh?

CAROLINE: But I don't get over. They make catcalls. Every night
they boo me, they whistle, and they laugh at me, just as you did
when you pulled my chair away.

FREDDY: Oh, that wasn't much!

CAROLINE: Not much! I'd like to know what is very much. You don't
know what it means to take your clothes off every night in front
of a lot of people that you don't even know. And then, when it's all

over, to stoop down and pick up your little old patch of a costume and run out with a bare ass through a crowd of people you don't even know, talking away and drinking . . . And no one even cares! They don't even look! And then there are those elegant ladies that stare at you as though you were a monster or something like that, just as though they weren't naked underneath their clothes! You don't know! You don't know! (*She hides her face in her hands.*)

FREDDY: You think you've got it rough because you don't know anything. Your humiliation is only skin deep. No one gets inside of you. They use you, yes, but in order to exhibit you like something in a shop window. Not me! They get inside of me, and they mix me up, they pull me inside out, they search me all over, they humiliate me . . . and then they pay me.

CAROLINE: But they love you.

FREDDY: Who?

CAROLINE: Your friend with the Impala . . . those ladies, the decent ones.

FREDDY: The decent ladies! Those respectable ladies use me like an old rag! And I have to pretend to admire them, to like them, to want them. They don't have to pretend anything! They pay! And as for Tito, he knows that he's the one who owns the Impala, and that he's the one who buys me my Palm Beach suits at ten dollars a yard. And it couldn't matter less to him if some days I feel tired or if he turns my stomach or if I should need some fresh air or just to breathe a bit and live . . . He owns the Impala, he has the money. Oh, he's ugly, he's disgusting, but he has the Impala, and he has the money . . . You know what I'm going to do? I'm going to save my money, and then I'm going to have my own car, and then I'll be the one who'll hire young boys just like myself—well built and with patched trousers—or pretty young girls like you with tears in their skirts.

CAROLINE: My father used to talk like that . . .

FREDDY: Your daddy too, huh?

CAROLINE: No! Don't be filthy! It's just that I remember when I was a kid. My mother was still alive then. My father was an artist . . .

he carved wood: a peasant dancing, a woman washing clothes, things like that. My father sold his carvings to an Italian who re- sold them in Santiago. The Italian really made a killing with those carvings . . . but he was smart . . . oh, he was smart! He paid my father very little. Just enough to keep us in food. That way he kept papa from going to Santiago to sell the carvings himself.

FREDDY: What are you getting at?

CAROLINE: That my father wanted to save some money just like you . . . have a little money put by so that he could go to Santiago. But he didn't intend to go carving . . . oh, no! He was going to get other men to do the carving and then he would pay them nothing and live the good life just like the Italian.

FREDDY: So?

CAROLINE: It didn't work out. He started to drink, the Italian got fed up, and the old man just bums around. He's even been in jail.

FREDDY: He didn't pull it off, that's all.

CAROLINE: No, that's not it. You think you can do it . . . and then you can't. Some people are born to take advantage and others to be taken advantage of. I'd give anything to have tons of money and go to a cabaret and sit at a table and make all those women that go to have fun staring at me . . . to make all of them take their clothes off, one by one! That would be my day! But no . . . it's nice to think about it, but it won't happen. Most of them will never be seen naked except by their husbands . . . and the doctor.

FREDDY: The husband, the doctor . . . and Freddy!

CAROLINE: They're not all like the ones you know.

FREDDY: Peas in a pod.

CAROLINE: What do you know about it?

FREDDY: If I don't, who does?

CAROLINE: Maybe it is the way you say. It would be a consolation . . . but it would be even better if it weren't that way. If there were some that were different. (*She lowers her voice.*) Listen . . . look at that lady. Do you think . . .?

FREDDY: For certain!

(*The Lady and the Gentleman, who have been pretending to pay no attention to the conversation of the young people, now face the young couple as they hear a direct reference to the Lady. Then later they return to their former posture of indifference.*)

CAROLINE: Sh! I think she's listening.

(*Freddy and Caroline continue speaking in a lower voice.*)

LADY: Are you going to allow that?

GENTLEMAN: What?

LADY: You heard.

GENTLEMAN: I'm deaf.

LADY: You did too hear.

GENTLEMAN: So I did, but they don't have to know that I did.

LADY: They've insulted me.

GENTLEMAN: Pretend you haven't heard.

LADY: But I did.

GENTLEMAN: People like us . . .

LADY: What about people like us?

GENTLEMAN: We don't know these things. It's another world.

LADY: You think so?

GENTLEMAN: What? What do you mean?

LADY: Don't be too sure.

GENTLEMAN: Of what?

LADY: That that man hasn't recognized me.

GENTLEMAN: Who? That one? It's the first time he's laid eyes on you.

LADY: How do you know?

GENTLEMAN: I know. That's enough!

LADY: I've had reasons enough to seek his . . . his services.

GENTLEMAN: You going to start that again?

LADY: Start what?

GENTLEMAN: The same old thing.

LADY: Have I ever spoken of anything to you?

GENTLEMAN: No.

LADY: Then why do you say "the same old thing"?

(*The gentleman starts to answer but is speechless.*)

Well, come on. Let's have it out. Come on! Out with it.

GENTLEMAN: You don't have to talk about it. I can tell from the way you look. Your silence.

LADY: You haven't satisfied me, ever. (*Pause.*) I said . . . you have never satisfied me.

GENTLEMAN: I heard you.

LADY: And what have you got to say?

GENTLEMAN: Nothing. I don't intend to discuss our private life in the middle of a highway at three o'clock in the morning.

LADY: Why not? They did.

GENTLEMAN: People like us . . .

LADY: People like us do not discuss their private lives. It's in bad taste. Right?

GENTLEMAN: You said it.

(*The Gentleman and the Lady remain silent, dignified, and still. Near the end of their conversation they have been unable to keep their voices down, and they have attracted the attention of Freddy and Caroline.*)

FREDDY: They're mad at each other.

CAROLINE: But they haven't fought. They're rich. They know how to behave. The only time they curse is when they're drunk. I'd like to be like her. She must feel so sure of herself.

FREDDY: You! Like her?

CAROLINE: Just to be able to look around like that, to feel that you own . . .

FREDDY: I've been in bed with more than twenty women like that.

CAROLINE: But even in bed I'm sure they are still the owners.

FREDDY: You're right. They've got money. They buy and we sell. And the customer always has the advantage. They can haggle. They can even return the merchandise.

CAROLINE: I bet that never happened to you.

FREDDY: Of course not! How are they going to return me to myself?

CAROLINE: Listen . . . if we were to behave the way they do . . . I wonder . . . would we feel the same way?

FREDDY: Where'd you get that?

CAROLINE: Haven't you ever tried it . . . with a smile?

FREDDY: You're off your nut!

CAROLINE: It's something I've learned from an old woman who used to live next door. Look, when you're sad, the best thing to do is to smile . . . smile even when you don't feel like it. And, well, you begin to smile, and the smile seems to . . . to take over inside, and your sadness goes away, and you feel happy. I think that if we were to try to . . . to imitate them, that is, we might feel equal.

FREDDY: That's crazy!

CAROLINE: Let's try it, anyway. Now, sit up like that.

(*They assume the position of the Gentleman and the Lady. Freddy begins to giggle. The giggles are contagious and Caroline catches them.*)

CAROLINE: No. No. You mustn't laugh. Let's see who can take it the longest.

(*They remain frozen in a caricature of the Gentleman and the Lady. Suddenly the Lady gets up and takes a step towards Freddy.*)

GENTLEMAN (*holding her back*): Where are you going?

LADY: I'm going to talk to him.

GENTLEMAN: What are you going to tell him?

LADY: I'm going to ask him for his telephone number.

GENTLEMAN: Are you crazy?

LADY: I suppose *you've* never paid for things like this.

GENTLEMAN: But . . .

LADY: It's not my fault.

GENTLEMAN: I suppose it's mine!

LADY: Yes.

GENTLEMAN: Very well. Let's talk.

LADY: But if it's so painful to you . . .

GENTLEMAN: Let's talk.

LADY: I'm listening.

GENTLEMAN: I won't talk alone. You too.

LADY: I've said my piece.

GENTLEMAN: And what else?

LADY (*after a short pause, she begins to disburden the repressions of many years*): It's been twenty years, day in, day out, night after night, no, no, it's twenty-five. Twenty-eight to be exact. I've waited. Oh, I knew that marriage was more than just that, but I also knew that marriage was that too. At least, for the most part. And so I waited. You had excuses, a headache, you were tired, you were sleepy, and time went by. Once in a while it happened like an obligation you had to fulfill, like paying taxes or . . . or some sort of duty. But you never made love. I've never known what it was to feel myself in the arms of a man who could make me forget . . . who could make me forget that I was myself. Sometimes when you came in late, I knew where you'd been, and I'd ask myself what made you go to other women, what you found in them, what was it that they gave you. (*She gestures toward Freddy and Caroline.*) At least they get paid for being humiliated. I've never had a penny's pay. I want my pay.

GENTLEMAN: You haven't told me anything I didn't know.

LADY: You knew?

GENTLEMAN: How could I help it?

LADY: Then why didn't you speak up, just once?

GENTLEMAN: People like us . . .

LADY: Yes, I know. How sorry it is to be like us!

GENTLEMAN: It's my turn to talk now.

LADY: Oh! So you do have something to say after all?

GENTLEMAN: Don't you know what it is?

LADY: No.

GENTLEMAN: Well, I'm ahead of you on that score. At least I knew what you were going to say.

LADY: Go on, then. Go on.

GENTLEMAN: A man must give his love, he must feel his love is wanted, needed. I was waiting, I kept waiting for a sign, something that would tell me you wanted me. But there you were in your nightgown, with your hair hanging every which way, and your fat stomach . . . claiming . . . claiming your right. There was never a sign, never. You had a husband, and he had to fulfill his duty. I came to you like some morsel to be devoured. I was some sort of official, not a lover. I did my duty, late and poorly, but I did my duty. And you never wanted me. You don't know what it means to feel unwanted!

LADY (*slowly, after a pause*): Was it necessary for our car to break down, and for us to take this taxi, and for the taxi to break down, and for these people to say what they have said about us, after twenty-eight years, was all that necessary to make us talk?

GENTLEMAN: It was.

LADY: We've wasted our lives.

GENTLEMAN: Tag! ... It's high time for us to be it.

LADY: It's too late.

(*Freddy and Caroline are tired of their pose, and they break out in laughter.*)

FREDDY: You laughed first!

CAROLINE: No, I didn't. You did.

(*They laugh together. Freddy stops laughing suddenly. Caroline follows suit.*)

FREDDY: You know?

CAROLINE: What?

FREDDY: I like you. Inside, you and I, we're very much the same.

CAROLINE: I'm not always like this.

FREDDY: Neither am I.

CAROLINE: I wish I had known you when you had patches on your pants.

FREDDY: I wish I had known you when you had a torn skirt.

CAROLINE (*feeling the Palm Beach of Freddy's suit*): *Five* dollars a yard.

FREDDY (*touching Caroline's skirt*): And you paid for this with the first money you made from dancing naked.

CAROLINE: It's getting late.

FREDDY: Yes. Very late.

CAROLINE: Well, what can we do?

FREDDY: We'll go on, just like before.

(*They remain still for a moment.*)

GENTLEMAN: What can we do?

LADY: We'll go on, just like before.

(*The four of them sit still.*)

DRIVER (*offstage*): All right, folks, come on, the car's fixed!

(*No one seems to hear him. No one stirs. The Gentleman seems to come to, gets up, and walks off with his head down. A moment later, the Lady does the same. And then Caroline. Freedy remains alone for a moment, turns, and then goes off whistling a sad tune.*)

The Exiles

*A bare stage against a sky cyclorama. After a moment, Hester en-
ters, pushed in a wheelchair by the chauffeur, Victor. Emily follows them somewhat listlessly. Hester is more than sixty years old.
Her clothes are definitely old-fashioned. Her face is a mass of
wrinkles in spite of the black velvet choker she wears to stretch
her skin. She uses a hearing aid. Victor is as old as Hester. He has
the stereotyped manner of the dull and dignified servant. His uniform is a mixture of the old coachman's uniform and that of a
chauffeur. Emily is about forty years old. Her bones are bigger and
her features are more coarse than those of Hester. The expression
on her face is tense and sour. It is obvious that to Emily this morning walk is part of a deadly routine.*

HESTER: Here, Victor. Stop here. We're far enough away now. Every
day it's twenty yards more. We're moving back, Victor, we're
moving back. Every day they take over another strip of the beach.
Every day the trip becomes longer, but thank God we've got a car
now instead of the old coach . . . Ah, Victor? Do you remember
when you came to us to be the coachman? (*Feebly to herself*)
Time flies, time flies . . . (*Again to Victor without looking at him*)
Now you're the chauffeur *and* the butler . . .! There were no butlers
in those days! Now? And you were much more comfortable,
weren't you? Oof, the ways of society! I remember that my cousin
Leon, who is very shrewd and given to politics, he used to say . . .
(*She laughs as she remembers and is sidetracked.*) He was very
clever, Leon! He died. (*A pause.*) You can go back to the car,
Victor. Come fetch me in an hour. (*Victor goes back to the car.*

*Hester looks at Emily, who has remained standing, looking on in-
differently.)* And you? What are you doing? Waiting for Victor
to go so that you can take your sunbath? For the life of me I can't
understand what pleasure there is in stretching out on the sand
for hours on end, baking in the sun. In my day . . .
*(Emily takes off her dress. Her swimming suit is an old-fashioned
thing, somewhat high in the bust and with a relatively long skirt.
She lies down on her stomach.)*
Of course, in my day, young ladies went to the beach, but naturally,
not to lie in the sun! Not to go swimming! We did, of course, sometimes, but cautiously, privately. The important thing was to converse, to enjoy society. We all knew each other. We knew who we
were. The beach was ours. I met your father at the beach. And oh,
how we talked, we conversed and conversed until we fell in love . . .
But . . . who bothers to talk now? Who converses? All they do is
squeal in the water or stretch out indecently in the sun like you.
I don't understand it, I can't understand it . . . *(Hester smells
something. She takes out a handkerchief and sniffs the air.)* Do
you smell that? Dead fish! So this is where they pushed us! To a
dump, to the dump where they dispose of dead fish! It's come to
this! And they've done it to me! To me! Oh, I remember when
they first started coming here. You weren't born yet. They used to
come on the early morning train on Sundays, and then they'd go
back in the afternoon. At first they only took up a distant corner
of the beach. We let them. They amused us! They were . . . oh . . .
picturesque. How we laughed at them, their clothes, their manners,
the way they tried to imitate us and couldn't. But they seemed to
grow, every Sunday there were ten more . . . I think they did it on
purpose. Slowly, surely, they crept closer to us. Then when there
too many of them we decided to stay at home on Sundays. No! No,
don't think that we agreed to do this by some sort of a . . . some
sort of a . . . What do they call it nowadays? Some sort of a . . .
a . . . an assembly! Nothing of the sort! Each one of us decided in-
dependently. We were good Christians, and those people had a
right to enjoy themselves at least one day a week. So it was almost
a duty to sacrifice Sunday to them. At least that's what your father

used to say. But I think he was wrong. There were other places
they could go. Viña belonged to us. It was ours! (*She addresses
Emily directly.*) Don't you agree, Emily? Emily! Answer me . . .!
Emily, I know you're not asleep, I know you're listening to me . . .
Answer me . . . who owns Viña?

EMILY (*without moving, and sounding like a tired echo*): We do.

HESTER: We do, of course, it's ours! And why, if it's ours, have they
pushed us into a place like this, a dump for dead fish? Why? Whose
fault is it? Whose? Before, when your father was alive, I used to
get up and I could see the sea from my window. And then, all of
a sudden, cement boxes, punctured cement boxes, began to get in
the way. I had to stand tiptoe and lean one way and another in
order to look at the sea. And then one day the sea disappeared.
There were just windows, convent windows that rose up to the sky.
Hundreds of little convents, thousands of windows that lit up at
night, and there they were: people, people no one knew, who looked
out and laughed and played (*she lowers her voice*) and made love
. . . I've told you, haven't I, what I saw in one of those windows?
And just think, you might have seen it!

(*Emily begins to do setting-up exercises. At first they are slow and
leisurely, but the rhythm picks up. Gradually, they become quite
energetic.*)

It's the foreigners who are to blame! We should never, never have
let them come into the country. Turks, Jews, Germans, Yugo-
slavians, Yankees . . . even Hungarians! Gypsies! In the old days
there were only Englishmen. They were the only foreigners. At
least they were the only ones we saw. They were so refined! Blond,
distinguished, and loyal subjects of the king. They played tennis
and spoke English, old-fashioned English, not the kind you hear
nowadays. Have I ever told you about Mr. Wotherspool? Mr.
Wotherspool! The trouble is that pride is a thing of the past. We've
allowed them to invade us! But I won't give up! I will not mix!
I'll die as I was born. (*She catches herself. Her voice drops.*) I'll
die. I have to die. Everyone dies. (*Then she regains some of her
assurance.*) I'll go to Heaven, and I'll tell St. Peter, "Here I come.
I've been a good Christian. I've kept the laws and all the sacra-

ments, and I've come to claim my place in Heaven. Back there on earth, they shunted me off into the fish dumps, but here, up here, I claim my rightful place." And St. Peter will say to me, "Come in, Miss Hester, come in and take your place at the righthand side of God All Powerful and Omnipotent . . . That's it, you've found your place. You see, they're all friends of yours. Look, look here, your dear husband and your old neighbors: Don Ramón, Don Estanislao, and Señora Matilde and Señorita Eulalia, who died a virgin . . ." I'd just like to see those foreigners get into a place like that. Those ragamuffins! Those tramps! I'd just like to see them get in there! I'd just like to see them in Heaven! (*She thinks a moment of her revenge. She smiles happily. Suddenly she has a disturbing thought.*) Emily . . .! Emily! Have you noticed? When we go to mass? On the mornings we take commuion? They go to mass too . . . They pray, and they take communion . . .! They're trying to get on the good side of God, Emily! They want to invade Heaven the way they did Viña. At first they'll be humble, then later on they'll begin taking it over, and the next thing you know they'll have taken our places at the right hand of God, the Father All Powerful. Emily! We've got to warn the priest! He's got to keep them out of church, he's got to deny them the sacraments, he must stop them from invading Heaven! Emily, you pay attention! I've said something new, something important, something different! I don't say things like this every morning! Listen to me! (*Emily continues doing her exercises.*) Stop it! Stop it! (*Hester throws her cane at Emily. Emily stops and looks at her mother.*) Why do you do exercises every morning?

EMILY: Do you want to know?

HESTER: No. No, I don't want to. I want you to listen to me. I'm afraid. We've got to warn the priest . . .

EMILY (*interrupting*): Do you want to know why I do exercises every morning?

HESTER: No! I want you to listen to me. There's a plot, a confabulation. There's another confabulation against us! It's a matter of . . .

EMILY (*breaking in once more*): You want to know why I take exercises every morning?

HESTER: I don't care. I want you to listen to me.

EMILY: I'm going to tell you why I take exercises every morning.

HESTER: I'm not going to listen to you. You won't listen to me, I won't listen to you!

EMILY: You asked me. For the first time in years you've asked me something.

HESTER: You listen to me! I'm your mother!

EMILY: I'm forty years old.

HESTER: You're an old maid. You're forty, you're forty, you're forty . . .

EMILY: I know. And I live every minute five times. Because I've dedicated every second of my life to one thing: I'm waiting.

HESTER: I don't care what you're waiting for. I was telling you that they're trying to butter up God, they're trying to push us out of Heaven just as they . . .

EMILY (*implacably*): I'm waiting for you to die.

HESTER: I can't hear you! (*She turns off her hearing aid.*) Without the hearing aid I can't hear anything. You know that very well.

EMILY: I don't care about your hearing aid. And I don't care if you do hear me. You've asked me a question. For the first time you've asked me a question. You taught me from the time I was a little girl always to answer one's elders. Well, I'm answering you, I'm answering you!

HESTER: I don't hear a thing, I don't hear a thing. La, la, la, la, la, la, la, la . . .

(*She forces a little song to demonstrate that she is not listening. The song continues into the next speech and fades out.*)

EMILY: I'm waiting for you to die. I'm waiting for you to die so that I can live! I know that I can't get away from you, you've brought me up like a little tame pet, and that's what I am. But when you die, everything is going to change. I've got to stay young. I've got to take care of myself. I exercise every day, every day, so my body will stay young. And then when you're dead, I'll be like a young pigeon, and I'll let the men put their hands into my blouse, and they'll feel my breasts, and they'll find them firm! I have to be ready when you die. That's why I take exercises, that's why I read.

All kinds of wonderful things happen out there in their world, over there where they are. And no one will hold it against me if I join them. When you die, I'm going to begin to live! To live!

(*Offstage we can hear a popular tune played through a portable radio. Emily looks in the direction of the music in sudden fear.*)

RUDY (*offstage*): God, it stinks around here!

CHARLIE (*offstage*): Yeah, I think this is where they dump the fish they can't sell.

RUDY (*offstage*): Hell of a place to come looking for clams!

EMILY (*turning suddenly to her mother*): Mama! Mama! Here they come! It's them! The summer people. We've got to get out of here ... right away! Mama! (*She discovers that Hester is asleep.*) Don't go to sleep now! Don't leave me alone! (*She looks around her desperately, searching for a place to hide from the danger that is approaching. She decides to lie down on the sand and cover her face.*) (*Rudy and Charlie enter. One of them wears a swimming suit, the other blue jeans. Rudy carries the portable radio.*)

RUDY: You're not going to find anything around here.

CHARLIE (*catching sight of Hester*): Hey, look! An old lady!

RUDY (*turning off the radio*): Where?

CHARLIE (*pointing to Hester*): Over there!

RUDY: Oh, for God's sake! A real old lady.

CHARLIE: What ya think?

RUDY: I don't know.

CHARLIE (*approaching Hester*): In a wheelchair, too.

RUDY (*going along with him*): She's asleep.

CHARLIE: She's deaf.

RUDY: How do you know?

CHARLIE (*taking the hearing aid and showing it to Rudy*): See the mike?

RUDY (*takes the microphone of the hearing aid and talks into it*): Hello, hello, hello ... testing, testing ... one, two, three ...

CHARLIE: What a bastard!

RUDY (*catching site of Emily, and nudging Charlie to get his attention*): Hey, look ...

CHARLIE: Another old woman.

RUDY: And what a crazy swimming suit!

CHARLIE (*walking around Emily, staring at her*): Hey, you know she's not too bad ...

RUDY: She deaf, too?

CHARLIE: I don't see any mike.

RUDY: Let's find out. (*He sits down next to Emily.*) Hey ... uh ... Mrs. ... uh ... (*He waits for a reaction. There is none. He gestures to Charlie that she is deaf.*)

CHARLIE: Maybe she's not married ...

RUDY: Uh ... Miss ... (*To Charlie*) Well, wrong again.

CHARLIE: I bet she's a mermaid.

RUDY: She's gotta be. I mean ... if she isn't a Miss or a Mrs. ...

CHARLIE: We got it! She's a mermaid under the spell of an evil wizard who's put her into a deep sleep until her Prince Charming comes along and speaks the magic words and gives her back her beauty and her youth.

RUDY: And I'm the prince to wake her up, eh? (*He kneels down next to Emily and speaks grandiloquently.*) Oh, my princess, my lovely princess, awaken from your legendary sleep. The time has come, my princess. I have no riches to give you, I bring thee love. The world is alive! Awake! The sun is shining. The moon that brings dreams to the lovers! You cannot go on hidden from the sun *and* the moon. You are rejecting God, who has given them to us. Awaken, awaken ...!

(*Emily sits up slowly and smiles at Rudy.*)

CHARLIE: Oh, shit!

EMILY: Forgive me, I was asleep.

RUDY: Forgive me, Ma'am. I didn't mean to wake ya up ...

EMILY: Miss.

RUDY: Forgive me, Miss ...

EMILY (*pointing at Hester*): My mother.

(*Rudy faces Hester and, seeing that she is still asleep, makes a deep bow. Emily looks at Charlie, expecting a formal introduction.*)

RUDY: Charlie, he's a friend of mine.

(*Emily and Charlie nod to each other. Emily turns to Rudy.*)

EMILY: Go on.

RUDY: Go on what?

EMILY: You were talking . . . (*Rudy is surprised.*) About the sun and the moon . . .

RUDY: Ah, so you did hear? That was a joke, Ma'am . . . I mean, Miss. (*There is an embarrassing pause.*)

EMILY: Forgive me. I'm not used to talking to strangers . . . (*Regaining her composure*) No . . . uh . . . no . . . I didn't mean . . . that . . . uh . . . please . . . don't be offended. You're not a stranger. I've introduced you to my mother, and you've introduced me to your friend. Uh, my name is Emily.

RUDY: My name is Rudy.

EMILY: Rudy? Rudolph, just like the actor?

RUDY: What actor?

EMILY: I'm not too sure. My mother used to talk to me of an actor whose name was Rudolph. All the women were crazy about him. They even fainted in the theater.

RUDY: I go to the theater a lot. But I don't know any Rudolph.

EMILY: Oh, not the theater. I mean those moving pictures . . .

RUDY: Oh, yeah, the flicks.

EMILY: Oh, you must know who I mean. He's famous. His last name is, uh . . . Valen . . . uh . . . no, no, not Valenzuela . . . Valentino! That's it.

RUDY: Rudolph Valentino? He's been dead for years.

EMILY: Dead? Oh, I'm sorry. I'm very sorry. Death is awful, isn't it, Rudy? I don't want to die, not yet. I've hardly been born . . .

CHARLIE: Hey, Rudy . . .! Let's get out of here!

(*Rudy turns to Charlie and makes gestures which indicate that Emily is crazy and that he wants to have some fun teasing her.*)

EMILY: I want so much to be alive. I wait day after day to *begin* living. And you *live*, don't you?

RUDY: Yeah . . . I'm alive.

EMILY: And what do you do? Tell me! Tell me all about it!

RUDY: I . . . uh . . . work . . . I work for . . . the . . . uh . . . Grace Line. I'm on vacation now . . . same as you.

EMILY (*with a note of superiority*): No. I'm not on vacation. I live in Viña. I was born in Viña.

(*Charlie has moved off, making ready to go. He looks impatiently at Rudy.*)

CHARLIE: Hey, Rudy . . .! I'm going to shove off!

RUDY (*getting up*): If you'll excuse me . . . my friend's calling me.

(*Emily suddenly grabs Rudy and holds him back.*)

EMILY: Oh, please! Don't go!

(*Rudy looks surprised.*)

(*Begging*) Please stay!

(*Charlie shrugs in disgust and goes off. Rudy comes back and sits beside Emily.*)

Do you converse?

RUDY: What?

EMILY: Yes, of course you do. I like to converse, I always converse . . . but not with people.

RUDY: Then who do you converse with?

EMILY: I pretend . . . I imagine that I converse. Yesterday I imagined something new. I pretended that I was in a hotel, in the restaurant of a very luxurious hotel. And you know who with? With a sweetheart! We were drinking champagne. Do you like champagne?

RUDY: I don't know. I only drink it at weddings and at New Year's.

EMILY: What do you drink in fancy restaurants?

RUDY: Gin . . . neat.

EMILY: What's that?

RUDY: Gin and uh . . . well, gin.

EMILY: Oh! I've never read about that. In novels one always drinks champagne. I don't know what champagne tastes like either. I don't go to weddings and New Year's parties.

RUDY (*impatient*): Charlie, my friend is, uh . . . he's waiting for me.

EMILY: Don't go! You can't go.

RUDY: Why not?

EMILY: You're the only man who knows me. Victor isn't a man! He's a chauffeur. You know all kinds of intimate things about me. You know things that no one else knows.

RUDY: Such as?

EMILY: Well, that I imagine that I converse . . . with lovers. Not even my mother knows that. She'd think that was wrong. She doesn't want to mix. And I do, Rudy. I want to mix. She's asleep now. Let's take advantage of it.

RUDY (*slyly*): So you want to mix?

EMILY: Yes. But I don't know how it's done. And there's so little time. She isn't dead yet. She's just asleep.

RUDY: Okay . . . (*He puts his hand on Emily's knee. She jerks back frightened.*)

You don't want to mix?

(*Emily recovers her composure with an effort and forces herself toward Rudy. She takes his hand and puts it back on her knee. She closes her eyes.*)

EMILY: It's difficult to . . . get used to.

RUDY: All I did was touch your knee.

EMILY: Be quiet . . . let me feel . . . let me feel it. I want to remember it.

(*There is a moment of silence in which Rudy looks at Emily half amused, half frightened. Charlie comes back. He has a dead fish by the tail. He holds it up for Rudy to see.*)

EMILY (*with her eyes still closed*): Rudy . . . kiss me . . .

RUDY: On the mouth?

EMILY: On the mouth.

(*Charlie creeps up to Rudy and hands him the fish. Rudy puts the fish against Emily's mouth, at first gently, and then rubs it against her face. Emily's first response is to squirm sensuously, but when she realizes what has happened, the boys break out in a laughter and run away. Emily looks about without understanding. She sees the fish and stares at it for a moment. Then she gets up and backs off in violent disgust. She goes to Hester and sits at her feet.*)

EMILY: Let's go, mother, let's go. We have to get away. We have to go back even further. They've come this far, they've invaded this part of the beach too! Further on, we'll be alone. I want you to tell me what Viña used to be like. I never heard you when you talked to me about Mr. Wotherspool, and now, I want to . . . I want to. I'm not going to do any more exercises, mama. There's no use, you understand? One can't begin to live all of a sudden. One begins litttle by little. And you didn't want me to, mama, because you love your little girl. You didn't want her to suffer. I understand now. We are different. We shouldn't mix. We can't. Listen to me, mama. Wake up! (*She shakes her gently. Hester's hand slips off the wheel chair and swings lifelessly. Emily looks at her in amazement. She takes the hand and lets it go. It swings again.*) So you've gone off? You're through waiting? You're seated at the righthand side of God the Father Omnipotent. You've found your place. You're no longer an exile? (*She rises and looks at her icily.*) I'll wait, mama. Just as you did. In your chair.

(*Victor enters.*)

VICTOR: It's twelve o'clock, Mum. Time to go back.

EMILY (*indicating Hester*): She's dead.

(*Imperturbably, Victor removes his cap.*)

Get rid of her.

(*Victor picks up Hester in his arms.*)

(*Pointing in the direction taken by Rudy*) Over there! Where they dump the dead fish, over there!

(*Victor goes off in that direction, carrying Hester's body. Emily remains alone. She picks up the fish with great delicacy and then sits down in the wheelchair. She puts the fish against her cheek.*) And so now I know what kisses are like. (*Slowly, and with a forced tenderness, she kisses the fish and then presses it against her bosom.*)